● *VIEW FROM THE BACK OF THE STAGE AT A GEORGE BENSON SHOW IN HARLEM*

MASTERS OF JAZZ GUITAR	The story of the players and their music

A BALAFON BOOK	First British edition 1999
	Published in the UK by Balafon Books,
	an imprint of Outline Press Ltd,
	115j Cleveland Street, London W1P 5PN, England.

ISBN	USA 0-87930-592-4
	UK 1-871547-85-7
	Printed in Singapore
Art Director	Nigel Osborne
Editor	Charles Alexander
Editorial Director	Tony Bacon
Production	Pip Richardson
	Print and origination by Tien Wah Press
	99 00 01 02 03 5 4 3 2 1

TONY RUSSELL   THE GUITAR BREAKS THROUGH

IT TOOK THE INVENTION OF ELECTRICAL RECORDING FOR THE GUITAR TO SHAKE OFF EUROPEAN GENTILITY AND TAKE ITS PLACE AS THE VOICE OF A NEW ERA AND A NEW WORLD.

Looking back from here, the guitar seems to have been the defining instrument of 20th century popular music. Yet at around the time that the 19th century put up its shutters and the 20th prepared to open for business, several other instruments vied for space in the music stores' windows. The guitar had yet to assert its domination over the piano, the violin or the banjo. The process of establishing that pre-eminence is entwined with the history of jazz – but not with jazz alone.

For some decades the guitar had lived a double life. At one stratum of society it was a favourite instrument of the middle-class drawing room. Young men and, more particularly, young women would acquire some skill upon it as a polite accomplishment, rather as Jane Austen's ladies, a century or so earlier, sought a respectable competence on the piano. With the rise of the Gibson and Martin stringed instrument companies in the later 19th century there was also a rapid growth in stringed instrument societies (often sponsored by Gibson or Martin) under such genteel names as the T.A. Miles Guitar and Ukulele Club of Knoxville, Tennessee, or the Silk City Plectral Sextet of Paterson, New Jersey. These societies formed guitar, banjo or mandolin orchestras, often using variants of the featured instrument, such as harp guitar, bass banjo and mandola.

At the same time, the guitar was a component of the string orchestras and mariachi bands of Mexico and the Mexican-Texan border and of the small 'serenading' groups of stringed instrument players in South Texas and New Orleans. Meanwhile, the surge of immigrants from Europe introduced fresh subcultures of guitar-playing that grew quickly in the ethnic enclaves of New York, Philadelphia, Boston or Chicago.

So the guitar had a place, or places, in society. But it had yet to find a prominent role in the recording studio. In an age when the sound of an instrument had to be filtered through the thick blanket of the pre-electric recording process, it was imperative that it should be loud and resonant. Whether picked or strummed, the wood-bodied guitar could hardly compete in this arena with the clangour of the banjo, whose vivid recordability quickly put it on a secure footing with the early record companies. Reliable studio practitioners like Fred Van Eps, Vess L. Ossman and Olly Oakley were especially in demand, and by the time of the Great War, they and scores of other banjoists in the United States, Britain and elsewhere had recorded hundreds, possibly thousands, of rags, marches, cakewalks, "coon songs" and light classical pieces.

The recorded guitar repertory, by contrast, was meagre, though the picture began to change in the early 1910s with the discovery that one type of

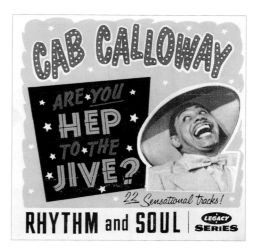

Guitarist Danny Barker with Cab Calloway's Cotton Club Orchestra in 1943 (above left). Originally a New Orleans banjoist, Barker became a leading New York rhythm guitarist. With Calloway from 1939 to 1946, he played guitar on recordings such as 'Minnie the Moocher'.

playing could be successfully transferred to the half-pound shellac discs of the time: the shimmering legato lines of the Hawaiian guitarist, playing with the instrument flat on the lap, making the strings sing by swooping up the fretboard with a steel bar. Hawaiian guitar troupes had begun to visit the United States in the 1890s; 20 years on, they were familiar on vaudeville bills and travelling shows. The influence of Hawaiian guitar playing, with its open tunings and its quivering sustained notes, would seep into American vernacular music everywhere, echoing and expanding the chance discoveries made by rural and small-town guitarists, black and white, as they experimented with knife-blades and broken-off bottlenecks.

In the smaller world of the recording studios, the Hawaiian revelation seemed, for a decade or so, to be regarded as Holy Writ. Guitar recordings of the 1910s and early 1920s, whether in the Hawaiian idiom or not, were almost always made in quasi-Hawaiian style. In 1921 the vaudevillean Sam Moore recorded 'Laughing Rag' and 'Chain Gang Blues' on an octochorda, an eight-string guitar of his own devising, played flat with a steel bar. Sylvester Weaver's 'Guitar Blues' and 'Guitar Rag' (1923), the first recorded guitar solos by an African-American musician, were likewise in the "slide" or "bottleneck" manner.

Also in 1923, Weaver participated with Sara Martin in the first records of blues singing accompanied by a solo guitar. Here he plays with his fingers alone, overcoming some of the deficiencies of the acoustic recording process by his big, booming tone and slow, deliberate picking. In the spring of 1924, Ed Andrews, a wholly obscure figure, followed a similar line on his 'Barrelhouse Blues', though using a 12-stringed instrument. Recorded in Atlanta, this appears to be the first Southern recording of an African-American singer accompanying himself on guitar.

Papa Charlie Jackson, an African-American vaudeville artist from New Orleans, who began recording in 1924, reached a slightly different solution, using the six-stringed banjo-guitar, a banjo with a guitar neck, to combine the volume of the former and the chordal richness of the latter while executing lively picking patterns.

It is a banjo-guitar too that is heard on the 1920s recordings of Louis Armstrong's Hot Five, where the New Orleanian Johnny St Cyr employs both banjoists' and guitarists' righthand techniques. (In doing so he thoroughly confused discographers, who have been unable to decide whether to list St Cyr as playing banjo or guitar. In a sense, he is doing both.)

References to banjo-guitars and 12-string guitars hint at the strategies necessary at that time to boost the guitar's level. As the English guitarist and guitar historian Ivor Mairants remarks, "The main aim of the guitar was to produce as big an acoustic tone as the instrument would project." Hence the big-bodied instruments of the early decades of the century, with their high action, and the thick, heavy picks required for them. Hence the 12-string model, and the 16-string harp guitar. Hence, a little later, the steel-bodied National and Dobro guitars, containing resonating cones that acted as amplifiers.

The adoption of the Western Electric recording process by most American record companies in 1925-6 rewrote the book on recording technique especially for the guitar, releasing it from imprisonment in the acoustic recording horn. Guitarists could now play without props, pick and fret with their hands, use dynamics for light and shade, accompany voices – including their own – without muffling the interplay of vocal and instrumental lines. Where acoustic recording had caricatured music, electric documented it, brought it to real rather than fictive life. The electric microphone was a gateway through which musicians jubilantly charged, to be heard properly for the first time.

Guitarist Bud Scott with Kid Ory and His Creole Jazz Band at the Jade Palace in Hollywood, California, in 1945.

One of the first through the gate was the guitarist Lonnie Johnson, another native of New Orleans, by birth at least, though by the 1920s he was based in St Louis. Johnson survived until 1970, but since he was always reticent about his past, surprisingly little is known about his early life and how he acquired his extraordinary powers. He came from an impressively musical family and could play several instruments: indeed, much of his early recording work with other singers was on violin, on which he developed a highly distinctive style. But for his first recording in his own name, 'Mr Johnson's Blues' (1925), he played guitar. OKeh, the company responsible, was not yet using the Western Electric process, and the sound of the guitar is somewhat thin and distant; it isn't until the following year's 'To Do This You Got To Know How' that we begin to hear Johnson clearly. Yet from the first it was plain that he represented a decisive step forward in guitar technique.

The present-day listener can eavesdrop on that progression as it took place. By 1927 Johnson was so considerable a star of the "race record" market (the name then given to the business of making records for the African-American audience) that he began to be treated by OKeh's producers as an attractive addition to records by other artists on their roster, even equally established ones. In December 1927 he joined Louis Armstrong's Hot Five at a couple of sessions, making cameo appearances on their recordings of 'I'm Not Rough', 'Hotter Than That' and 'Savoy Blues'. Though St Cyr, the group's regular guitarist (or banjoist), kept his seat, Johnson, figuratively speaking, blows him out of it. This is no rhythm player being granted a solo chorus, but a lead musician claiming his place in the front line.

Seconds into 'I'm Not Rough', Johnson announces his presence with a forceful flatpicked tremolo. Later he contributes a singing single-string solo and sinuous accompaniment to Armstrong's vocal chorus: St Cyr can be faintly heard, stolidly chording in the background. On 'Hotter Than That' Johnson dances an intricate two-step round Armstrong's scat chorus before playing call-and-response with him: for all one can hear of St Cyr he might as well have stayed at home. He is more evident in 'Savoy Blues', laying a firm, unflashy low-register line for Johnson's solo. Nevertheless, to hear these three sides is to hear the turning of a page. St Cyr was a well respected musician, and not an old man: he was 37, and had a good few more playing years in him. Johnson was only a few years younger, if at all (the most likely of three cited birthdates seems to be 1894), but in approach, technique and even temperament he belonged to another era, a Model T Ford to St Cyr's horse and buggy.

Having proved that he could play alongside Louis Armstrong and not be hidden by his shadow, Johnson took on the challenge of working with a whole orchestra, sitting in first with the Duke Ellington Orchestra and then with The Chocolate Dandies. The Dandies' 'Paducah' put him on the familiar ground of a slow blues, where he played two lovely, light, swinging choruses, but his solos in the same band's 'Star Dust' and in Ellington's rocket-speed 'Hot And Bothered' proved that he was not disconcerted by different musical structures.

In November 1928, less than a year later, Johnson sat down in an OKeh studio with another of the company's artists. This man was a well-known figure in his own right, but that fact had to be concealed, because he was also white: according to the bizarre racial etiquette of the day black and white musicians were not supposed to appear on records together. Still, any musician or sharp-eared enthusiast of hot music would have known immediately that the player quaintly billed on the labels of these startling guitar duets as Blind Willie Dunn (a name nobody had heard before) was really... Well, he was really Salvatore Massaro, but nobody had heard of him, either, except his family and boyhood friends. Musicians knew him, and already revered him, as Eddie Lang.

Eddie Lang accompanying Bing Crosby in the 1932 movie The Big Broadcast.

That two musicians as prodigally yet matchingly gifted as Johnson and Lang should have been near-contemporaries is one of those happy accidents that make the history of jazz such a tantalising affair. That they should have recorded together was no accident at all but a considered decision by someone at OKeh's New York office, very likely the producer/promoter Tommy Rockwell. Johnson was the biggest-selling guitar artist in the company's blues catalogue and Lang was well known to jazz fans for his work with Red Nichols and the Jean Goldkette Orchestra. But the notion of recording them as a duet may well have been prompted by musical as much as commercial motives. It's difficult to imagine a producer hearing the two together and not wanting to get them into a studio.

Their compatibility was not founded on similar backgrounds. Lang was born, probably in 1902, into Philadelphia's Italian-American community, the son of an instrument-maker and guitarist who brought him up to play guitar, banjo and violin. In his teens he played the dance music of his community, mazurkas, polkas and waltzes, often in the company of a schoolfriend of the same age, named Giuseppe, or Joe, Venuti, who played violin. They went on to join dancebands, developing – off the stand more than on it – the exuberant yet always precisely integrated improvisational interplay that they would unveil in New York's radio and recording studios in the late 1920s. In 1926 they made their first recording as a duet, a sideways look at 'Tiger Rag', titled 'Stringing The Blues'.

In the next four or five years they, and collaborators like Jimmy Dorsey and Adrian Rollini, would virtually invent a new kind of jazz – "chamber

Lonnie Johnson at the Fairfield Hall, Croydon, during his 1963 British tour.

jazz" is one of the names applied to it – that crystallised the vivacity of the expert hot player in a polished setting.

But Venuti & Lang were not a kind of jazz Laurel & Hardy, effective only when together. Lang had begun to draw attention to himself as a superlative rhythm guitarist as early as 1924, on recordings with the Mound City Blue Blowers, and after that with Red Nichols' Five Pennies. In 1927 he began to record guitar solos, and by the time of the meeting with Lonnie Johnson he had laid down such influential tracks as 'Eddie's Twister', 'Perfect', 'Add A Little Wiggle' and 'Church Street Sobbin' Blues'.

What Lang presented to a delighted public and a despairing company of fellow guitarists, when he sat down with his archtop Gibson L-5, was an array of skills never previously encountered in one player: a huge sound, solid yet never cumbersome; a gorgeous, resonant tone; a fine sense of dynamics; speed; a complete command of the chordal vocabulary.

The jazz historian Richard Hadlock observed details like these: "The changing of fingers on the same fret to produce a fresh attack, interval jumps of a tenth to simulate the effect of a jazz piano, parallel ninth chords, flatted fifths, whole tone scalar figures, smears, unusual glissandi, harmonics, harplike effects, consecutive augmented chords, and relaxed hornlike phrasing." All that in one piece, 'Eddie's Twister'.

In a spell of less than 11 months Lang and Johnson recorded ten guitar duets. (There were also two duet accompaniments to the blues-singer Texas Alexander, and two joint appearances in a pick-up group with King Oliver and Hoagy Carmichael, billed as Blind Willie Dunn's Gin Bottle Four.) It is hard to overestimate the importance of this handful of discs.

"The intermingling of their two styles," writes Ivor Mairants, "became the basis of jazz guitar phrasing for years to come out ... The slurred triplets that were first heard from Lang and Johnson are still the stock-in-trade of guitar phrasing out... The playing is hard hitting, free from any rhythmic inhibitions and provides a perfect basis for jazz blues played on the guitar."

Historical importance aside, this is also music of enormous charm, whose power to excite the listener has scarcely dimmed in the seven decades since it was made. In particular, fast pieces such as 'Hot Fingers' and 'A Handful Of Riffs', with Johnson's virtuoso cascade of pulled-off triplets, have a vivacity seldom heard in studio recordings.

The layout of the performances is almost always the same. Johnson takes the lead part – on what appears to have been a 12-string guitar adapted to a 10-string, the first (E) and second (B) strings being single and the others in the usual pairs – while Lang supports with chords and moving bass lines. Thanks, however, to the recording balance, or perhaps to the players' deference to each other, Lang's underpinning often has as much presence in the mix as Johnson's superstructure.

In any case, describing the parts in such terms fails to bring out the complexity of their texture. In 'Bull Frog Moan', for example, Lang's squelchy bass figures are an essential part of the pattern, lending the slow blues tune most of its froggy character, while in sections of 'Blue Guitars', 'Midnight Call (Blues)' and 'Blue Room (Blues)', Lang takes over the lead. With these momentous recordings behind them, Lang and Johnson went their different ways. Johnson returned to continue his long career as a blues singer, and Lang went back to his collaboration with Venuti, and on to radio, recording and movie work with Bing Crosby, one of his greatest admirers. He was to die unexpectedly, in 1933, when complications set in after a routine tonsilectomy.

Beside such innovators as Lang and Johnson the majority of jazz guitarists of the 1920s and early 1930s – men like Ellington's Fred Guy, say, or Fletcher Henderson's Clarence Holiday – tend to seem pale journeyman figures. The occasional individualist is spotted, such as Cal Smith, who played crisp single-string lines with several of the jugbands from Louisville, Kentucky.

Others are more elusive, for instance the enigmatic Edwin McIntosh "Snoozer" Quinn (1906-1952), of whom reputable judges said that if he had chosen to make more of his gift, he would have rivalled Lang. A native of McComb, Mississippi, he was recommended to Paul Whiteman by two of that leader's bandsmen, Bix Beiderbecke and Frankie Trumbauer, which in itself tells us something about his talent. He can be felt, more than heard, on a few of Whiteman's recordings, but only stayed with the band for a matter of a few months. Most of his short career was spent in obscure bands in Texas or Louisiana, and the only sides that tell us much about his jazz capabilities were cut near the end of his life on primitive equipment in a New Orleans hospital to which he was confined with tuberculosis. They are undeniably impressive: another "what-if" story.

By the early 1930s technological progress had completed the redesigning of the dance orchestra rhythm section. The old formation, fixed for years as piano, banjo and tuba or sousaphone was succeeded by one in which guitar replaced banjo and the upright string bass was substituted for the brass bass. Both banjo and brass bass disappeared almost totally from jazz until they were restored by revivalist New Orleans-style bands in the 1940s. The guitar-centred rhythm section of the 1930s gave jazz a new fluidity of movement, put an elasticity in its step and refined the concept of swing.

Eddie Lang's innovative guitar skills and versatility are documented on this compilation of solo, duo, small-group and orchestral performances from 1927 to 1929.

RICHARD COOK

MASTERS OF RHYTHM

OVERLOOKED, UNDERVALUED AND SOMETIMES ALMOST INAUDIBLE, THE GUITAR AT THE HEART OF THE RHYTHM SECTION WAS NONETHELESS CRUCIAL TO THE DEVELOPING RANGE AND COMPLEXITY OF JAZZ AS IT MOVED INTO THE ERA OF THE BIG BANDS.

The sophistications of 1930s jazz were suited to the guitar in every way but one: as an acoustic instrument, it just wasn't loud enough to compete with the rest of the band.

This situation that would continue for many years (when Bobby Hackett first took up a job with the Glenn Miller orchestra, it was as a guitarist, rather than his accustomed trumpet and cornet. Hackett would strum in front of a closed microphone and remembered being completely inaudible). But in every other respect, the guitar was an important part of the new rhythm sections of jazz in what came to be the swing era. Just as the string bass replaced the less flexible tuba and sousaphone – which soon became synonymous with a hick mentality, and entirely wrong for jazz, as an urban, upwardly-mobile phenomenon – so the guitar added a lightness and resonance which rendered the plunk of the banjo obsolete.

Players such as Eddie Lang had begun the change in the previous decade. But the two-beat dance orchestras of the 1920s themselves had to change to allow the guitar a greater freedom. By following the evolution of one notable band through the 1920s and 1930s it is possible to hear how the guitar released itself into a position of genuine and often catalytic importance. Like most of their contemporaries, the Fletcher Henderson Orchestra initiated a stiff and reluctant relationship with jazz in the early 1920s. But through the solicitous impact of Louis Armstrong, Don Redman, Coleman Hawkins and others, the group evolved into the major black band on the East coast by the middle of the decade. Its eminence ebbed away in the 1930s, with the departure of many of its star soloists and Henderson's own laissez-faire attitude to bandleading. But it remained a powerful and often exciting group on record, and several of its 1930s discs can equal the best created by earlier groups. Its long-time banjo player Clarence Holiday moved only cautiously towards the guitar – he was still playing banjo on records as late as 'Sugar' (October 1931) – and the group's subsequent holders of the guitar chair took a more significant role. Of the four principal players, Bernard Addison is especially interesting.

Addison had previously been working with Louis Armstrong in New York, where he made the prototypical switch from banjo to guitar, and he clearly got on well with the tenor saxophone master Coleman Hawkins, who would use him as a sideman a decade later. Addison's style, clean but formidably propulsive, is at its most characteristic on the 1933 Vocalion 'Yeah Man', a Horace Henderson chart which involves a string of supercharged soloists, each nimbly supported by Addison: listen to the way he throws in an unexpected double-time strum behind Coleman Hawkins. He has a more surprising role on

Freddie Green in 1955 (left). His three-and four-note chords throbbed at the heart of Count Basie's rhythm section for 50 years from 1937. Count Basie's The Atomic Mr Basie album from 1957 (CD reissue above) features the superb writing of Neil Hefti, and is a big-band classic. Freddie Green's guitar, beautifully recorded, drives the band along on the fast tempos and sets the mood for the ballad 'Lil' Darlin' with a harp-like introductory arpeggio.

another Horace Henderson arrangement from the same year, Hawkins' theme 'Queer Notions', where he plays a melodic counterpoint to the riffing horns in the opening chorus and suggests the harmonic inquisitiveness of the composer's idea elsewhere in the record.

If Addison was a more than capable figure, he was only one of many. Some of the major bandleaders seemed to use their guitarist purely as an extra, and not especially individual, thread in the rhythm section: there's no better example of this than Fred Guy in the Duke Ellington Orchestra. Ellington either wasn't interested or couldn't find a striking role for Guy, and when the guitarist retired from the band in 1949, Ellington never saw the need to replace him. His principal function was as a rock-solid timekeeper in a band which had its share of players who sometimes liked to rush things along.

In that sense, Guy resembled the most famous big-band guitarist of them all. Freddie Green joined Count Basie's band in 1937 and stayed for the best part of 50 years. He exemplifies the selflessness which came to be the swing orchestra's staple requirement from a guitarist. A southpaw, never granted a soloist's spotlight, he simply played an apposite chord on each beat of the bar, his light strumming eventually becoming such a signature touch that it was as inimitable as Basie's minimalism and Jo Jones's deft swing. You can hear him on what was only his third recording date with Basie, in August 1937, meshing handsomely with the rest of the rhythm section behind Jimmy Rushing on 'Good Morning Blues'. As recording standards improved, the guitar assumed a resonance in studios which it had trouble finding on the bandstand: Green is unobtrusive, but he can be heard.

The problem of volume is central to the guitar's development in jazz in the 1930s. One answer came in the "resophonic" guitars, often known today by the name of one of their principal makers: Dobro. By fitting a resonating metal cone inside the body of an acoustic guitar, a louder, even brasher tone could be twanged out of the instrument. Eddie Durham, who came from Texas and toured with several of the major territory bands, eventually came to work with both Basie and Jimmie Lunceford. He was an early user of the resophonic. In Europe, Django Reinhardt used an instrument made by Selmer which had an extra sound chamber inside the body of the guitar: this helped him get the extraordinary ringing tone which became his trademark. But it was clear that genuine amplification was the only way the guitar was going to hold its own. The breakthrough came when Gibson introduced their ES-150, an electric arched-top guitar with a pickup that introduced the particular sound that most associate with 'jazz guitar' to this day. The reverberant open tone approximates the resonance and fullness of an acoustic instrument, while introducing the weight and attack made possible by amplification. Although it would be many years before solidbody guitars were introduced, this was the point when the guitar became modern as far as jazz was concerned.

That innovation, though, led the way for the guitar to assume a meaningful soloist's role rather than a louder presence in a big-band. It would take Charlie Christian to intitiate that next step. In the meantime, big-band guitarists still played a backroom part in the impetus of the orchestra. Allan Reuss was one who took up the electric instrument readily enough, and he found a persuasive way of combining chordal delivery with an harmonic insight that would point towards the jazz of the 1940s. As ever, Reuss is seldom prominent on recordings but contributes a notable feel to all of his various rhythm sections. One of the rare occasions when he steps into the limelight is on Jimmy Dorsey's 1942 Decca 'Sorghum Switch', a Jesse Stone theme which sounds very like one of Glenn Miller's more assertive pieces. Reuss opens and closes the disc with a subtle string of chords that plays off against the lowering brass. For the rest of the tune, he is all but invisible.

Few of these guitarists had pretensions to moving to the front of the bandstand or doing much more than taking seriously their important but comparatively uneventful place. Yet a handful of players did adapt the rhythm player's style to a more central position. Carl Kress and Dick McDonough had already played on many important sessions in the 1920s, as part of the fertile and prolific group of New Yorkers which dominated much of the studio work in that decade; along with Eddie Lang and Andy Sannella, they were the most in-demand of guitarists. In the ensuing decade, they didn't alter their styles so much as mould their environments to suit themselves: and they even began working together as duettists. McDonough, who came from Brooklyn, was three years older than Kress, who was from Newark. As ubiquitous as they were, they are not much remembered today by the wider jazz audience since none of their individual tracks has attained the eminence of Lang's solos and duets. But the music is worth rediscovering.

Kress, in fact, was the partner in two of Lang's final duet recordings, 'Feeling My Way' and 'Pickin' My Way', from 1932. With McDonough, he cut five duets, and there are six solos made for Decca in 1939. The duets, dating from two sessions in 1934 and two in 1937, are graceful, a little neutral in feel,

Allan Reuss laying down the chords in 1938. He played rhythm guitar with the bands of Benny Goodman, Jack Teagarden, Paul Whiteman, Jimmy Dorsey and Lionel Hampton.

but played with the kind of apologetic virtuosity which seems to have been the natural bent of both men. 'Chicken A La Swing' starts out as a nimble chase piece before surprising with its sudden slow middle section, which concludes with some very Lang-like bent notes before a reprise of the original theme. 'Heat Wave' is an ingenious arrangement of Irving Berlin's song that features rubato playing, changing leads, the deftest of counterpoint and the cleverest of endings. These are surprisingly little-known tracks. So are two 1934 transcriptions featuring McDonough by himself. A duet with bassist Artie Bernstein, 'The Ramble', has something of the old-time feel of the novelty and rag players of perhaps a generation earlier, the formal variations of the tune worked through impeccably, and a solo treatment of 'Honeysuckle

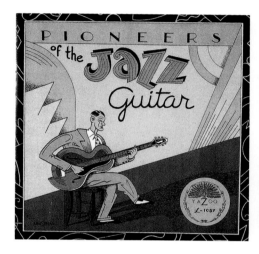

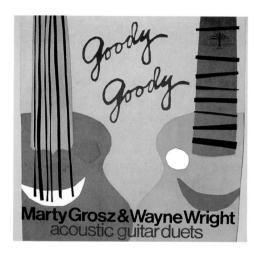

Rose' shows McDonough's elegance: satisfied with keeping the melody to hand, he thrums along its path, just slightly varying the attack in each chorus, and again suggesting the valued precision of his forebears. It is rare to find such a guitar solo in jazz recordings.

McDonough, although destined for an early death (he succumbed to pneumonia in 1938) had a somewhat higher profile than Kress by dint of his bandleading: there were 12 sessions for ARC in 1936-7 by an eight- or nine-piece group which included, at various times, Bunny Berigan, Adrian Rollini and Artie Shaw. The records are mostly somewhat unremarkable but the best of the soloists bring them to life, and although Kress's involvement is uncredited, there are moments when he seems to be present. He is definitely there on a group of 1937 transcriptions which feature an intriguing glimpse of two rhythm guitarists at work together in a swing band. McDonough leads and takes the lion's share of the solos, but there are openings for Kress to swap phrases and generally do more than play second fiddle. Always the undertow of crisp, encouraging chords lifts the rest of the band.

Kress, who died in Reno in 1965, while still working, was a shrewd man who took pains to explore different avenues in his approach to the guitar. In the 1920s, his move from banjo to guitar began (as for many others) with the adoption of a four-string model. When he switched to a six-string in the 1930s, he kept the C-G-D-A tuning of the tenor banjo on his top four strings, and added low strings in fifths, making his basic tuning Bb-F-C-G-D-A. Kress realised that the A-string could sound unflatteringly high and tetchy in the rhythm section, and was particularly interested in using his Bb-string as something that could work in close tandem with the bassist in a group. In the

Pioneers Of The Jazz Guitar (left) is an invaluable collection of guitar duos from the 1920s and 1930s, including Carl Kress & Dick McDonough, Lonnie Johnson & Eddie Lang, Kress & Lang, John Cali & Tony Guttuso, as well as solo performances from McDonough and Nick Lucas. On the late-1920s Ellington collection (centre) from the band's spirited Cotton Club period, Fred Guy plays banjo with Teddy Bunn joining on guitar for 'Oklahoma Stomp'. Guy later mainly played guitar, but when he retired in 1949 Ellington dropped guitar from the band. Marty Grosz & Wayne Wright's Goody Goody (above) from 1979 features acoustic guitar duets from two masters of early chordal styles, including re-creations of Carl Kress & Tony Mottola duets. Wright also played rhythm guitar in the Ruby Braff-George Barnes Quartet.

A fervent advocate of the unamplified guitar, Marty Grosz (right) regularly performs jazz repertoire of the 1920s and 1930s with skill and wit.

McDonough transcription of 'Wang Wang Blues', you can hear how he uses that contrast to particularly imaginative effect. He often experimented with different tunings but, like McDonough, he remained fundamentally a rhythm man, seeing little need to take a soloist's role.

George Van Eps, who died in 1998 at age 85, had the admiration of several generations of guitarists for a style that was, like that of the men discussed above, founded on a rhythm player's vocabulary. From a musical family – his father Fred was one of the great masters of the banjo era – George played his first professional engagement at age 11 and spent half of the 1930s with different bandleaders and half as a Hollywood studio pro. In the latter capacity, he had time for teaching and thinking about his own playing, which resulted in both an important text for guitar players and a new seven-string instrument, a variation of which he would use for the rest of his life. By adding a seventh string, he gave himself the capacity to play his own bass lines, the kind of approach which Kress had worked on with six strings. Despite numerous appearances on record with Benny Goodman, Red Norvo and others in the 1930s, Van Eps has never been much noticed by most jazz followers. But guitar specialists always acknowledge his harmonic mastery in particular, a facet which became much clearer on some of his later recordings. He worked in jazz festivals in the 1960s, 1970s and 1980s, and in the 1990s he made three albums with Howard Alden, with the younger guitarist proving a likeable partner for the old professional.

Some of the music is a bit insipid at slow tempos, but on the best of their albums, *13 Strings* (Concord), a sympathetic rhythm section frames the two players and shows Van Eps's timeless swing chording to particular advantage. It makes an interesting companion piece to 'Bughouse', a 1935 track with Red Norvo, one of the rare instances of the period in which Van Eps gets some solo attention. Although it's more of a break than a true solo, sandwiched as it is between Norvo and Johnny Mince, it epitomises Van Eps's swing, chordal dexterity and hamonic curiosity in a few bars.

Once Charlie Christian came along, the guitar and its exponents moved entirely away from this kind of playing, and though the effectiveness of swing guitar remained a constant, players hungered for the kind of solo opportunities which Christian's language had begun to make available. As with everything else in jazz, though, there is always scope for a revival, and the style is dormant rather than extinct. In recent years, with the kind of enlightened revivalism which has brought back large areas of jazz repertory and style, rhythm playing has been particularly enhanced by the knowing contributions of Marty Grosz.

Grosz has been in jazz for longer than perhaps he cares to remember, but he has become widely known at festivals and in clubs for an approach to repertory that is part affection, part wry amusement. Grosz tends to specialize in unleashing bewilderingly obscure tunes on his audience, but his own guitar playing, executed on a proudly unamplified acoustic, is based on chords and rhythm, a perfect vehicle for the kind of small-band swing which he delivers on records that tend to rejoice in titles such as 'Songs I Learned At My Mother's Knee And Other Low Joints'.

Bucky Pizzarelli is a near contemporary of Grosz's, but seems to have been around for much longer through his long association with the orchestra of Vaughan Monroe and his studio and TV work, which found him often glimpsed in high profile, non-jazz company, such as *The Dick Cavett Show*. As with Grosz, though, it wasn't until comparatively late in his career that he began accruing attention as a jazz guitarist. He was a close attendant of Benny Goodman's in the 1970s (an association that continued until Goodman's death), playing in a manner that, ironically, owed more to the pre-Christian vocabulary.

Pizzarelli has, like Van Eps, adopted the seven-string instrument, with the low A-string employed for bass counterpoint, and put a personal spin on the swing-rhythm language of his forebears. He has recorded some excellent duets with his son John, which are interesting in the way that they manage to sound up-to-the-minute without admitting any boppish leanings in the delivery, and a particularly adroit encounter can be heard on a recently-discovered session with Zoot Sims, *Elegiac*, recorded live in 1980. In the exposed format of a sax-guitar duo, Pizzarelli comes up with his most ingenious chording, muscular dialogue and rhythmic alacrity.

Bucky Pizzarelli is a master of the chordal guitar approach first developed by the likes of Eddie Lang, George Van Eps, Carl Kress and Dick McDonough.

BRIAN PRIESTLEY

SOLOISTS OF THE SWING ERA

IN THE ERA OF BIG-BAND SWING, JAZZ GUITARISTS BORROWED IDEAS AND PHRASING FROM BLUES PLAYERS AS THEY STRUGGLED TO GIVE THEIR INSTRUMENT A STRONG SOLO VOICE TO MATCH ITS ACKNOWLEDGED HARMONIC AND RHYTHMIC IMPORTANCE.

Teddy Bunn backstage at Harlem's Apollo Theater in 1939, where he was appearing with The Spirits Of Rhythm. Not just a rhythm player, Bunn brought blues and jazz sensibility to his single-line solos.

The music of the swing era was once described as "Everybody trying to play like Louis Armstrong", and it's true that the big-band style largely consisted of arrangements based on Armstrong's phraseology. For guitarists – just like pianists, to some extent – things were not so simple.

From the late 1920s onwards, those guitarists who wished to expand their role had to take into consideration the tradition and nature of their instrument. Not only were they thought of by other players as being rhythm-accompanists first and foremost, but they were often heard in groups where they were the only person laying down the chords. Whereas pianists (when in a group without a guitarist) could continue chording with their left hand while improvising a solo with the right, guitarists often tried to alternate both functions on the same fretboard. It was either that or abandon the chordal element altogether, which would have seemed a precarious adventure, given the rudimentary nature of most bass-players' contributions at the time.

In practice, jazz guitarists found much encouragement and specific examples to follow in the work of the 1920s bluesmen. Blind Lemon Jefferson (1897-1930), the first widely popular blues singer on record to accompany himself on guitar, was enough of a stylistic pace-setter for a string of later players to claim they had acted as his "eyes". Beginning in the winter of 1925-6, Jefferson had a recording career of less than four years before his untimely death, but cemented a style in which his two-bar vocal phrases received rudimentary chordal backing while the two-bar gaps were filled with single-line responses. In this way, he not only influenced every blues singer-guitarist who came after, but indirectly numerous jazz guitarists too.

The leading exponent of the 1930s, Teddy Bunn (1909-78), was a case in point. Bunn himself was capable of singing blues lyrics, though with a rather unsuitably bland voice, and he also did studio work backing blues-singers during the late 1920s and early 1930s with Victor and the late 1930s with Decca. It's his work in jazz contexts which has kept his name alive, although his crisp picking and clear acoustic tone show the influence of Lonnie Johnson (whose recording career began at the same time as Jefferson's) and the jazzy bounce of bluesman Blind Blake's guitar work.

Apparently, Bunn's earliest professional work was in the backing group of a calypso singer (West Indian immigration to the US increased significantly in the 1920s). An indication of his early promise is the fact that his first issued jazz recording was as an added starter with Duke Ellington's band in 1929, in a role previously filled on a couple of sessions by none other than Lonnie Johnson. He may have been picked on spontaneously by Duke (Bunn was already at the studio to record with blues singer-pianist Walter "Fats"

Pichon) but he was featured in short solo spots on three of the four tunes Ellington recorded that day. In each case, he plays single-note lines of a notably bluesy character, sometimes dialoguing with others. Some time after, possibly the following summer, he briefly toured with Duke's band as a replacement for the latter's banjo-player, Fred Guy, who by contrast never soloed and concentrated on rhythm-section work.

Teddy's own instrument at this period was a banjo-guitar, strung like a guitar but with a banjo-like body, and the articulation of his notes was always achieved with his right thumb and without the aid of a plectrum. Some of his studio work in 1930 was with one of several "washboard bands" that became popular with black audiences as the Depression took hold (and were also

Teddy Bunn on guitar in 1937 with the John Kirby Sextet at the Onyx Club in New York's 52nd Street (left). The band included Frankie Newton (trumpet), Pete Brown (alto sax) and Buster Bailey (clarinet). Bunn contributes several sparkling single-string solos on the tracks by the Hot Lips Page Trio on this compilation (above) of large- and small-group sessions.

popular with record companies because they were cheaper than the established black artists). Their mixture of blues and ragtime influences, and their combination of jazz horn-players with "found" instruments such as washboards and kazoos, led the way to the late 1930s jump-bands and 1940s R&B. One of these record dates in 1932 (without Bunn, as it happens) included members of an unclassifiable group that came to be known as the Spirits Of Rhythm. When Teddy replaced their previous guitarist, the stage was set for them to become the most popular group on New York's 52nd Street after the repeal of Prohibition in late 1933.

Basically, the Spirits were a close-harmony vocal quartet whose leaders, Wilbur and Douglas Daniels, accompanied themselves on the tiple, a kind of Mexican ukulele. But the chief attraction for more hip listeners was vocalist Leo Watson who, as well as singing with the rest of them, indulged in zany vocal improvisations while imitating the action of a slide-trombonist. (The humour of Watson's approach may have been an inspiration for the later work of Slim Gaillard [1911-91] whose vocals were usually backed by his very

adequate guitar playing.) The trouble with the Spirits' records, and their live performances too, was that Bunn was only given the same amount of solo space as the Daniels brothers' tiples, sometimes even less. However, their up-tempo version of 'I Got Rhythm' shows him in full flight, with romping single-string lines rhythmically reminiscent of Coleman Hawkins-style saxophonists.

Naturally, popular success meant that Teddy stayed with this winning team, though he left for a period in the late 1930s to concentrate on record sessions and his own groups, before rejoining the Spirits. His studio dates in the intervening period included not only blues sessions but several all-star jazz groups, featuring some or all of the horn-players Tommy Ladnier, Mezz Mezzrow, Frankie Newton and Sidney Bechet. The first three of these were organised in the winter of 1938-9 by the visiting French critic Hugues Panassie and, although Bunn's space is limited, he does not sound outclassed in such fast company. In the spring of 1939, he recorded twice for the new Blue Note label's all-star group, The Port Of Harlem Jazzmen, the second of these occasions featuring Bechet again. The most memorable outcome was a version of 'Summertime', which became Blue Note's first hit single, and which was effective partly because of the low-register counter-melodies that Bunn improvised behind Bechet's majestic lines.

Doubtless because of this hit, Teddy appeared twice more for Blue Note the following year, on a piano-less quartet date with Bechet and the next day completely unaccompanied. The latter departure, highly unusual for the period, was slightly undercut by Bunn's blues vocals on two tracks, but these take up little of the playing time and the instrumental work is a convincing compromise between sophisticated blues phraseology and jazz improvisation. The other two pieces are even more impressive, featuring completely assured playing on an up-tempo 12-bar sequence ('Guitar In High') and a version of 'King Porter Stomp', both alternating single-string lines with chordal punctuation.

Interestingly the Spirits Of Rhythm, reunited with Bunn, appeared on both radio and records for Lionel Hampton in 1940. In the broadcast, the guitarist has no solo space but plays the same unison riffs on 'Flying Home' which Charlie Christian previously recorded alongside Hampton. In the studio two days later, whether or not at Hamp's request, Bunn is suddenly heard using electric guitar for the first time, and sounding strangely close to Christian. Not only had Teddy paid close attention following the latter's appearance on the national scene a year earlier, but had paved the way for many of Christian's innovations. Sadly, the Spirits Of Rhythm's subsequent move to the West Coast, where less recording was taking place, led to Teddy's work being soon overlooked and, by the end of the 1940s, he moved into R&B and then rock-n-roll. He worked with, among others, Louis Jordan after the latter's heyday, but obscurity and recurrent illness meant that he never made a comeback or received due acknowledgement for his achievements.

One of the many who described the Spirits as "the swingingest group I ever heard" was guitarist Al Casey (b.1915), quite a compliment considering the fact that he played during the same period with pianist Fats Waller And His Rhythm. Despite joining Waller at the tender age of 17, Al was himself one of the swingingest accompanists and section-players of the era, and he remained with the group from 1933 to 1942 with only 18 months' break, when he worked with Teddy Wilson and others. Of course, the jivey atmosphere and

Al Casey with bassist John Levy and drummer Denzil Best (opposite). Casey's long career began with Fats Waller, with whom he played from 1933 to 1942. A great rhythm player, Casey also developed a distinctive chordal soloing style.

general mayhem of Waller's group was similar to a more jazz-oriented version of the Spirits Of Rhythm but, with the attention afforded to the hornmen and Fats's vocals and piano, there was little space for Casey as a soloist.

When given the opportunity, Al specialised in a style that emphasised series of extremely mobile three-note (sometimes four-note) chords with successive top notes forming an improvised melody-line. These chorded solos on a small minority of Fats's many records, usually brief and only achieving prominence on his 1941 feature number 'Buck Jumpin'', earned Casey a reputation among fellow guitarists. But it's an open question whether it was his own idea to feature them so exclusively during this period, or perhaps the bandleader's desire for textural contrast, since the Waller group's first record session in 1934 finds Al playing single-string backings to Fats's vocal before introducing his patented chording in his own solo. Revealingly, perhaps, several Waller broadcasts find him using more single-string lines in his solos, one of which switches rather too abruptly to the chordal approach after only a few bars.

On the other hand, Casey also took part in one of the aforementioned Hugues Panassie sessions (led by Frankie Newton) and one of Lionel Hampton's all-star dates, in each case reverting to his speciality. Yet, on the 1943 recording of Coleman Hawkins and the Esquire All Stars and a 1944 Earl Hines trio date in memory of the recently deceased Waller, he played amplified and in a very Christian-influenced style, even joining in the boppish theme of 'Mop Mop' in unison with the horns. Despite leaning in this modern direction, however, Al seemed old-fashioned to the beboppers and was soon gravitating towards R&B. Fortunately, this led to studio work and, in particular, during the late 1950s and early 1960s he had a lengthy association with saxophonist King Curtis. An informal live recording of them together finds Casey playing in a wide variety of appropriate styles on a solidbody electric instrument.

As a result of this exposure, in 1960 the guitarist made the only two US albums under his own name, including a revival of 'Buck Jumpin''. He continued working on the borderline between swing-era jazz and R&B and, despite some time out of music during the 1970s, has pursued a career as visiting soloist, making at least three LPs in London and recording as recently as the mid-1990s in Germany. Although some of this touring work is predicated on nostalgia for the Fats Waller sound, we must be grateful that he has remained active and continued to find an audience for so long.

Another guitarist whose career started in the 1930s, and for whom session work occupied the majority of his career, was the Chicago native George Barnes (1921-77). Barnes began learning the piano as a child, but in the Great Depression his family lost their house and possessions, so the only instrument available was an $8 Sears-Roebuck guitar. His father taught George, who was soon good enough to support the family, forming his own quartet at 14 and starting to record a year later.

Most unusually for a white musician at this period, Barnes became a regular on many sessions of early Chicago blues, with such artists as Big Bill Broonzy and Blind John Davis. He spoke with unashamed pride of the fact that Hugues Panassie, who insisted on racial identification of the performers he wrote about, invited Davis to France in the 1950s and later told Barnes, "I had to find out from a blind black man that you're white." George not only benefited from personal coaching by Lonnie Johnson, but he was one of the

Les Paul in 1987 (opposite) playing the guitar that bears his name. His jazz chops were sharpened by jamming with Art Tatum in the early 1940s, but it was his innovative multi-tracked guitar recordings that brought him commercial success. This 1990s reissue of Les Paul Trio recordings (above) features lightning chromatic runs, slick swing phrasing, Django-style flourishes, string-bending and glissandi. Radio transcriptions from 1947, they showcase Paul's commercially-aware electric guitar style: a virtuosic blend of swing-jazz and country music, the guitar technique of Reinhardt and the harmonic thinking of pianist Art Tatum.

first to record on electric guitar, for instance on Broonzy's version of the Leroy Carr song 'The Night Time Is The Right Time' in May 1938.

Later that year, such freelance recording ceased as Barnes became, at 17, one of the youngest players in the country to be a radio-station musical director, working for NBC in Chicago and then ABC after army service during World War II. At 30, he joined the New York staff of Decca Records as instrumentalist, arranger and conductor and, although also involved in much out-and-out pop material, he worked memorably with the Yank Lawson-Bob Haggart band and with Louis Armstrong's group. George also found time to fit in some live work, for example in duos with Carl Kress and subsequently Bucky Pizzarelli, and from 1973-5 a two guitars, bass and cornet quartet with

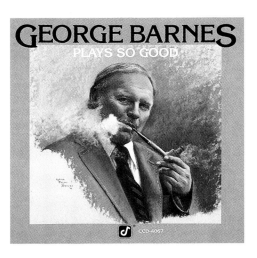

Duets with ALBERT HARRIS and recordings with
THE IVOR MAIRANTS GUITAR GROUP

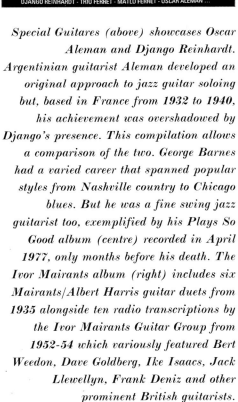

Special Guitares (above) showcases Oscar Aleman and Django Reinhardt. Argentinian guitarist Aleman developed an original approach to jazz guitar soloing but, based in France from 1932 to 1940, his achievement was overshadowed by Django's presence. This compilation allows a comparison of the two. George Barnes had a varied career that spanned popular styles from Nashville country to Chicago blues. But he was a fine swing jazz guitarist too, exemplified by his Plays So Good album (centre) recorded in April 1977, only months before his death. The Ivor Mairants album (right) includes six Mairants/Albert Harris guitar duets from 1935 alongside ten radio transcriptions by the Ivor Mairants Guitar Group from 1952-54 which variously featured Bert Weedon, Dave Goldberg, Ike Isaacs, Jack Llewellyn, Frank Deniz and other prominent British guitarists.

Ruby Braff, which produced six memorable albums. With the alternately mellow and excitable brass of Braff, Barnes's sharp-toned single-string lines left the second guitarist to play the chords and functioned much as a clarinet, the instrument of Jimmie Noone who had employed him as a teenager. He also made a late album with Joe Venuti but, sadly, Barnes's alcohol consumption hastened his premature death from a heart-attack.

Les Paul (b.1915), a name to conjure with in both the guitar world and the record industry, also started out on piano. He too did musical-director work for Chicago radio-stations, both before and after his trio toured with Fred Waring's popular Pennsylvanians from 1938-41. When he moved to Los Angeles in 1943, his experience of hanging out in Chicago with Art Tatum and violinist Eddie South paid off in his new trio, which began recording for Decca and for radio transcription programmes. The clear tone of his single-string work and the humour of his special effects, such as an occasional exaggerated vibrato or gruff bass-register phrases, set a clear precedent for the innovative multitrack records that made his name a few years later.

Les's home studio, where he single-handedly created these, gives new meaning to the phrase "garage band". The arranging talent he displayed is almost as impressive as the playing, for Paul often created four or more simultaneous musical layers. A bass-guitar sound was achieved by recording at fast tempo and then slowing the playback to half-speed, when the melodic lead and a full harmony part were overdubbed, with the addition of a "piccolo-guitar" sound recorded while the speed of the rest was halved again. Often, these upper parts would include some minimal improvisation, on pieces such as 'Walking And Whistling the Blues' and the early 'Hip-Billy Blues'.

But the best evidence of Les's long-forgotten jazz ability, and his admiration for Django Reinhardt, is on the first Jazz At The Philharmonic concert in 1944, where he improvises at greater length than on any studio recording.

Oddly enough, the musical wit and harmonic sophistication of Les Paul's one-man-band records is foreshadowed by a series of guitar duets recorded for radio transcriptions in 1941. At this period, the new duet partner of Carl Kress was the young Tony Mottola (b.1918), who had been recommended by Kress as a staff musician for CBS Radio. Both guitarists played electric and carefully spread advanced chords between the fingers of the two players, so that these tracks, with their "tempo changes, modulations, the juxtaposition of up-tempo themes with ballad interludes, big-band syncopations [and] three-part harmonies" (to quote Richard Lieberson's liner-notes) mark a clear advance on Kress's earlier duets.

Mottola soon confined himself to studio work, and writing and playing for numerous television shows. But the theme of multiple guitar groups can also be heard in the case of a British-based studio musician, the legendary Ivor Mairants (1908-97). Born in Poland but brought up in London from the age of six, Mairants came up through all the best British bands of the period and was working with Roy Fox when he made his first freelance recordings in 1935-6. These included six duets with the younger guitarist Albert Harris, who had filled Mairants's previous berth when the latter joined Fox, and was later replaced by Mairants with the Ambrose band when he (Harris) moved permanently to the US in 1938.

Their acoustic duets, three written by Mairants and three by Harris, naturally reflect the influence of the Carl Kress-Eddie Lang and Carl Kress-Dick McDonough sessions, but are rather more straight-ahead ('Spring Fever' being based on 'China Boy' and 'Yankee Doodle Plays A Fugue' hardly living up to its title). Intriguingly, the two also took part in a 1935 recording which was rejected – probably on technical rather than musical grounds – with four guitars simultaneously, an ambition that subsequently resurfaced on separate albums by George Barnes and Tony Mottola, and which Mairants later pursued with a 1950s BBC series by his Guitar Group. This played intelligent arrangements, usually featuring three electric guitarists blended with a reedman and accordionist and including such session musicians as Ike Isaacs, Dave Goldberg and Bert Weedon.

In surveying the swing-style soloists, we should not forget that based in Paris during the 1930s was the Argentinian virtuoso Oscar Aleman (1909-80). He too did his share of backing work, for instance in live performances by American star Josephine Baker and in recording sessions, but his excellent jazz work was overshadowed by the reputation of Reinhardt, though Aleman allegedly considered himself the better player. Not until 1938 was he properly featured on disc, first in a jam-session with Danish violinist Svend Asmussen and then solo, following up with a group of trio records the next year.

Hearing these sides is a reminder that he was certainly influenced by Reinhardt but, whereas the latter used a pick, Aleman employed all his fingers in the Spanish style. He returned to Buenos Aires when Paris was occupied by the Nazis and, although he later produced much "easy listening" music (as did Barnes and Mottola), performances of standards by his 1940s Quintetto De Swing demonstrate why the Argentine scene was eventually to produce such musicians as Lalo Schifrin and Gato Barbieri.

Ivor Mairants recorded guitar duets with Albert Harris in the mid 1930s and was featured guitarist with many of the leading British swing bands of the time. His guitar instruction books influenced a whole generation of young players.

MAX HARRISON

DJANGO REINHARDT

A MANOUCHE GYPSY, DJANGO REINHARDT WAS A SKILLED BANJOIST AND GUITARIST AT 18 WHEN A FIRE IN HIS CARAVAN CRIPPLED HIS LEFT HAND. AFTER RECUPERATION AND INTENSE GUITAR PRACTICE HE EMERGED TO TRANSFORM THE INSTRUMENT – AND JAZZ – FOREVER.

So protean a figure was Jean Baptiste "Django" Reinhardt that he can be viewed in several ways. In a book about jazz, it is best to approach him as the first major figure in that music who was not American. Yet his seemingly intuitive – if not quite immediate – mastery of jazz arose through his being a Gypsy, specifically a Manouche. Space is lacking to discuss his racial or family antecedents yet something should be said about Romany, the Gypsy language. It has many dialects, reflecting the territories through which a particular group of Gypsies travelled. In rather the same way their music absorbed aspects of many other musics. This suggests parallels with jazz, which has also assimilated much from other styles, thereby providing a foundation for Reinhardt's grasp of jazz improvisation.

Nomadic peoples escape documentation but his birthday is taken as January 23rd 1910, in Belgium. Yet that signifies little, marking only a pause which Reinhardt's particular group of Gypsies made during their incessant travels by horse-drawn caravan. These were eventually abandoned and his family settled in a shanty town of a Gypsy encampment outside Paris. That is where the great guitarist spent the rest of his youth.

He was always interested in music and finally got his hands on a banjo. Rather than proving a false start, this was advantageous to his eventual highly idiosyncratic command of his real instrument. Given a heightened endowment of Gypsies' inborn musicality, he soon mastered the banjo and at about 12 was performing in various Paris locations. His first recording sessions, in 1928 at the age of 18, were with an accordionist and someone playing slide-whistle: these show him already an extremely capable performer. Yet this is street music, compelling us to ask what brought him to jazz and to becoming an original, creative virtuoso of the guitar.

First, in the year of his initial recordings, came a disaster. Returning from work in the small hours of November 2nd 1928, he had an accident with a candle and quickly the caravan became an inferno. His burns were such that he was bedridden for 18 months and for considerably longer had nightmares about the fire. Far worse, his left hand was so damaged that it seemed unlikely he would play music again, least of all on a stringed instrument. What Reinhardt then did was nearly as much a feat of genius as almost anything found in his subsequent music.

He completely redesigned his playing technique on a new, seemingly far more limited basis. To this end, and to help pass the time during convalescence, some of his fellow Gypsies gave him not a banjo but a guitar. It would have been remarkable if he had put together an averagely serviceable playing method yet he went much further, and in an almost entirely new

Django Reinhardt during his 1946 American trip playing a borrowed archtop guitar. In spite of his visibly deformed left hand, his technical command of the instrument was truly awesome.

direction, arriving at a unique virtuoso technique. After the fire, his third and fourth fingers were locked at the first joint and although this greatly restricted their movement he still could reach certain chord shapes with all four fingers. For his extraordinarily agile single-string playing he obviously used his two still-normal fingers. With that left hand disabled he needed to bring his right hand more into things and the chromatic runs of which he was so fond were managed by co-ordinating one shift of a left-hand finger on the fretboard with one upward or downward stroke of the right-hand wrist, these being repeated for each note of the scale. His initial banjo technique with its fast wrist-rolls was surely crucial here, being reflected in the ripping-rolling syncopated tremolos so characteristic of his guitar work. Though he was perfectly capable of playing finger-style he normally used a plectrum on the guitar, his pick being very thick for large volume and strong attack.

We have no idea how Reinhardt went about discovering his new method or how long he took to master it. He seems never to have been interviewed on the subject and though he was always ready to show what he could do he may not have been able to explain it verbally. It is a grim thought that his crippling accident was ultimately beneficial to Reinhardt, impelling him to an approach on the guitar which he otherwise scarcely would have taken and leading to a musical originality he might not otherwise have attained.

The first recordings of him on the guitar, in 1931 and 1933, mainly accompaniments to singers, are not much closer to jazz. After recovering from the accident, he travelled to the south of France to work with his younger

The Quintette du Hot Club de France in Paris, August 2nd 1939. After their recording for Decca in London later that month, violinist Stephane Grappelli remained in London while guitarist Django Reinhardt (second left) returned to Paris just days before the outbreak of war.

brother Joseph. Here he encountered records which focused his interest on jazz, which until then he had only listened to fleetingly in Paris.

We have little idea about which titles Reinhardt heard, yet there is reason to believe that numbers by Louis Armstrong, Duke Ellington and Joe Venuti were included. It is also reasonable to guess that with Venuti was Eddie Lang who, together with Lonnie Johnson, pioneered the guitar in jazz. Here then was the second factor which, along with his accident, and building on his Gypsy heritage, shaped Reinhardt's singular artistic personality. Jazz not only gave direction to his musical development but, such are the mysteries of human psychology, also unlocked the seemingly inexhaustible powers of invention demonstrated by his subsequent records.

Back in Paris he continued to record accompaniments to singers, but his discography proves that he was now in contact with some of the pioneer French jazzmen who had started emerging in the 1920s. Reinhardt can be heard in unequivocal jazz circumstances on 'Black Panther Stomp' by Patrick et son Orchestre and Michel Warlop's 'Blue Interlude and Presentation Stomp'. It is clear from these 1934 performances, with his guitar driving all before it, that a major figure had arrived.

This being so, he attracted the attention of famous American visitors, an instance being a 1935 session by Coleman Hawkins and Warlop's large band. In particular this produced a beautiful reading of 'Stardust' from the tenor saxophonist with just a Reinhardt-led rhythm section. American jazzmen understood perhaps better than anyone that what he offered was entirely new, and from then on he was always in demand whenever distinguished visitors recorded in Paris. Dates with Reinhardt by Hawkins, Benny Carter, Dicky Wells, Eddie South and by permanent expatriates like Bill Coleman resulted in performances which rank among the classics of jazz on disc and, in the cases of South and Wells, the finest records of their careers.

Some of the most notable of these sessions took place in 1937 and for some years before that there had been talk of Reinhardt fronting his own band. Yet he was remote from having a bandleader's temperament. Very much a Gypsy, aware he had a reputation in the non-Gypsy world, he yet found that sphere strange, its values and expectations difficult to grasp. For example, he possessed little sense of time and was often very late for engagements. Other musicians wanting to play with him often had to search long and hard. Yet, as occasionally happens, the problem solved itself.

There is no room to detail the chain of accidental circumstances which led to the founding in 1934 of the Quintet of the Hot Club of France or how its singular all-strings instrumentation was decided. The combination of violin, solo guitar, two rhythm guitars and bass must then have seemed unlikely yet in practice turned out exceptionally well balanced, with a character all its own. Such diverse performances as 'Oriental Shuffle' and 'Mystery Pacific' demonstrate how it gave rise to a whole range of sounds and textures that were fresh to jazz.

There was, however, a problem between Reinhardt and Stéphane Grappelli. It is obvious from their records how well they got on musically, yet in all other respects they were opposites. They never trusted each other and were rivals for so long as Reinhardt lived. It would be foolish to underrate Grappelli. He was the clear-headed, well-organised individual who made sure the Quintet met its obligations, who, often at the cost of enormous trouble, headed-off the worst consequences of Reinhardt's fecklessness and got him to the club, the concert, the recording date more or less on time.

But attempts have been made of recent years to suggest Grappelli was the equal, even the superior, of Reinhardt, which is nonsensical. Grappelli did what he did for the Quintet because, as he always said later, no matter how maddening Reinhardt's behaviour, there was no question that he was a unique being, a genius.

Grappelli's music nowhere pretends to the emotional power, the brilliant originality, the sense of constant discovery that we hear in Reinhardt's finest improvising. Perhaps the guitarist's dissatisfaction with his partner was not just because of Grappelli's role as the Quintet's disciplinarian. He may have felt that Grappelli's contributions were too consistently elegant, too measured,

The first recording session of The Quintet of the Hot Club of France in December 1934 produced four classic tracks, three of which feature on this 1957 EP (left): 'Oh, Lady Be Good', 'I Saw Stars' and 'Dinah'. During a 1937 session, Django was asked to record two pieces entirely solo. With no time to prepare, 'Parfum' and 'Improvisation' (centre) were created on the spot. Both are masterpieces, complete compositions of immense beauty, emotional depth, and technical brilliance. Django played electric guitar on these radio broadcasts from 1947-1950 (above). While his style remained totally personal, he had clearly assimilated some of the rhythmic and harmonic ideas of Charlie Christian and the early bebop pioneers.

to balance the force – sometimes wildness – of his own solos. Certainly Reinhardt's playing still reflected the freedoms of Gypsy music.

To the basic influences of his native tradition were added his personal response to the blues and to the sort of spontaneous linear variations created by American musicians like Coleman Hawkins. An unaccompanied solo such as 'Echoes Of Spain' reflects a non-jazz mode of improvising: European, perhaps with Arabic elements. This point is underlined by the violent flurries of chords and dramatic tremolos found in many of his faster solos, these hinting at a Spanish, maybe even north African, source. And who can say whether his "bending" of melody notes owes more to the blues or to flamenco?

Older Continental jazz hands, people who were around when the Quintet was founded, maintained that the violinist Reinhardt actually wanted in the band was not Grappelli but Michel Warlop. On listening to him and the guitarist on 'Christmas Swing' or 'Sweet Sue' this is plausible, Warlop's playing being driven by a virile temperament and conveying a feeling of genuine risks being taken. Luckily Reinhardt and Warlop several times recorded together and the results could be exceptional, as in the violinist's 'Taj Mahal'. This is a sensitive composition and arrangement by Warlop with oriental overtones which show both him and Reinhardt in an unusual light. How beautifully the violinist controls the level of eloquence in his solo, allowing it to rise thus far and no further!

Although such encounters add to our understanding of Reinhardt's gifts the Quintet remained central to his and Grappelli's activities. The September 1939 outbreak of World War II found them in London. Reinhardt went home immediately, the others soon following, except Grappelli, who remained in London and started an independent career which lasted for decades.

Back in Paris Reinhardt too began a new path. His entry into a long period of intense activity was helped by the existence of a pool of excellent French jazzmen, yet it was ultimately due to quite other circumstances. In 1940 France was defeated and the northern part of the country occupied by the German army. The Germans, at least the Nazis, utterly rejected jazz, yet far from being extinguished it enjoyed a popularity in Occupied France that had no European precedent.

This can be seen in part as a reaction against the gloom of defeat and occupation, but has never been explained completely. All competent jazz musicians were extremely busy and Reinhardt, already famous, became a national figure, rather as did Sidney Bechet in France during the 1950s. Most significant in the present context is that Reinhardt made numerous records, including some of his most interesting and little known.

Inevitably he reorganised the Quintet of the Hot Club of France. Now unequivocally the leader, perhaps not unhappy about Grappelli's absence, he abandoned the all-strings formula, removed one of the guitars and added drums. This obviously changed the group's sound and textures greatly and he supplanted the violin with a clarinet. In fact a succession of clarinettists passed through the band. Hubert Rostaing was first and 'Crepuscule' may be cited as an almost arbitrary sample of the many delightful records made by this edition of the Quintet. Indeed there were many new things Reinhardt wanted to try.

For a start, he sometimes added a second clarinet, this giving him two clarinets, two guitars, bass and drums. Sometimes the second clarinet was Alix Combelle, whose tenor saxophone added yet another voice to the texture, as in

Stephane Grappelli was "rediscovered" in the 1970s and a new generation of audiences worldwide embraced his vivacious and romantic style. British guitarist Martin Taylor (above right) toured and recorded with him for 11 years from the late 1970s and later invited the violinist to record with his own group, Spirit Of Django.

Although different to Django Reinhardt in background and temperament, Stephane Grappelli was a stimulating and inventive musical partner for the maverick Gypsy guitarist. Born in 1908, his mother died when he was young and by the age of 15 Grappelli had to make his own way in the world. He began his career playing in a cinema band and, captivated by the music of Louis Armstrong and Bix Beiderbecke, turned to jazz for his inspiration. He met Django in 1931 and the Quintet was formed two years later.

'Oiseaux des Óles'. This, like 'Crepuscule', was a Reinhardt piece and though he had contributed many ideas to the old Quintet's repertoire it was during the war that he emerged decisively as a real composer. He would spend hours at the piano exploring harmony. "The chords, that's what I like best," he said. "There you have the mother of music. That's why I love Bach so much!" Charles Delaunay, who knew Reinhardt well, wrote that despite his often boorish antics "he was humble where important things were concerned and was always attentive when confronted with a work of art, listening in silence and never venturing to criticise".

The trouble was that Reinhardt could neither read music nor put it on paper and so was dependent on others to write his pieces down. This method has been used by great composers after going blind – Handel and Delius, for example – and allowed them to continue producing fine work. Yet it is bound to be somewhat inflexible. It was hard for Reinhardt to achieve much beyond short big-band pieces such as 'Nymphéas' and 'Féerie'. He dictated many similar items to musicians like Gérard Lévèque, at one time the Quintet's clarinettist. Such scores were dictated line by line off Reinhardt's guitar, which speaks of a well focused musical imagination. Usually they were recorded under the name Django's Music.

And he wanted to undertake larger works, for instance a lengthy treatment for full symphony orchestra of his 'Manoir de Mes Rêves'. This was presumably also to employ chorus, because it was supposed to include a setting of Jean Cocteau. The text was apparently never written but a performance was certainly planned in Paris. It never took place, though, and the full score, on which Lévèque had done so much work, simply disappeared.

Reinhardt also had a long-standing ambition to compose a mass. He did manage to get this performed, even though it was evidently incomplete. Delaunay wrote that its originality greatly impressed musicians who heard it, but no comment is possible because, again, the score vanished. He cherished other hopes too, which if realisable might have taken him further beyond jazz. There have been other such cases, such as Charlie Parker's wish to study with Edgard Varèse and Stefan Wolpe. Yet Reinhardt, like Parker, was never one to study anything except his instrument. Given his ambitions, however, it would have been better if he had learnt not only to read music but to study the technique of composition.

Invariably the response to this is that such "academic" activity would have defiled the "purity" and "innocence" of his inspiration. But such knowledge and skill would have allowed him to give richer form and substance to his teeming musical ideas, beyond improvised guitar solos and laboriously dictated numbers for big band. We can only speculate as to what we lost.

His prodigious creative activities continued throughout the war years, their quality and quantity unaffected by such external events as the allied landings in Normandy or even the liberation of the French capital. True, the latter meant he could record with American musicians again, but they were markedly inferior to those with whom he had worked in Paris in the 1930s. Titles exist by what was called on the original labels "Django and his American Swing Band", actually the big-band of Air Transport Command, stationed at Orly.

Most of the scores, though played with almost ferocious efficiency, followed the standard formulae of second-rank American Swing and lack the individuality of the pieces Reinhardt had painstakingly dictated to Lévèque. A performance like 1945's 'Swing Guitars' is just about recognisable as what the Quintet had recorded a decade before. For the best results it was advisable for Reinhardt to solo throughout, as on the version of Jimmy Lunceford's 'Uptown Blues' taken from a 1945 Salle Pleyel concert. Large band recordings by his all-French ensemble called Django's Music, such as 'Artillerie Lourde' and 'Place de Broukère', however, retained their distinction.

During those war years and after, he recorded with many other groups large and small, under such names as Alix Combelle, Philippe Brun, André Ekyan and Noel Chiboust. On some of these Reinhardt is less prominent, yet his presence is always felt even when he does not solo.

Immediately after the war, the chief event was supposed to be his visit to America. This was something to which he had looked forward for most of his life and he anticipated it would be the climax of his career. In the event it was something like the opposite. He was expected to appear with Duke Ellington's band and arrived extraordinarily late for their first concert – in Carnegie Hall. Ellington, not a man easily ruffled, had to offer an embarrassed apology to the audience for the guitarist's non-arrival, shortly after which Reinhardt strolled on to the stage, deigning to play at last. Later, in Chicago, he and the Ellington band did make a few inconsequential recordings but there is no space here to speak of Reinhardt's unhappy response to America or what this and his initial expectations of the experience tell us about his character.

Despite what might almost be called the systematic indiscipline of his life, it did seem that, with the war over, he would return to earlier professional obligations. Grappelli, still in London, made the first move and it was in London they were reunited, early in 1946. There were even a couple of Decca recording sessions, using the old Quintet instrumentation but with sturdy performances by British musicians. The two principals were clearly on their mettle after several years apart, but matters could never be the same again.

On returning to Paris, Reinhardt often used the clarinet version of the Quintet instrumentation, sometimes with Rostaing, at others with Michel de Villiers, Maurice Meunier or Gérard Lévèque. Yet there were also many more recordings with Grappelli, particularly a long 1949 series taken in Rome with an Italian rhythm section. Jazz was changing, however, as it always does, and Reinhardt was well aware of the fact. He had played Selmer-Maccaferri guitars since about 1937 and after his American visit he fitted a bar pickup to his instrument and used a simple valve amplifier. It was only during his final years, from about 1950, that he went fully electric.

During the late 1940s and early 1950s his style of improvisation was increasingly affected by bop, which, although blessed and cursed as a revolution in jazz was in reality, on rhythmic and harmonic planes, a final intensification of swing. Certainly Reinhardt took to it instinctively. Obviously it did not suit his erstwhile partner, or many of the Quintet's old fans, who asked him, "Why don't you play the way you used to with Grappelli?" But Reinhardt was impatient with such attitudes, being, as his most vivid solos make clear, committed to the present.

Feeling himself somewhat misunderstood, he appeared less in public in his last few years. More or less retired to the village of Samois-sur-Seine, he spent time fishing, painting, playing billiards. Yet Reinhardt still enjoyed performing with French musicians of the modern persuasion at places like the Club St Germain in Paris. There the present writer heard him with Bernard Hulin (trumpet), Hubert Fol (alto), Raymond Fol (piano), Pierre Michelot (bass) and Pierre Lemarchand (drums), a quite boppish group. The guitar improvising was as zestful as ever, and it might be added that at his final recording session, in April 1953, Martial Solal, the great French pianist of the next generation, was present. None of the music represents either participant near his best yet one has the impression of a torch being handed on.

A month later Reinhardt left us. On the morning of May 16th he finished playing at the Club St Germain, caught a train to Avon, the station nearest to Samois, and walked some three miles across the fields. There he had a drink at the local bar and then, quietly and quickly, lost consciousness. He was taken to the hospital at Fontainebleau but soon was gone. On May 19th 1953, the following Tuesday, he was buried at Samois. Selfishly but reasonably, we regret all the music the world lost as a result of Django Reinhardt's death at the early age of 43. Yet his manner of departing is surely to be envied.

DAVE GELLY # CHARLIE CHRISTIAN

IN A RECORDING CAREER LASTING LESS THAN TWO YEARS, CHARLIE CHRISTIAN PIONEERED THE USE OF THE ELECTRIC GUITAR IN JAZZ, ESTABLISHED A FORMIDABLE REPUTATION AS A SOLOIST AND PLAYED A PART IN THE CREATION OF BEBOP.

Charlie Christian at the Waldorf Astoria Hotel, New York, in 1939. Christian was born into a family of musicians who made their living playing music in the streets, but he also received a good foundation in music at school in Oklahoma City. The tenor sax style of Lester Young was an early inspiration and influenced his approach to playing jazz on the guitar.

Jazz history is full of major artists who died young, but Charlie Christian had the shortest career of all. His entire recorded output was achieved within a period of less than two years, between 1939 and 1941. Even more astounding is the impact he made in that brief time, and his lasting effect on jazz guitar style. To this day, despite all that has happened over more than half a century since his death, an echo of Charlie Christian can plainly be heard in the work of virtually every jazz guitarist.

This is partly because of the instrument he played. The guitar had always suffered from the disadvantage of being a quiet instrument. In the jazz rhythm section it acted as half of a kind of composite instrument, guitar-and-bass. The great guitar-bass partnerships of the swing era, such as Basie's Freddie Green and Walter Page, acted as the heartbeat of the band. Listeners and dancers were scarcely aware of their presence, but if they had faltered for an instant the entire organism would have collapsed. Guitar solos were virtually impossible in such circumstances. Only in small bands in small rooms, or on radio or records, did the guitarist get a chance to shine.

Musicians had been experimenting with ways of making the guitar louder since the 1920s, by using metal resonators and other devices. But from the early 1930s they had concentrated increasingly on electrical means. Eddie Durham was an early jazz experimenter in this field. First he placed a microphone close to the soundholes, but that picked up all the surrounding noises, too. Next, he tried fixing the microphone inside the guitar with the help of a wire coathanger. This was better, but the results were uneven and there was a tendency to cause the howling noise known as "feedback". Durham, like Charlie Christian, was working on an amplified rhythm guitar, of the type normally found in swing bands. This is not to be confused with the steel guitar, as played by Floyd Smith with Andy Kirk's Clouds Of Joy. He had a feature number, 'Floyd's Guitar Blues', which he played on an amplified steel guitar, held horizontally, sliding a metal bar along the strings in the Hawaiian manner.

The problem of amplification was finally solved by the invention of the electro-magnetic pickup, in which a string vibrating in a magnetic field causes an electrical current to alternate at the same frequency. The system was perfected by the Gibson company in 1936 and one of the first commercially produced electric guitars, the ES-150, made its trade debut in their 1937 catalogue.

The importance of Charlie Christian to this story is that he already had in his head a fully formed conception of what the electric guitar would do. He heard it as a distinct voice, not just a loud guitar playing guitar-type music but a new instrument, playing single-line solos, like a saxophone or trumpet, with a clear, warm, bell-like sound. So when the ES-150 finally came along he had a whole new musical language ready for it, waiting to be used. Charlie Christian "invented" the electric guitar in the same way that Coleman Hawkins "invented" the tenor saxophone: he was the first to play it with complete authority, and everyone else followed his lead.

Charles Christian was born in Dallas, Texas, on July 29th 1916, into a family of musical entertainers. His father, Edward Christian, was a blind musician and singer of a type common in black American communities at the time, an honourable calling in a tradition with roots in West African culture. Charlie's older brothers, Clarence and Edward, played various string instruments and the family earned its living as a band of strolling players.

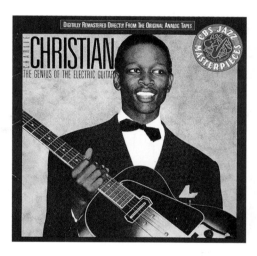

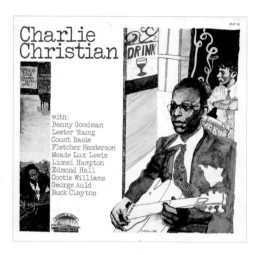

The early lives of most jazz musicians born in the first half of the 20th century are obscure. They came mostly from the poorer sections of society, from one-horse towns or city ghettos where daily life went by unremarked and unrecorded. But, by sheer chance, we know quite a lot about Charlie Christian's boyhood. When he was five, the family moved to Oklahoma City, where the boys attended the Douglass School. Among their fellow students was the future novelist Ralph Ellison, who was later to write that classic of black American literature *Invisible Man*. Ellison's younger brother sat in the same class as Charlie and the two families knew each other well. The picture of their life that Ellison draws, in a 1958 *Saturday Review* article about Christian, is far removed from the squalor and ignorance of popular mythology.

"In the school which we attended," wrote Ellison, "harmony was taught from the ninth through the twelfth grades, there was an extensive and compulsory music appreciation programme, a concert band, an orchestra and several vocal organisations." Clarence Christian had a fine tenor voice and took a leading role in the operettas which the school regularly put on. Ellison also reveals that Charlie and his brothers spent a lot of time in the school's woodwork shop, making their own musical instruments. It may have been poor by American standards, but the community in which Charlie Christian grew up was a striving and cultured one. Catfish Row it wasn't.

Throughout the 1920s and 1930s touring bands travelled the endless dusty roads of the south-west, from Kansas City to Tulsa, Wichita, Texarkana and down through Texas to San Antonio and beyond. Oklahoma City lay in the centre of this vast territory and bands were forever passing through, calling

Charlie Christian's recording career may have lasted less than two years, but his playing was extensively documented from the time he arrived in New York in 1939, and most of his work has been reissued on CD (three examples from many, above). Christian turned out classic solos with Benny Goodman's Sextets and Septets on swing themes such as 'Air Mail Special', 'Seven Come Eleven', 'Wholly Cats' and a 'Smo-o-o-oth One'. On his feature 'Solo Flight' with the Goodman Orchestra, Christian's playing has all the relaxed creativity of tenor-sax star Lester Young. But it is the longer tracks recorded by an admiring fan at late-night jam sessions at Minton's Playhouse that reveal the guitarist's sustained inventiveness and rhythmic brilliance over chorus after chorus of pure improvisation.

in, playing a few dates, picking up and dropping off musicians. It was here, in 1929, that Ellison recalled first hearing the great saxophonist Lester Young, then little more than a teenager, jamming at a shoeshine parlour and causing a sensation with his smooth, agile, endlessly inventive improvisations. Two years after that, Charlie left school and began working with bands. He was at an impressionable age: Lester's sound and approach had a lasting effect upon him and profoundly influenced his own playing.

But jazz was not the only music the young Charlie Christian would have heard. In those days, the population of the western States was still a patchwork of recently-settled ethnic groups, each with its own style of music: German polkas, Irish ballads, "hillbilly" tunes, revivalist hymns. Most pervasive of all was the language of the blues, which flourished vigorously in the south-west and spread its accents far beyond the limits of the black community.

Then there was radio, which brought the popular music of the big cities to the remotest part of the country. "This was the era of radio," Ralph Ellison recalled, "and for a while a local newspaper gave away cheap plastic recordings of such orchestras as Jean Goldkette's along with subscriptions." Goldkette ran one of the leading white dance bands of the day, through whose ranks passed some fine players, including the great cornettist Bix Beiderbecke.

So Charlie Christian, growing up at a time and in a place where jazz was developing with unprecedented vigour, enjoyed a rich and varied musical education.

Clarence Christian formed his own band, the Jolly Jugglers, in which Charlie played both guitar and bass before moving on to a series of other jobs with travelling bands. Exactly when he played with which band during the 1930s is impossible to pin down, although he was certainly a member of Alphonso Trent's orchestra in 1938.

It is also impossible to know just when he began experimenting with guitar amplification, but he was certainly doing so in the mid-1930s, because people remembered hearing him play amplified guitar. Guitarist Mary Osborne recalled standing outside a cabaret in Bismarck, North Dakota, in about 1934 and hearing what she thought was a tenor saxophone being played into a microphone. On going inside, she discovered that it was Charlie, playing a guitar with a microphone attached to it.

Mary Osborne was not the only one to notice the young Charlie Christian. His name increasingly came up in musicians' gossip as a player to watch out for. That was how reputations began in those days, especially for those working a long way from the entertainment centres of New York, Chicago and Los Angeles; but to consolidate a reputation a musician would have to move to one of these centres or join a nationally known touring band. Charlie's opportunity came when news of him reached record producer and jazz promoter John Hammond.

It was Hammond who, a few years earlier, had discovered Billie Holiday singing in a Harlem dive and brought Count Basie's band from Kansas City for its New York debut. He was permanently on the lookout for jazz talent and would go to great lengths to track it down.

In the early summer of 1939, Hammond was due to fly from New York to Los Angeles to supervise a recording session by his brother-in-law, Benny Goodman. The reports about the sensational young guitarist in Oklahoma City had been arriving thick and fast and he determined to make a detour, to hear for himself. Hammond posted a letter to Charlie, care of the Ritz Cafe, Oklahoma City, and set off on the tortuous, 20-hour flight.

"Staggering out of the plane, beat and airsick," Hammond wrote in his memoirs, "I looked around for a cab, but I was set upon by six guys in a decrepit Buick. The entire band was there to escort me first to the hotel and then to the Ritz Cafe.

"Charlie used amplification sparingly when playing rhythm but turned it up for his solos, which were as exciting improvisations as I had ever heard on any instrument, let alone guitar. Before an hour had passed I was determined to place Charlie with Benny Goodman," he wrote.

Goodman's radio show had a budget allowing for a different guest soloist each week and Hammond calculated that this would cover Charlie's air fare to California and a Union-scale fee. Together they set off, arriving in time for the recording session and hoping that they could persuade Goodman to audition Charlie when the session was over.

"Benny was too preoccupied to pay him the slightest attention. All that he could perceive was a country bumpkin in a cowboy hat, tight, pointed shoes and a purple shirt with matching bow tie, and he thought it unlikely that such a kid could produce any memorable music. I couldn't even get Benny to listen to him."

Goodman's band was opening that night at the smart Victor Hugo Hotel in Beverly Hills. Blacks were not admitted as customers, and the management was distinctly unhappy about the fact that the band contained two black musicians. Nevertheless, Hammond smuggled Charlie in via the kitchen, waited for the band to take an interval, crept onto the stage and set up Charlie's guitar. When Goodman returned, to play a set with his quartet, there was Charlie, in purple-shirted splendour, all ready to play.

There was not much that Benny could do about it, without causing an unseemly fuss in public, so he called the first tune, 'Rose Room'.

"After the opening choruses, Benny pointed to Charlie to take a solo, and the number, which ordinarily lasted three minutes stretched out to 45! Everybody got up from the tables and clustered around the bandstand, and there could be no doubt that perhaps the most spectacularly original soloist ever to play with Goodman had been launched."

What was so special about Charlie Christian's playing? In the first place there was the novelty of the sound. In Charlie's hands, if it sounded like anything else at all, it resembled the cool tenor saxophone sound of Lester Young.

But Charlie's appeal as an artist went far beyond mere novelty. He was one of those rare individuals who seem somehow to be made out of music. The lines that flow from him with such grace are like the flight of birds, free and unforced, emerging without any apparent effort. Yet every note is minutely judged, every phrase has a rhythmic charge and turns at some harmonically apt point. And the sheer, unhesitating precision of his playing is a wonder in itself. Everything about a Charlie Christian solo is so deliciously, intoxicatingly right that it is impossible not to laugh with pure pleasure.

Goodman hired Charlie on the spot, incorporating him into his sextet (later septet), the small group of soloists drawn from the full band which was a feature of every show. He soon proved to be much more than a virtuoso soloist. His experience with south-western bands, many of whom did not bother much with written music, had left him with a marvellous facility for

Eddie Durham was trombonist, guitarist and admired arranger for Count Basie and other top bands. From the early 1930s he experimented with various ways of amplifying the guitar, including resonator instruments as well as placing microphones in soundholes. Durham recorded on electric guitar with Basie and the Kansas City Six as early as 1938.

devising instant themes, riffs and backing figures. These sextet and septet recordings of 1940-41 sound different from other Goodman small-band records because they are largely, in all but name, the work of Charlie Christian.

It is possible to hear one of these pieces evolving on a test recording that fortunately survives. On March 13th 1941 the septet was due to record at Columbia's New York studios. Benny had not yet arrived, the engineers were testing the equipment and the musicians were warming up. Out of the random scatter of notes and phrases comes Charlie's guitar, swinging purposefully. Soon a little riff begins to emerge, the piano fits an accompaniment and everybody joins in. Eventually the engineer calls "Stand by, ten seconds" and the music vanishes. Later on the same day, the full septet recorded that same riff, tidied up and entitled 'A Smooth One'. It became one of Goodman's most popular small-band numbers.

Altogether, Charlie recorded around 25 numbers with the Goodman sextet and septet, plus a few with the big-band, including his feature, 'Solo Flight', where he has rather more space than usual to stretch out. The two exuberant takes of 'Solo Flight' convey his fluent style to perfection. At the same time, he was able to record the occasional session in other company. There is a strange but lovely set with clarinettist Edmund Hall, pianist Meade Lux Lewis (playing celeste, of all things) and bassist Israel Crosby, on which Charlie plays acoustic guitar. He can also be heard playing acoustic rhythm guitar on several small-band sessions led by Lionel Hampton. An unsuspected rarity surfaced in the 1970s – a single unissued session by a trial version of Goodman's septet with Lester Young playing tenor saxophone. Apparently, Goodman originally wanted Lester as a member of the band, but the two simply could not get along. The only other examples of Lester and Charlie playing together are three numbers recorded at a Carnegie Hall concert in December 1939.

In his brief career Charlie never once recorded as leader, despite the fact that, by the end of his first full year in the Goodman spotlight, fans had voted him Top Guitarist in *Metronome* magazine's annual poll. He seems to have been genuinely unconcerned about that kind of success. But he did have another, more intense musical life.

In October 1940 a new nightclub, Minton's Playhouse, opened at the Hotel Cecil on 118th Street in Harlem. Monday nights, the usual night-off for musicians in regular jobs, soon became established as jam-session nights. It was at Minton's that the new jazz generation began hatching the musical revolution that became known as bebop. Thelonious Monk, Dizzy Gillespie and Charlie Parker were among the leading lights, and so was Charlie Christian. He was the most regular attender of all, arriving early and not leaving until the last note had been played. Minton's manager, the former bandleader Teddy Hill, could not get enough of the young genius who had landed so unexpectedly in their midst. "Where did he come from?" he kept demanding in wondering tones. Hill bought a brand-new guitar amplifier and kept it at Minton's for Charlie's exclusive use.

Luckily, another Minton's regular was a young fan named Jerry Newman, who owned a portable disc recorder (this was before the days of tape), and used it to capture some of the Monday-night music, especially Charlie's contributions. The recordings which survive are invaluable, because they catch Charlie in full flow, improvising at far greater length than on any commercial recording. Each of Charlie's solos would take up a whole side of a conventional

12-inch, 78 rpm record. The four surviving pieces, incomplete and rough though they are, show that Charlie was not really a bebopper, despite the presence of Monk and drummer Kenny Clarke in the rhythm section, but, like Lester Young, an advanced and subtle exponent of classic swing.

At the start of 1939 Charlie Christian was earning $10 a week at the Ritz Cafe, Oklahoma City. By the end of the year his income had jumped to an average $250 a week. He was 23 years old, voted America's top guitarist, featured soloist with the King Of Swing, and having the time of his life. "Everybody loved Charlie," recalled swing journalist Bill Simon. "The chicks all mothered him and the musicians kidded him good-naturedly." Temperance and early nights were clearly not on the agenda. Like all happy young people, Charlie simply assumed that he was immortal, but his time was running out.

He was taken ill in June 1941, while on tour with Goodman. It turned out that he had contracted tuberculosis early in life. The disease had lain dormant but now flared up thanks to his hectic new lifestyle. Charlie was sent to Seaview Sanitorium on Staten Island. Count Basie's doctor kept an eye on him, Teddy Hill came every week, bearing fried chicken and other delicacies, well-meaning cronies brought gifts of whisky and dope. He began to improve, but was finding life dull. One night he slipped away with some pals for a spot of off-limits carousing, caught a chill and died on March 2nd 1942.

Without the electric guitar Charlie Christian might never have found his voice and realised his genius. Equally, without Charlie Christian the electric guitar might have remained a mere curio in the attic of musical history.

Charlie Christian with Georgie Auld (tenor sax), Benny Goodman (clarinet), Cootie Williams (trumpet) and Artie Bernstein (bass) at the nucleus of Goodman's small band that recorded 'Wholly Cats', 'Benny's Bugle' and 'Breakfast Feud', immortalised by Christian's swinging guitar solos.

SWING TO BOP

THE BRIEF BUT EXPLOSIVE CAREER OF CHARLIE CHRISTIAN
LASTED LONG ENOUGH FOR HIS INFLUENCE TO SPREAD
THROUGHOUT THE JAZZ WORLD. PLAYERS IN BIG BANDS AND
SMALL GROUPS ALIKE SOON EMBRACED BEBOP AND THE
ELECTRIC GUITAR.

The pervasive influence of Charlie Christian continued unabated through the 1940s and well into the following three decades. To some extent, it continues today.

Christian's exceptional technique, his innovative ideas and his use of the electric guitar, would have a positive effect on both established practitioners and aspiring younger players. His musical vocabulary shared much with that of the great tenor saxophone stylist Lester Young, and his approach to improvisation, like Young's, would prove to be important in the emergence and development of jazz's greatest revolution: bebop.

Of the numerous Charlie Christian disciples to become influential from the 1950s onwards, the two most important were Barney Kessel (b.1923, Muskogee, Oklahoma) and Mitchell Herbert "Herb" Ellis (b.1921, Farmersville, Texas). Kessel and Ellis had similar musical backgrounds, embracing jazz and blues. Even though the two Mid-Westerners acquired their early professional experience with a variety of Swing Era bands – large and small – they were also deeply affected by the New Music being created by such as Charlie Parker, Dizzy Gillespie, Thelonious Monk and Bud Powell. Both would also interact with a natural ease – and no stylistic obstacles – with most, if not all, of the champions of bebop.

Barney Kessel bought his first guitar at the age of 12 and was playing with a local black group two years later – the only white musician in the band. Although Muskogee was a small town, many touring bands passed through the area and Kessel would jam with these musicians after hours. At the age of 16 his destiny was shaped by the profound experience of meeting and jamming with his hero Charlie Christian, whose music he knew from recordings and broadcasts with Benny Goodman. Within a year, he had left Muskogee for Los Angeles, determined to make his career in music.

There, Barney Kessel worked initially as a dishwasher, doing the occasional casual gig, before his ability and enthusiasm landed him the guitar chair with the Chico Marx Band. Under the direction of Ben Pollack, this band was formed to accompany the Marx Brother in his stage shows and it included several leading jazz musicians. A good electric guitarist was always in demand by bandleaders, and by 1947 Barney had played in the big bands of Charlie Barnet, Hal McIntyre, Benny Goodman and Artie Shaw. Even before this, in 1944, he had been on hand to appear in *Jammin' the Blues*, an Oscar-nominated movie short, alongside such luminaries as Lester Young, trumpeter Harry Edison, and drummer Sidney Catlett. But for an eager youngster like Kessel, the single most important event in his developing career took place in 1947: a chance to record with Charlie Parker, at what would later be

*Herb Ellis in London during the 1960s
(above left). Ellis is in inspired form on
Nothing But The Blues from 1957
(above), digging deep into his blues roots,
aided and abetted by Roy Eldridge
(trumpet) and Stan Getz (tenor sax). This
CD reissue includes four bonus tracks also
featuring Dizzy Gillespie, Coleman
Hawkins and Ellis's long-time boss,
pianist Oscar Peterson.*

acclaimed as a classic bebop session. Kessel's Christian-based guitar sounded not at all out of place, supplying distinctive introductions, accompaniments and fills. Parker allocated him generous solo space and his relaxed, yet positive, contributions (including the four takes needed to complete 'Relaxin' At Camarillo') reveal a confident and accomplished improviser.

But the event which would ultimately make Barney Kessel both a national and international name took place in 1952, when he joined the Oscar Peterson Trio for a Jazz At The Philharmonic tour that embraced 14 countries. This, in turn, led to recordings with Peterson and a score of illustrious jazz names recorded and presented in concert by Norman Granz. Oscar Peterson was a brilliant pianist and his Trio, which also featured bassist Ray Brown, was one of the hottest properties in jazz. In the 1950s and 1960s, Kessel became a mainstay of Los Angeles' television, radio and recording studios. He was particularly in demand to accompany top jazz vocalists such as Sarah Vaughan, Ella Fitzgerald and Anita O'Day. His guitar introduction and backup on Julie London's 1955 recording of 'Cry Me A River' is legendary.

Apart from one album for Atomic Records in 1945 and the compilation album *Swing Guitars*, for which Oscar Moore, Tal Farlow and he each contributed four tracks, Barney did not record in his own name as a leader until November 1953. The 1950s and 1960s were to prove a fruitful period, in which he cut some of the finest recordings of his career for Contemporary Records. *To Swing Or Not To Swing, Some Like It Hot*, and *Let's Cook!* are probably the best, but the overall standard of performance is high. Kessel's chord-melody skills are to the fore on ballads, which he interprets with beautifully stated harmonies, but ever-swinging solo lines, blues-tinged inflections and imaginative accompaniments also characterise his style. Barney was by now the best-known and most popular jazz guitarist in the US, winning the jazz guitar polls year after year in magazines such as *Down Beat*, *Esquire*, *Playboy*, *Metronome* and *Melody Maker*. This led to a series of superb "Poll Winners" albums for the Contemporary label, with bassist Ray Brown and drummer Shelly Manne, showcasing the guitar trio format and demonstrating how well the guitar could substitute for piano in a jazz setting.

In 1968, Barney Kessel left the studios to make a European tour as part

On the classic tracks on Nat King Cole Trio 1943-1947 (1994 CD reissue, above) Oscar Moore defines the role of the guitar in a piano trio, laying down solid rhythm, providing chordal stabs and single-string fills, playing unison lines with the piano, and unfolding perfectly-shaped solos. Herb Ellis is featured in 1998 at age 76 in Hamburg, Germany, on Burnin' (centre), swinging just as hard as he did at 36. The trio album Poll Winners Three! from 1960 (right) with bassist Ray Brown and drummer Shelly Manne illustrates Barney Kessel's all-round mastery. He displays imaginative introductions, delicate chordal-melody on the ballad 'Easy Living', driving solos at up-tempos, and rousing chordal "shout choruses".

of Guitar Workshop (with Jim Hall, George Benson, Larry Coryell and veteran Elmer Snowden). The following year he moved to London, to live and work in the UK and Europe. By late 1970, he had returned to the US to resume his busy studio-plus-gigs schedule in the United States, including playing on the soundtrack of four Elvis Presley movies. But the life of a studio musician was no longer so attractive to him and he opted to make jazz his priority. In 1974 Kessel was invited to form a guitar trio to tour Australia, for which he teamed up with Herb Ellis and Charlie Byrd. This formula was an immediate success and The Great Guitars, as they became known, toured world-wide for almost two decades, recording several albums. Barney also toured the US and Europe as a solo act with local rhythm sections.

In 1992, following a Great Guitars tour of Australia, Kessel suffered a stroke, leaving him partly paralysed, wheelchair-bound, and unable to play the guitar or even to speak. With typical determination, Barney patiently worked to reduce his disability, working on his speech until he was able to resume his one-to-one teaching.

Herb Ellis's career differed from Kessel's in that at first he played with local Texan bands but not, as he has firmly maintained, with country, hillbilly or Western Swing bands. After graduating from North Texas State University, he found his career in music developed more slowly than he would have wished. His first break was with the Casa Loma Orchestra (1944), switching to the Jimmy Dorsey Orchestra (1945-1947). Together with two ex-Dorsey colleagues – pianist Lou Carter and bassist John Frigo – Ellis then formed Soft Winds, an instrumental-vocal combo that enjoyed a measure of nationwide success. Two of its jointly composed originals – 'Detour Ahead' and 'I Told Ya I Love Ya, Now Get Out' – proved popular favourites.

In 1953, following the break up of Soft Winds, Ellis replaced Barney Kessel in the Oscar Peterson Trio. He has often remarked that he truly came of age during that six-year stint. Certainly, his Charlie Christian-inspired solos demonstrate a newly-found maturity. The often complex interplay between guitar and piano, particularly during the typically whirlwind arrangements of the Trio, plus his basic rhythm guitar duties, all presented additional challenges. During this time Ellis introduced what he calls his "bongo rhythm" – generating a percussive sound by tapping the body of his Gibson ES-175 guitar – which helped to compensate for the absence of a drummer.

With the Trio, Herb recorded prodigiously. He also took over from Kessel as house-guitarist for Norman Granz's labels, supporting a veritable *Who's*

Al Casey on guitar with Fats Waller And His Rhythm at an RCA Victor recording session, New York, 1938.

Who of the most important jazz players of the 1950s and 1960s. He also toured globally with Granz's Jazz At The Philharmonic troupe; and there were further separate tours, at home and abroad, for the Peterson Trio. During this halcyon period, with its marathon record sessions, Herb Ellis was occasionally invited to make albums under his own name. The finest of these remains *Nothing But The Blues* (1957), with the leader firmly and dynamically back to his roots. Apart from the authenticity of his blues statements, there is a consistency throughout which even he hasn't quite surpassed, before or since.

Ellis spent most of 1959 with Ella Fitzgerald; something he would repeat from time to time until 1962. But for more than 16 years from 1956, now married and wishing to cut back on touring, he worked primarily as a studio guitar player in and around Los Angeles, spending much of his time inside television studios, as part of the resident bands of top shows such as those of Steve Allen (1961-1964) and Regis Philbin (1964-1965). In 1971 he started to perform with Joe Pass: they were two great players with compatible, but different, styles. This happy musical union is immortalised on the excellent albums *Seven Come Eleven* and *Two For The Road*. Turning his back on commercial studio work in the early 1970s, Herb strengthened his jazz profile by a string of albums for Concord Jazz, and occasional solo tours, but it was his work with The Great Guitars from 1974 onward that won him a new generation of jazz listeners, who enjoyed the same qualities that he had brought to the Oscar Peterson Trio in the early 1950s: his vibrant, hard-swing style, always carrying the message of Charlie Christian and his own blues background, and tinged with his debt to Charlie Parker.

Of the best swing era guitarists whose own styles evolved from the Christian mould, three would work at various times as sidemen with vocalist Nat King Cole. Oscar Frederic Moore (1912-1981) was arguably the most famous. Throughout his career, Moore's elegantly-articulated single-string playing and tasty chordal work earned him the respect and admiration of fellow guitar players. Although most of his life in music revolved around Cole, with whom he spent the years 1937 to 1947, he did perform with equal distinction with Art Tatum, Lionel Hampton, and others. After leaving Cole, he spent some years with brother Johnny Moore as a member of The Three Blazers, but his career was to remain low-key. Adhering to the Christian approach, Moore became intrigued with bebop without ever making the fundamental change from swing to bop. Still, it was Leonard Feather who perceptively pointed out Moore's use of a ninth chord with a flattened fifth at the conclusion to the Cole Trio's recording of 'That Ain't Right' (Feather called it "a daring innovation" for 1941).

Moore's replacement with Cole was Irving C Ashby (1920-1987). A New England Conservatory graduate, he had already built up a healthy reputation – playing solos and rhythm-guitar – with the first Hampton big band, with Jazz At The Philharmonic and Gene Norman Presents Just Jazz concerts and through numerous gigs and jam sessions in and around Los Angeles. Spending three years with Nat King Cole from 1947, his name became widely-known: something which continued when he worked with the Oscar Peterson Trio in 1952 and joined the first Jazz At The Philharmonic trip to Europe. In the 1960s Ashby withdrew from music to concentrate on outside activities.

Dizzy Gillespie, along with scores of other top musicians, admired the playing of the superbly gifted John Elbert Collins (b.1913). Collins' impeccable technique, his sophisticated harmonic sense and supreme versatility enabled him to perform with enviable ease in the company of some of the greatest jazz players, including Dizzy Gillespie, Count Basie, Benny Carter, Lester Young and Fletcher Henderson, in a career that spanned six decades. His infinite good taste also made him a favourite among vocalists such as Ella Fitzgerald, Frank Sinatra, Nancy Wilson and Carmen McRae.

Collins first played with a band led by his mother and went on to gain rich professional experience with virtuoso pianist Art Tatum (1934), and the fiery Roy Eldridge band (1936-1939). Other combos which benefited from his presence included those led by bassist Slam Stewart (1946-1948) and pianist Billy Taylor (1949-1951). But it was his long spell with Nat King Cole (1951-1965) that sealed his professional reputation although, as Collins admits, guitar solos became an increasing rarity during the later years. That his was a lasting talent can be gauged from his contributions to recordings by Snooky Young (1979) and Carmen McRae (1984).

Albert Aloysius Casey (b.1945) will be always remembered principally as the longest-serving guitar player with Fats Waller's famous "Rhythm" combo: he spent a decade (1934-1943) with the great pianist-vocalist, and his most famous recorded solo ('Buck Jumpin'') was made with Waller in 1941. Even so, Casey's musical career ranged reasonably far and wide, working and recording with some of the finest in the business: Billie Holiday, Chuck Berry, Earl Hines, Teddy Wilson and, during the 1970s and 1980s, with such as Helen Humes, Jay McShann, Milt Buckner and the Harlem Blues & Jazz Band. In addition, his Christian-influenced guitar was heard during the post-Waller period with the likes of Charlie Parker, Lester Young and Dizzy Gillespie, particularly during his own Trio's residency at the Downbeat Club. Although for years he had favoured acoustic guitar, he went electric with the R&B outfits fronted by King Curtis and ex-Hampton drummer Curley Hamner. Albert Casey returned to jazz full-time in 1973. His blues-based single-string and chordal playing was a welcome sound on the jazz scene.

Lloyd "Tiny" Grimes (1917-1989) shared an affinity for both blues and jazz with Al Casey. A former pianist and dancer, he was a four-string tenor guitarist whose first exposure came in 1940 with The Cats & The Fiddle, a combo which combined out-and-out jazz with novelty. The following year he moved to California where at a jam session he met Art Tatum. Obviously impressed, Tatum asked him to join the new trio with bassist Slam Stewart. Even though he always rated his three years with Tatum as his career highlight, Grimes was honest enough to admit he hadn't the technical skills

John Collins at Associated Redifussion Television Studio, Wembley, England, in October 1960. A fine accompanist, Collins worked with vocalists Nat King Cole, Bobby Troup, Ella Fitzgerald, Frank Sinatra, Sammy Davis Jr, Carmen McRae and Nancy Wilson.

for what must have been an awesome task. Grimes' other claim to fame was to invite Charlie Parker to make his first recording after leaving the Jay McShann big band in 1944 with a Grimes quartet.

Grimes' Rocking Highlanders combo attained some popularity, both on 52nd Street and elsewhere, but folded when he moved out of New York in 1947. After spending the 1950s in Philadelphia, he was back in New York the following decade, for regular work. He visited Europe with Milt Buckner in 1968 and Jay McShann in 1970 and appeared at the Nice Jazz Festival in 1980. For the remaining years of Tiny Grimes, life, his direct, swinging, guitar style kept him gigging more or less full-time.

Acknowledged by her peers as much for her admirable versatility as for the excellence of her expertly-placed single-string solos, Mary Osborne (1921-1992) was renowned also for her positive rhythmic abilities. One of the few female guitarists to make the jazz big-time, Osborne found her jazz direction after she had heard a youthful Charlie Christian with the Alphonso Trent band. She even managed to talk with the man who, from that night, would become her all-time musical idol. It was after that Charlie Christian gig, in her native Bismarck, North Dakota, that she changed to amplified guitar. For about a year she performed regularly on Pittsburgh radio station KDKA, thereafter touring with various bands, including one led by violinist Joe Venuti. In the early 1940s she arrived in New York with Winifred McDonald's combo, staying on when that band broke up in 1945.

Throughout the late 1940s she was active on the 52nd Street scene and could be heard with such high-flying artists as Coleman Hawkins, Mary Lou Williams, Beryl Booker, Mercer Ellington and Wynonie Harris. She recorded with her own combo at this time but turned freelance following the group's break-up in 1949. In 1968, she and her trumpeter husband Ralph Scaffidi moved to Bakersfield, California. Osborne taught both jazz and classical guitar and played jazz gigs in the Los Angeles area, including a concert at the Hollywood Bowl (1973). Her appearance at the 1981 Kool Jazz Festival was warmly received. It was Osborne's last major gig, and in the same year she recorded the final album under her own name.

STAN BRITT # THE BEBOP MASTERS

AFTER A SLOW START, AND DESPITE ITS GREAT TECHNICAL DEMANDS, BEBOP SOON CAME TO BE ONE OF THE DOMINANT STYLES OF JAZZ GUITAR. EVEN SO, IT WAS NEVER AN EASY CAREER PATH TO FOLLOW, AS THE MIXED FORTUNES OF SOME OF ITS GREATEST EXPONENTS GO TO SHOW.

The bebop guitarist Barry Galbraith once said jazz guitar is "nothing to mess with unless you're serious". While most practitioners of the art, however talented or quick to learn, might tend to agree with this statement, it must have been especially true for those who, like the talented Galbraith himself, committed themselves to the bebop cause.

Bebop, the new language of jazz that evolved during the 1940s, presented a new level of complexity to its mainly youthful aspirants. Its harmonies, melodic lines and rhythms were sophisticated and demanding, both intellectually and in terms of sheer technical skill, for many instrumentalists.

For guitarists it required a high level of technical competence and a radical review of the standard approach to playing the instrument. This may explain, in part at least, why there were precious few bebop-based guitar players during the movement's formative years. And somehow, despite the gradual move from acoustic to amplified guitar, the instrument failed to achieve the same kind of impact as trumpet or saxophone: certainly, in terms of the sheer excitement generated by the likes of Gillespie and Parker.

The pioneering work of bop-influenced guitarists such as Barry Galbraith only began to attract a reasonable audience at the tail-end of the 1940s. It would take until the middle of the next decade before bop guitar (or even bop-derived guitar) would elevate the new stylists of the era to a deservedly high status or foster a growing number of highly individual players in their own right. Only from the mid 1950s did the early bop pioneers of the guitar exercise a truly positive – even profound, in some cases – influence on their contemporaries, as well as on a new generation of aspirants.

It is a curious fact, perhaps, but all the leading masters of bop guitar were white. Bearing in mind that bebop started among black musicians, the lack of a leading black bebop guitarist in the 1940s might explain the late emergence of bebop guitar. Nevertheless, a handful of white guitarists did manage to work alongside some at least of the major figures, mostly on record dates.

Bebop's most famous figurehead, Charlie Parker, became the guitarists' major inspiration – as indeed he was to practically all other aspiring instrumentalists in the 1940s. Even though their experiences alongside this undoubted genius were sporadic, the inspiration afforded to such as Bill De Arango, Arv Garrison, Mundell Lowe and Remo Palmier would be profound - as they would attest, many times over, in later years.

William "Bill" De Arango and Arvin Charles "Arv" Garrison shared not only a native state and a youthful interest in bop. They also had regrettably short careers in the limelight.

A former Dixieland guitarist, Bill De Arango (b.1921, Cleveland, Ohio)

Mundell Lowe worked with the bands of Ray McKinley, Mary Lou Williams, Fats Navarro and Benny Goodman in the 1940s and 1950s and recorded with Charlie Parker, Buck Clayton and Lester Young. His success as a composer and arranger for film and TV interrupted his performing career for several years from the mid 1960s.

arrived in New York after his US Army service, and his fluent guitar lines could soon be heard on 52nd Street with tenor saxophonist Ben Webster. In 1945 he had a golden opportunity to appear on what was to become a classic bebop record date under the leadership of Dizzy Gillespie. Even though solo space was limited, his beautifully articulated contributions to 'Ol' Man Rebop' and 'Anthropology' showed just how quickly – and well – he had begun to absorb the bebop language.

Yet even with this kind of promise of things to come, a substantial career failed to materialise. He recorded just one album under his own name, *Bill De Arango*, released in 1954. By 1948, he had returned to his hometown. In the 1960s and 1970s he ran his own music shop, and for the last 50 years has played locally. At Gunther Schüller's suggestion, De Arango recorded again in the mid 1990s for GM Recordings, and showed just how much he had kept in touch with post-bop developments in the succeeding years.

Arvin Charles "Arv" Garrison (b.1922, Toledo, Ohio) had a similarly brief involvement with the New York jazz scene in general and 1940s bebop in particular. His first important period covered 1941 to 1948, when he fronted his own trio. In 1946 that became the Vivien Garry Trio, led by the bass player to whom he was married. Garrison's star shone brightly in that year after he took part in West Coast recording dates headlined by Dizzy Gillespie, Charlie Parker and Howard McGhee. The Parker date was the most important, with Garrison also playing alongside Lucky Thompson, Miles Davis and Dodo Marmarosa. His solos on such numbers as 'A Night in Tunisia' and 'Yardbird Suite', like those by De Arango with Gillespie, give a positive indication of his bebop appreciation. But, like De Arango, this promising career was never fulfilled. By the mid-1950s he was back in Toledo, where he continued to gig, right up until his premature death in 1960.

The careers of Mundell Lowe and Remo Palmier proved very different. Both spent much time as studio-session players. They would also perform in the highest company – including that of Parker.

Mundell Lowe (b.1922, Laurel, Mississippi) started his career after leaving home at 13. In New York, his obvious playing ability and enviable musical versatility quickly enabled him to become perhaps the most in-demand guitarist in the Big Apple. During the late-1940s, and through the 1950s, his credits included work with Billie Holiday, Lester Young, Red Norvo, Charles Mingus, Helen Humes, Stan Getz and Charlie Parker. His beautifully unhurried approach, elegant tone and cleanly-picked single-string playing can be appreciated, even at stratospheric tempos, on Parker's famous Rockland Palace recordings. One of the great accompanists, his skills are featured on the classic Sarah Vaughan album *After Hours*.

The 1960s found him inside TV studios, first in New York and then Los Angeles. Writing commissions increased significantly for TV and movies, obliging him to cut back on live performances, although he continued to record. He did manage to fit in a performance at the White House with Peggy Lee, several tours of Japan with Benny Carter, and a 1974 tour of Europe with singer Betty Bennett, but composing remained Lowe's priority until the early 1980s when he decided to concentrate again on a performing career. In 1983 his quartet Transit West, with Sam Most on saxophone and flute alongside bassist Monty Budwig and drummer Nick Ceroli, appeared at the Monterey Jazz Festival. Since then Mundell Lowe has performed world-wide as a solo artist and with the Andre Previn Trio in Japan (1992), North America (1993) and Europe (1995).

Remo Palmier (b.1923) grew up in New York City and started playing the guitar at the age of 10. He had his initial exposure to jazz guitar from the recordings of Django Reinhardt and Charlie Christian. He had painted from an early age, but his intention to make that his career was subverted by his growing interest in jazz.

After a period of intense music study, he landed his first full-time professional job with pianist Nat Jaffe's Trio in 1942. His rapid development and sure-fingered, Christian-based work came to the attention of a succession of jazz notables, including Coleman Hawkins (1943), Red Norvo (1944) and Billie Holiday. Further exposure came when Palmieri (he spelt his name with a final "i", in those days) appeared with another famous jazz vocalist, Mildred Bailey, during her 1944 CBS radio series. He was also a regular with pianist-composer Phil Moore's band at Cafe Society.

Palmier had been a convert to bebop from the moment he first experienced the music of Dizzy Gillespie and its other pioneers. Like fellow guitarists De Arango and Lowe, he assimilated the vocabulary and structures of bebop in an impressively short time.

A signal honour came when he was invited to record in the company of Dizzy Gillespie and Charlie Parker, at a session which produced three classic bebop sides - 'Groovin' High', 'Dizzy Atmosphere' and 'All The Things You Are'. In the same year Palmier accepted an invitation to become house guitarist on *The Arthur Godfrey Show* at CBS radio, a position he held for almost 30 years. This placed his jazz career in abeyance until 1972, when he

Jimmy Raney at the Pizza Express Jazz Club in London during 1985. Raney's musical partnership with saxophonist Stan Getz in the early 1950s established his credentials both as a sophisticated jazz guitarist and as a resourceful composer. In spite of an erratic career, there are many fine recordings of his work.

appeared with his Quartet in a New York jazz club.

Two years later he joined the Benny Goodman Orchestra for several major concerts. In 1976 he recorded a duo album with Herb Ellis for Concord Jazz and two years later he finally recorded his first album as a leader: *Remo Palmier*. Since then, Palmier has continued to work in the studios and play the occasional jazz gig.

While there is little doubting the individual talents of the above quartet – or, indeed, some others, still to be remembered – few would disagree that the two major figures of the genre were Talmadge Holt "Tal" Farlow (b.1921, Greensboro, North Carolina; d.1998, Sea Bright, New Jersey) and James Elbert "Jimmy" Raney (b.1927, Louisville, Kentucky; d.1995, Louisville).

During their respective lifetimes, Farlow's awesome, but well-deserved, reputation among both aficionados and the general jazz public invariably scored over his long-time friend Jimmy Raney. In terms of absolute technique, Farlow's exquisite fireworks and close attention to detail probably shaded the other man's undoubted all-round expertise. Yet Raney's contributions to the bebop area of jazz guitar are second-to-none. In terms of direct influence on their own work, there was no dispute – Charlie Christian to begin with, then Charlie Parker. Farlow, though, had another original signpost – the pianistic genius of Art Tatum. Both guitarists, however, shared a permanent desire to crank the amplification down, not up. Superior technique notwithstanding, neither man lacked real warmth or the powers of basic communication.

Farlow's professional career began at the relatively late age of 22; Raney was already working with local Louisville bands at 15. But, as with Raney, Farlow's long and distinguished career was interrupted from time to time by periods of self-imposed semi-retirement. Indeed, after marrying for the first time in 1958 and relocating to Sea Bright, New Jersey, an on-off work pattern ensued for almost 20 years. Raney, too had a fairly lengthy

interval of near-retirement (between 1964 and 1972) after returning to Louisville from New York.

In his virtual semi-retirement, Tal Farlow often reverted to sign-painting, the trade to which his banjoist-guitarist father had apprenticed him after school days. For a time he even had his own sign shop. Despite this low professional profile, however, he never stopped playing the guitar.

Self-taught, and a Christian devotee after hearing the Texan on radio broadcasts with Benny Goodman, Farlow found his first gig outside his home town as a member of pianist Dardanelle's combo. Once in New York, he heard at first-hand the many and marvellous sounds which came about nightly, in and around 52nd Street, including bebop and, of course, Charlie Parker. A similar event took place during Jimmy Raney's developing career. For him, it happened during his two-month tenure with the Jerry Wald band. His conversion to bebop was immediate, helped no little by Wald's pianist, Al Haig – soon to become an integral part of the New York bebop scene.

After returning to Louisville to rethink his whole musical strategy, Raney relocated to Chicago, where his career proper started. Here he was heard by, and played with, Tiny Kahn, a most talented, if ill-fated, drummer, arranger and composer. Kahn warmly recommended Raney to Woody Herman. Equally impressed, Herman added the guitarist to the line-up of the Second Herd. Raney's stay with Herman lasted less than a year: the on-the-road existence physically exhausted him, and his allocation of solos was meagre.

One significant result did transpire, however. Stan Getz, a major soloist with the Herd, became a fan of Raney's playing. A month after leaving the band, Raney was invited by the tenor saxophonist to participate in a record date for Bob Shad's independent Sittin' In With company. Even though the fully-fledged bebopper was still emerging, his beautifully structured lines complemented Getz's own flowing parts. What would become a unique tenor-and-guitar partnership was cemented in 1951, when Getz formed a new Quintet with Al Haig as its pianist.

Proof that Jimmy Raney had now been elevated to the upper ranks of guitarists in post-World War II jazz was vividly demonstrated that October, when the Getz Quintet was recorded in live performance at Boston's once-famous Storyville Club. Each of the five members plays well above himself, the group driven along in peerless fashion by its temporary drummer, Tiny Kahn. The rapport and interplay between the leader and his guitar player were extraordinary, particularly on items such as 'Move', 'Jumpin' With Symphony Sid', 'The Song Is You', and two compositions by Raney – 'Signal' and 'Parker 51'.

With his impressive reputation firmly established, Raney left Getz in 1952. A studio reunion with Getz – this one under Raney's name – took place the following year. Once again the tenor-and-guitar rapport is in focus at all times. The individual highlight is one of the finest recorded versions of Monk's 'Round Midnight'.

Tal Farlow's initial New York exposure came through the combos of Marjorie Hyams and Buddy DeFranco. But his big-time breakthrough arrived in 1949 when he joined the Red Norvo Trio, on Mundell Lowe's recommendation. With Norvo, Farlow's exceptional talents were given full reign. The leader's predilection for ultra-fast tempos obliged the guitarist to work hard on his technique, and soon he was using his huge hands to move with lightning speed over the strings, executing even the most intricate

The Red Norvo Trio (above) with Red Norvo (vibes), Tal Farlow (guitar) and Charles Mingus (bass). The Trio introduced Farlow's talents to a wide jazz audience from 1949. Tal Farlow (opposite) went on to record a series of outstanding albums for Blue Note and Verve, but withdrew from the jazz scene for several years from the mid 1960s. The most influential of the bebop-inspired guitarists who emerged in the late 1940s, Farlow had a technical brilliance and unfettered musical brilliance that set new standards for all subsequent jazz guitarists.

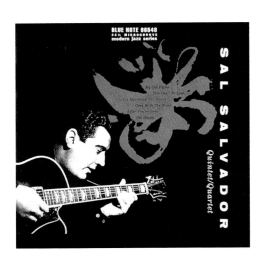

Sal Salvador made his name with the Stan Kenton Orchestra. This recent CD reissue showcases his lively boppish style on small-group tracks from two albums, Sal Salvador Quintet and Kenton Presents Sal Salvador, recorded in 1953 and 1954.

passages with ease. His facility with artificial harmonics enabled him to execute bell-like double-octaves in a manner few other players would attempt, and he would even perform chorus after chorus using only harmonics. The dazzling interplay between Farlow and Norvo became one of the Trio's recognisable trademarks. Farlow and Norvo would be reunited in the same Trio setting in 1954 and 1955 – he had left Norvo for the first time in 1953 – and in the early 1980s the pair got together again in Trio format, for tours both in the US and abroad.

It was during the 1950s that Farlow began to record under his own name, first with Blue Note, then with various Norman Granz-owned labels, including half-a-dozen for Verve: their consistency alone would have made him a legend. His creative powers were probably at his peak during the late 1950s. Albums such as *Autumn In New York*, *The Swinging Guitar Of Tal Farlow* and *This Is Tal Farlow* amply document the ability of this player to re-harmonise a song with the most sophisticated chord melody arrangement and then follow it with several choruses of inventive, swinging improvisation.

Through the years, Tal Farlow kept a fairly active schedule – although, sensibly, he could never have been accused of over-working. Indeed, after his semi-retirement in 1958, Farlow's mellow-sounding guitar would not be heard outside his home town of Sea Bright, New Jersey, until the late 1960s, either in person or on record. But when he resumed playing in the 1970s, Farlow's career enjoyed a new lease of life.

After Norvo ceased touring, in the 1980s, Farlow continued to work as a solo act, sometimes travelling with a trio, but generally performing with local rhythm sections. Extensive touring until the mid 1990s, when deteriorating health forced him to cut back, won him new audiences in many countries, captivated by his harmonic brilliance, the depth of his musical resources and his undimmed enthusiasm for simply playing music.

Following his success with Stan Getz, Jimmy Raney's career really opened up in the 1950s and 1960s. He, too, worked as a member of the Red Norvo Trio, for two years – personally recommended by his close buddy, Tal Farlow. With Norvo, he made his first visit to Europe, in 1954. He worked with, among others, pianist Jimmy Lyon from 1955-1960. At that time he also appeared, offstage, with a combo that starred in the Broadway production of *The Thurber Carnival*.

From 1964 to 1972, Raney disappeared from the jazz scene. Like Farlow, he took a long sabbatical, returning to Louisville where he played only occasional local gigs and undertook some teaching. After a welcome appearance at the 1971 Newport Jazz Festival, his long overdue comeback started the following year. Apart from a Carnegie Hall Recital with Al Haig in 1974, Raney lugged his guitar and amp overseas to Japan and Europe, sometimes as a solo performer, but also with Al Haig, and as a duo with his guitar-playing son, Doug Raney (b.1957).

Happily, there are several excellent recordings from this period including *Solo* (1976) which, intriguingly, features his unaccompanied as well as overdubbed use of an F guitar (tuned a fifth lower for some performances). There is a notable collaboration, in free jazz style, with Hungarian-born guitarist Attila Zoller from 1979, a series of fine albums with Doug Raney, and several that capture him with first-rate rhythm sections, weaving his intricate lines with clarity and harmonic subtlety through the chord changes of jazz classics and standards. Jimmy Raney suffered a stroke in 1993 and

Chuck Wayne (second left, above left) with the Phil Moore Group, New York, 1945. This recent album (above) features previously unissued tracks from 1957 and 1958 by two burning bebop guitar players, recorded during rehearsals. Billy Bean dropped out of the jazz scene, but John Pisano pursued a successful career in the studios and in jazz. Pisano's skills at accompaniment are clearly demonstrated on Joe Pass's 1963 album For Django.

died two years later. For bop specialists Sal Salvador, Barry Galbraith and Chuck Wayne, their reputations extended beyond their first-class instrumental and performance abilities. All three would become highly-respected tutors of their chosen instrument and over several years would publish instructional guitar music books which have proven invaluable study material for thousands of aspiring young jazz guitarists.

Chuck Wayne (1923-1997) was born Charles Jagelka in New York City and originally played mandolin in a Russian balalaika band. A self-taught musician, Wayne's introduction to the guitar came at 16. Joining clarinetist/saxist Joe Marsala's popular combo at the Hickory House from 1944 to 1946, his versatility and reliability led to invitations to record with top names, including Jack Teagarden, Lester Young, Coleman Hawkins, Marsala and – most significantly – Dizzy Gillespie. When Billy Bauer decided to leave the rip-roaring Woody Herman First Herd, he recommended Wayne to take his place. Unable to read music, he busked his parts until he managed to learn to read adequately.

After Herman disbanded, things really started to move. From 1949 to 1952 he was a founder member of the George Shearing Quintet and their distinctive piano-vibes-guitar sound introduced Chuck Wayne's guitar style to an international audience. He became Tony Bennett's musical director for four years in the mid-1950s and composed and performed the music for Tennessee Williams' play *Orpheus Descending* on Broadway in 1957. Chuck also spent a long period as a staff musician at the CBS studios and had a regular spot on the Ed Sullivan Show, but he still found time to study guitar and to play the occasional jazz gig.

Wayne returned to more regular jazz activity in 1973 with the Chuck Wayne-Joe Puma guitar duo. A noted teacher with a disciplined approach to guitar technique, he held a post at Westchester Conservatory for several years from the mid 1960s and also taught privately. In later years the onset of Parkinson's disease prevented him from continuing as a studio musician and he concentrated instead on teaching, with rare jazz appearances only.

Salvatore "Sal" Salvador (b.1925, Monson, Massachusetts) was influenced initially (and unsurprisingly) by Charlie Christian, after first becoming attracted to jazz by the music of trumpeter Harry James. His first guitar studies, on acoustic, focused on the styles of pre-Christian players like George Van Eps and Dick McDonough. But after hearing Christian, he switched permanently to the electric instrument. Further study involved correspondence courses with Oscar Moore and Hy White, and personal tuition from Eddie Smith.

His guitar-playing buddy, Mundell Lowe, recommended Salvador, then age 24, as staff guitarist at Radio City Music Hall, in New York. After further study, he worked with the combos of Terry Gibbs and Eddie Bert and a unit called the Dardanelles. Then Mundell Lowe and Salvador put together their own combo. Sal also served as house guitarist for Columbia Records, supplying backgrounds for top-selling vocalists Frankie Laine, Rosemary Clooney, Tony Bennett, and Marlene Dietrich.

Sal Salvador's highest jazz profile yet came during a two-year period spent touring and recording with the Stan Kenton Orchestra. He was featured on Kenton presentations of standards ('There's A Small Hotel'; 'Sophisticated Lady') and 'Invention For Guitar & Trumpet' and 'Frivolous Sal', two showcases written by Bill Holman. There was also a most rewarding small-group partnership with pianist Eddie Costs, which started in 1954, and an exciting, one-off appearance with altoist Sonny Stitt, at the 1958 Newport Jazz Festival, which was immortalised as part of the celebrated *Jazz On A Summer's Day* movie.

From 1958 to 1963, Sal Salvador fronted his own big band. Although it never achieved a high profile, it was admired, not only by its members but by those who heard it live or on record (for example on *Colors In Sound* or *Beat For This Generation*). Associated for many years with the guitar-maker Gretsch, he helped design, and later played, the Gretsch Sal Salvador model. During the 1970s, he and fellow guitarist Allen Hanlon worked successfully in the guitar-duo format, and he re-formed his big band for a while in the 1980s. In more recent years, he has been busy as a teacher, producing guitar instruction books and undertaking his duties as Head of the Guitar department at the University of Bridgeport.

Between 1955 and 1960, Barry Galbraith is reputed to have been the most recorded guitarist on the New York recording scene. Like so many of the players in this chapter, the former banjoist could produce exactly what was required in practically any situation. His brilliance made him constantly in demand from 1941, when he first took up residence in New York.

Joseph Barry Galbraith (1919-1983) was born in Pittsburgh, Pennsylvania. His career began with successive jobs with solo performers such as Art Tatum, Red Norvo, Babe Russin and big-band leaders Hal McIntyre and Teddy Powell. A significant move was his membership of the Claude Thornhill Orchestra – Galbraith worked with this unique outfit between 1941 and 1942, and, again, after army service, between 1946 and 1947. Thornhill's highly-gifted arranger, Gil Evans, was on staff in both periods. He and Galbraith struck up a lasting friendship and mutual admiration for each other's talent, which no doubt led to Evans' use of Galbraith's guitar on his classic album, the forward-looking *Into The Hot*, which included 'Barry's Tune', a feature for Galbraith's guitar at its most inventive and exciting.

But "straight" jazz gigs would take a second place for much of Galbraith's post-Thornhill years. From 1947 to 1970 he was in constant demand as a studio musician, working mostly for the NBC and CBS networks. His discreet, flexible playing would be heard in support of a veritable *Who's Who* of jazz-influenced music, including Billie Holiday, Ella Fitzgerald, Sarah Vaughan, Michel Legrand, Barbara Streisand, Tony Bennett, Peggy Lee, Wayne Shorter, Tal Farlow and many others. For the rest of his productive life,

Barry Galbraith taught privately in New York, was a faculty member at New York City College, and was the author of numerous widely-acclaimed guitar music books (available originally through his own Vista Publishing company, later republished by the jazz publisher Jamey Aebersold). Both Joe Puma (b. Joseph J Puma, 1927, New York City) and William Frederick "Billy" Bean were talents in their own right, yet like so many other performers never quite made the kind of impact their particular approaches to jazz-guitar deserved.

Puma came from a guitar-playing family – his father and his two brothers played the instrument. He worked first as an aircraft mechanic and then as a draughtsman, until his rapidly-growing interest in music in general and jazz in particular determined him to become a professional musician. For five years, from 1948, his reputation grew as he worked with various small groups, including that of pianist-singer Cy Coleman in 1951, and later with the bands of Artie Shaw and Don Elliott. From 1954 to 1956 he played guitar for Peggy Lee, then formed his own combo in 1957, and was heard with Lee Konitz in 1958. From 1960, he toured as musical director for Morgana King.

In 1974 he was back in New York and performing and recording with Chuck Wayne in a fondly remembered guitar duo. Like several of his New York contemporaries, his career in the studios has obscured his jazz talents. But he still does club dates, often as a duo with guitarist Al Gafa.

Like Puma, Billy Bean (b.1933, Philadelphia, Pennsylvania) came from a musical family: his father played guitar and his mother was a pianist. From a young age, Bean was a familiar figure on the local Philadelphia scene. His major breakthrough came, at 23, when he became a member of the Charlie Ventura Quartet.

Two years later, in 1958, he moved to California, where he operated as a freelancer, in and around LA. Bean interacted with such locals as Bud Shank, Paul Horn, Buddy Collette and Calvin Jackson, and visitors like Buddy DeFranco. His technique was on a par with most of his contemporaries. But in terms of emotional excitement and drive, he left many behind. Indeed, only a small handful of bebopping guitarists produced the kind of fierce, hard-swinging playing that has always suffused his work, especially up-tempo.

Billy Bean's precious few recordings offer proof of his exceptional talent. Most have been long deleted, especially the quite astonishing two-guitar performances by Bean and John Pisano, a superb team during the late 1950s, documented on two prize albums for American Decca in 1957 and 1958: *Take Your Pick* and *Making It*. Thankfully a collection of Bean-Pisano duets was released on CD in 1999 by the British label String Jazz Recordings, as *Makin' It Again*. These document the rehearsals of the duo, together with some quintet and sextet tracks, which Pisano taped in preparation for the actual recordings. Bean's superb wide tone, his unerring, swinging lines and ceaseless flow of ideas are well represented. Sadly, though, health problems have kept Billy Bean's musical career dormant for more than 20 years.

All of these players – Farlow and Raney in particular – contributed to the developing role of the guitar in jazz, not merely by applying to the guitar the ideas of Charlie Parker, Bud Powell and Dizzy Gillespie, but also by extending its expressive range with their own innovations. In the late 1930s the role of the guitar was still primarily confined to four-in-the-bar rhythm. Charlie Christian began the process of change and the bebop guitar masters continued it. By the early 1950s the guitar had truly arrived in the front line of jazz.

THE COOL SOUND

***GUITARISTS WHO ADOPTED THE COOL APPROACH IN THE 1950S
PRACTISED A REFINED, THOUGHTFUL STYLE WITH THE
EMPHASIS ON MUSICAL ELEGANCE AND CRAFTSMANSHIP.
INTERESTINGLY, THE FIRST GREAT EXPONENT OF THE STYLE
DID NOT EVEN CONSIDER HIMSELF A JAZZ MUSICIAN.***

"Cool" was one of the vogue words of the 1950s, not just in music circles but in all walks of life. In jazz it meant restrained, relaxed and understated. It often manifested itself as playing slightly behind the beat, eschewing the obvious and generally using tone-colours distinct from those employed by such soloists as Coleman Hawkins, Louis Armstrong and Roy Eldridge.

In the world of jazz guitar, cool playing meant producing very melodic linear improvisations allied to a total grasp of harmony and the cultivation of a smooth, clear tone throughout the range of the instrument. To achieve these essential elements it was necessary first to possess the very highest level of musicianship, and there was no better craftsman anywhere in the field than Johnny Smith.

John Henry Smith Jr was born in Birmingham, Alabama, on June 25th 1922 and was only five years old when he became fascinated with the guitar. His father played five-string banjo but guitar was John's first and lasting love. Initially he was frustrated by the lack of a guitar teacher or instruction manuals; determined to master the instrument, he taught himself to play. Many outstanding and individual jazz soloists have fallen back on the empirical method for the same reason as Smith and emerged with wholly distinctive sounds. In 1935 the Smith family moved to Portland, Maine; Johnny was 13 and good enough to play in local bands.

In 1942 he joined the USAAF (he was already a student pilot) and ended up in a band which needed a cornet player rather than a guitarist. In six months he had learned the cornet well enough to be given the position of first cornetist. After his discharge from the Air Force in 1946 he went back to Portland to play both guitar and trumpet on local radio as well as playing in clubs at night, but the pay was never very good. He went to New York to work as an arranger at NBC and in 1947 he became a member of the NBC orchestra. For eight years he worked with the orchestra as guitarist, trumpeter, arranger and composer.

Although he had been greatly influenced by Django Reinhardt and Charlie Christian at the outset (he learned Django's solos from record and actually met the Gypsy guitarist when he came to the United States in 1946) Johnny did not consider himself to be a jazz musician. Nevertheless, he made his first record as leader in March 1952, in the company of Stan Getz, Eddie Safranski, Sanford Gold and Don Lamond. One title from that date, 'Moonlight In Vermont', was a turning point in Smith's career despite its short duration. The song (a big hit for singer Margaret Whiting years earlier) has an unusual construction, comprising an AABA[1] form made up of 6-6-8-8 bars. (The A[1] section is the same as A plus a two-bar tag.) The melody in the middle-eight (the B section) is economical but there is a host of beautiful chord changes.

'Vermont' was made for the Royal Roost label (frequently abbreviated to Roost Records) and the company signed Smith to a long-term contract during which time he produced around 20 albums. Roost was later absorbed by Roulette which reissued several of Johnny's LPs. Most of the albums featured solo guitar or a trio; two backed Smith with strings playing arrangements the guitarist wrote himself. There was a great appeal to Smith's graceful, melodic treatment of superior tunes. Not only the record-buying public but hundreds of guitarists found the music entrancing. The dextrous fingering, the perfection of the manner in which he ran chords and arpeggios, all contributed to the acclaim for Johnny's work. The Gibson company built a guitar to his design and marketed the model with his endorsement.

He continued to work at NBC until 1958 when, following the death of his wife, he decided to leave New York to be near his young daughter. In 1982 he told Robert Velin of *Guitar Player* magazine: "I got the best glimpse of New York I ever had – it was out the rear view mirror of my car, which was heading down the New Jersey Turnpike. I always hated New York, but I loved the work there, and I was extremely lucky to work with so many great musicians and arrangers."

One album he made in 1953 placed him in a different context. He took part in the studio jam session which produced *Jazz Studio One* for American Decca. For contractual reasons he appeared on the album under the pseudonym "Sir Jonathan Gasser", and opened the long 'Tenderly' in inimitable fashion with a beautiful exposition of the theme. One interesting aspect of the music is the way he and pianist Hank Jones share the support duties behind the soloists (Joe Newman, trombonist Bennie Green and saxists Paul Quinichette and Frank Foster). Some years later he made a fine quartet LP for Verve, again with Hank Jones: their harmonic understanding is remarkable. Smith moved to Colorado Springs in 1958 and three years later opened his music store there. He still does occasional concerts, and did a world tour with Bing Crosby as a member of the Joe Bushkin Quartet in the 1970s. The group made an album in London on which Johnny was featured throughout 'Sunday Of The Shepherdess', a Scandinavian folk song known variously as 'Ack Varmeland Du Skona' and 'Dear Old Stockholm'.

Recordings by Django Reinhardt were an inspiration to Jim Hall in his formative years as a guitarist. So too was the work of such tenor saxophonists as Lester Young, Coleman Hawkins and Ben Webster, whose playing influenced him in the creation of horn-like solos on his instrument. Born James Stanley Hall on December 4th 1930, in Buffalo, New York State, he moved with his family to Cleveland, Ohio, in 1946 and it was in Cleveland that he began playing in local bars. He entered the Cleveland Institute of Music and graduated with a bachelor of music degree, but halfway through working towards his master's degree he decided to leave school and head for Los Angeles. The year was 1955, and he started to take lessons from the California-based classical guitarist Vincente Gomez.

At the same time he was making contact with locally-based jazz musicians and was chosen as the replacement for Howard Roberts in drummer Chico Hamilton's trio. Almost by accident Chico's group became a quintet, with the unusual instrumentation of guitar, bass, cello, drums and Buddy Collette playing flute and reed instruments. The music was deliberately low key, a true jazz equivalent of chamber music. The band was recorded one summer

Jim Hall's probing, sensitive musical mind makes him the ideal musical partner, and his associations with Jimmy Giuffre, Sonny Rollins, Paul Desmond, Ron Carter, Art Farmer and – more recently – Pat Metheny, have all produced recordings of remarkable beauty. For many, Intermodulation from 1966 (above), an intense musical dialogue with pianist Bill Evans, is one of the highlights of Hall's long career.

A study in concentration: Jim Hall (guitar) and Steve Swallow (bass) recording with the Art Farmer Quartet for BBC Television in London, 1964 (opposite). Undercurrent from 1959 (above), the first collaboration of pianist Bill Evans and guitarist Hall, finds them unconcerned by the absence of bass and drums, exchanging solo and accompaniment roles at will, pursuing and developing ideas as they emerge, and exploring the harmonies of standards such as 'My Funny Valentine' and 'I Hear Rhapsody' as creative equals.

evening at the Strollers club in Long Beach with Jim Hall taking his first solos on record and introducing one of his compositions, 'Spectacular'. Hall remained with Hamilton until the beginning of 1957 and appeared on several of Chico's albums, on the Pacific Jazz label.

Pacific Jazz was owned and run by Dick Bock, a man with an extraordinary ability to spot burgeoning talent. He employed Hall on the session which produced the ground-breaking album *Grand Encounter* with John Lewis and Percy Heath from the Modern Jazz Quartet, tenor saxophonist Bill Perkins, Hall and Chico Hamilton. Jim found a soulmate in Lewis and the manner in which their playing interlocked is best exemplified in the restrained treatment of 'Skylark'. Just before leaving Hamilton's quintet Hall made his first album as leader, again for Pacific Jazz, a wholly delightful trio set with the highly individual piano of Carl Perkins and the brilliant bass playing of Red Mitchell. The reader is warned that a reissue of this LP during the 1960s had drummer Larry Bunker dubbed on to the original trio recording; there was never any need for a drummer, good though Bunker is.

After Hamilton's quintet Hall joined a new trio formed by multi-saxist Jimmy Giuffre completed by bass player Ralph Peña. This was the group that recorded the first version of Giuffre's folksy 'The Train And The River' but Jimmy felt that an instrumentation pivoting around a strong bass line restricted the freedom of expression he wanted and by January 1958 the bass had been replaced by the valve trombone of Bob Brookmeyer and the trio had relocated to the East Coast. Hall now had to discover and perfect a new role for himself.

Brookmeyer and drummer Dave Vailey had joined the Giuffre trio in the summer of 1957 for record dates which produced the enjoyable *Traditionalism Revisited* album (for Pacific Jazz). But with no bass or drums to lay down the time the new Giuffre unit was breaking new ground and Jim Hall was called upon to provide the function of a complete rhythm section while at the same time joining Bob and Jimmy in three-part inventions.

That the guitarist solved the problems of his new status is an historical fact; in so doing he also reached a turning point in his career. His sensitive work with the minimum of musical colleagues singled him out as a very special kind of musician. From then on he was in great demand from leaders of other small groups and it is true to say that Hall's finest work has been with groups no larger than a quartet. He learned a lot from his time with the Giuffre Trio for the leader elected to play a wide range of music, including free-form pieces with no key signature or defined rhythmic pulse, the kind of music pioneered in the late 1940s by pianist Lennie Tristano and his students. Perhaps significantly Hall formed a duo with Lee Konitz, arguably Tristano's best pupil, which worked successfully in 1960 and 1961.

Jim's task with the Giuffre Trio and with some of the later groups he played in was to become virtually transparent, in musical terms. His understated style of playing, great knowledge of harmony and a truly compositional approach to improvisation marked him out as a master musician. Whitney Balliett wrote a profile of him for *The New Yorker* in which he referred to Hall as having "a grace and inventiveness and lyricism that makes him pre-eminent among contemporary jazz guitarists and puts him within touching distance of the two grand masters – Charlie Christian and Django Reinhardt".

Towards the end of 1961 tenor saxophonist Sonny Rollins, a musician Hall had admired for years, emerged from a self-imposed exile with the desire to

form a new group. He contacted the guitarist and the first new album Rollins made (in January and February 1962), entitled *The Bridge*, was greeted with ecstatic praise by those who were anxious to hear the "new" Sonny. The conjunction of Hall (still looked upon as a West Coast musician by many) and the muscular, strong sound of Rollins' tenor was a revelation and provided Jim with the most important addition to his musical track-record.

In May 1962 he took another giant artistic step when he recorded a duet album with pianist Bill Evans for the United Artists label (later reissued on Blue Note with four additional tracks). Entitled *Undercurrent*, it comprised six of the most intimate, inventive items of music of the decade. Harmonic clashes, usually involving passing chords, can result when pianists and guitarists play together but there is an uncanny empathy between Evans and Hall as they create superb improvisations, a triumph which was repeated four years later for the Verve label with *Intermodulation*.

Jim Hall has carved out a unique niche for himself in the jazz pantheon. His work with Art Farmer's quartet (1962-1964), the string of albums he made with the late Paul Desmond (with Gerry Mulligan added on some) and his own duos (with Ron Carter on bass) and trios all point to a man who has carefully honed his skills to the point where he can perform brilliantly given the right company. A tape exists of his appearance at New York's Fat Tuesday club in April 1979 paired off with Bob Brookmeyer for some brilliant and spontaneous abstract interpretations of songs such as 'Fly Me To the Moon', 'You Stepped Out Of A Dream' and 'Prelude To A Kiss'. Music such as this defies categorisation and is beyond the confines of jazz as most people perceive it.

Although Ed Bickert has confined most of his musical activities to his native Canada his life has run parallel with that of Jim Hall for parts of their careers. Born Edward Isaac Bickert on November 29th 1932 in Hochfield, Manitoba, Ed grew up in Vernon, British Columbia, and took up the guitar at the age of eight. Both parents were musicians: his father played violin while his mother was a pianist. At the age of 11 young Bickert was sufficiently competent to join his parents in a country dance band. "Some of the first things I played were polkas, Viennese waltz-type things, foxtrots, two-steps and schottisches – just the kind of music people out in the country danced to, not country music as we know it today from Nashville, he has said."

Ed's father liked a broad spectrum of music including The Ink Spots, The Mills Brothers, Count Basie and Duke Ellington. These were the early jazz influences on Ed, followed by an admiration for Oscar Moore with Nat King Cole's trio and the records of Les Paul. There were also the guitarists in the big touring bands from the western Canadian cities, one of whom, Gordie Brandt, made a big impression on Bickert: "He was a high energy player with a lot of facility and daring and speed. I was always more of a laid-back player but I enjoyed being that close to someone who played that well."

In 1952 Ed left home for Toronto where he met up with the local guitar players, but he decided he was not yet ready to join that league of musicians. Instead he worked at radio station CFRB as an engineer, studying music in the evenings and gradually easing himself into the jazz scene. He became influenced by Barney Kessel and Tal Farlow and by 1955 was working and recording with units such as the Moe Koffman Quartet: he was on the original recording of Koffman's hit tune 'Swingin' Shepherd Blues'. He played with leading Canadian jazzmen including Rob McConnell, Phil Nommons and

Hagood Hardy. Later he worked regularly with bass player Don Thompson and drummer Terry Clarke, two of the finest players Canada has produced since Oscar Peterson.

Although he has spent a great deal of his working life as a first-call studio musician, Ed's interest in jazz has remained the chief focus of his music. Visiting American soloists such as Frank Rosolino, Red Norvo and Milt Jackson returned home with glowing reports of Bickert's artistry, and Paul Desmond was moved to have his performances with Ed at Toronto's Bourbon Street club in 1975 recorded for release on an American label. The mellow sound of Bickert's work with Desmond echoed Paul's pairing with Jim Hall more than ten years earlier. It is probably no coincidence that Bickert has

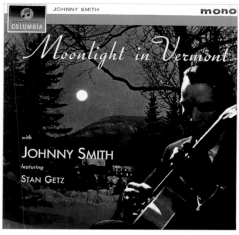
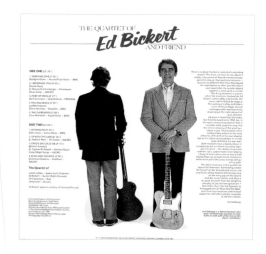

expressed his admiration for Hall's playing or that Jim has frequently worked with Ed's Canadian colleagues Don Thompson and Terry Clarke.

In the early 1980s Bickert commenced a series of recordings for the Concord label starting with a live date at Toronto's Bourbon Street with American visitors Scott Hamilton, Warren Vache and Jake Hanna. There has been a consistently high level of playing throughout the Concord series, especially so on *Third Floor Richard* by an all-Canadian trio (Bickert with Terry Clarke and bass player Neil Swainson) plus American guest pianist Dave McKenna on four of the 11 tracks. As with many Bickert albums, the programme is made up principally of standards (including a couple of rare Duke Ellington pieces). "I certainly identify with some of the older tunes," he says. "Perhaps I'm reacting to a lot of things that have been going on in the past few years. Pretty things are out; it has to be hip, energetic and sometimes just straight-ahead energy. A lot of those things are just not part of my personality."

A man who would probably echo those sentiments is the fourth of the "cool" players, Ted Greene. Born in Hollywood on September 26th 1946, Greene took up the guitar at the age of ten and studied briefly with George Van Eps. He has lived in Woodland Hills, Los Angeles, for some time and has devoted much of his working life to teaching and organising guitar seminars. He has made a particular study of chords and the way they are voiced: he is the author of four books including one entitled *Chord Chemistry*. Although not known to the wider audience he is rated very highly by fellow guitarists and has produced his own *Solo Guitar* album for the PMP label.

Johnny Smith recorded a string of remarkable albums for the Roost label which remain largely unreleased on CD, including The Johnny Smith Foursome (left). Smith's close-harmony chord-melody interpretation of standards, performed in a relaxed manner with a beautiful, clear sound, is the hallmark of his style. The Johnny Smith/Stan Getz version of the dreamy ballad 'Moonlight in Vermont' became a hit in 1952 – a rarity in jazz – but there are many other gems on the reissue of the original album (centre) such as the up-tempo Smith original 'Jaguar'. Two of Canada's finest guitarists feature on The Quartet of Ed Bickert And Friend Lorne Lofsky from 1985 (above). Bickert's subtle chordal style, with a harmonic sense reminiscent of pianist Bill Evans, has featured on record with Paul Desmond (alto sax), Ruby Braff (cornet) and Rob McConnell's Boss Brass.

J O H N   F O R D H A M # INFLUENCE AND CONFLUENCE

JAZZ DID NOT DEVELOP IN ISOLATION, EITHER FROM THE REST OF MUSIC OR FROM THE REST OF THE WORLD. SOME OF THE KEY PLAYERS OF THE 1950S AND LATER BROUGHT INFLUENCES FROM COUNTRY MUSIC, FROM CENTRAL EUROPE AND FROM THE CARIBBEAN.

Buddy Rich, a man whose wit was as fast as his drumming, was once on his way to the operating theatre, a place he visited with some frequency in later years, when he was asked whether he was allergic to anything. "Only country & western music," he is supposed to have replied.

Jazz and country or folk musicians, and their respective fans, have tended to inhabit separate worlds until recent years. There have been practical as well as sectarian reasons for this. Jazz music is traditionally instrumental, improvised, unsentimental and sometimes wilfully unpredictable. Folk music is built around popular singers, communal emotions, familiar melodies and shared experience. But there are points of contact which the diehards of either side have conveniently glossed over.

Jazz, which has often assumed an artistic status above folk music, grew out of a folk music itself, and just as readily embraces flexible rules, imprecise notes and personal expression. And since the popularity of American jazz since the 1920s has made it the basis of an international language, it has inevitably merged with other folk musics, something increasingly widely recognised in the "world-music" era. This expansion of the jazz influence has resulted in a number of guitarists entering the jazz firmament, whose influences go far beyond a Chicago R&B club or the bebop flurries of 52nd Street.

In jazz guitar history, there have been a number of elusive figures whose careers and interests have prevented their consignment to the convenient filing cabinet of a single genre. Among guitarists with country & western roots, the Nashville session star Hank Garland and the short-lived and reclusive Canadian Lenny Breau have been two of the most innovative and influential – and overlooked. Two guitarists from Hungary, Gabor Szabo and Attila Zoller, have made an impact on the American jazz world with approaches that have shown profound understanding both of their own stringed-instrument tradition and that of America. A Caribbean guitarist, Ernest Ranglin, has been both a resourceful and celebrated jazz improviser and a specialist in the rhythms and phrasing of reggae and ska, and has often brought the musics of the West Indies and the United States together. And New York-born Billy Bauer, though closer by apprenticeship and geography to the main lines of American jazz, has sidestepped many of the implications of those traditions, developing an understated and sometimes almost abstract finger-style technique quite different from the plectrum-flickering, single-line approach of the bebop players.

One of the most remarkable jazz guitarists to have emerged from the American country & western tradition, maybe the more remarkable for the brevity of his creative career, is Hank Garland. Garland was a South Carolina guitarist who supported the Everly Brothers and Elvis Presley as a Nashville studio player, but whose jazz career might have been formidable had not a road accident stolen years from his career and much of his remarkable skill.

Hank Garland was born Walter Louis Garland, at Cowpen in South Carolina, on November 11th 1930. Inspired by the guitar sounds on the Carter Family's 'Wildwood Flower', he badgered his father into buying him a guitar and took lessons from the age of six. Hearing electric guitars on his local radio station, the boy initially experimented by attaching his instrument directly to the mains, a venture that nearly ended his career there and then. In 1945 Hank Garland graduated to an electric archtop guitar with a Gibson amplifier, and when Paul Howard, leader of the Georgia Cotton Pickers band (a pioneer

of the electric guitar's acceptance in country bands) heard him playing in Alexander's Music Store in Spartanburg, he offered him a job. In his first show, the teenager's playing brought the crowd to its feet. Paul Howard christened Garland "Baby Cotton Picker" after the show. "Kid," Howard said, "you have a job here as long as I got one."

In the short run, though, Howard was wrong. At 15, Garland was too young to join the union, and his professional employment broke child-labour laws. He was obliged to wait another year before joining Howard full time.

Garland admired Jimmy Wyble, guitarist with the Texas Playboys, who was influenced by Benny Goodman's star guitarist, the young bebop pioneer Charlie Christian, as was Billy Byrd, another country player Garland encountered in the 1940s. All this awakened Garland's interest in jazz, just as his career was taking off in the fledgling Nashville studio world.

From 1948, Garland, Chet Atkins, Harold Bradley and Grady Martin became legends as studio musicians who could play songs they'd never heard before, invent an appropriate backing on the run-throughs and lift the quality of the music as much as the celebrity whose name was to be on the label. This elite drew country stars from all over the southlands to Nashville to record.

Chet Atkins introduced Garland to the music of Django Reinhardt, and he became obsessed with Reinhardt's flying runs and ornate flourishes. "He was one of those guys you could play a lick to and he'd come back like an echo," Atkins recalled. Jazz lines began to appear in Garland's country solos, and he began experimenting with different guitars and amplifiers, as well as practising constantly and jamming in jazz clubs after studio hours. He even wrote a hit tune, 'Sugarfoot Rag', in 1949: the B-side to Red Foley's

Nashville studio guitarist Hank Garland recorded Jazz Winds From A New Direction (left), his celebrated jazz album, in 1960. The following year a car accident left him badly injured, preventing him from continuing his professional career. George Benson cites Garland as an early inspiration. The Living Room Tapes (centre) is an informal document of the talents of finger-style guitarist Lenny Breau who created a highly personal style by bringing together elements of Chet Atkins's technique, McCoy Tyner's piano chords and an appreciation of the jazz guitar masters. Wranglin' (above) is a live recording from the early 1960s that reveals an outstanding talent. Ernest Ranglin plays melody and chords simultaneously like a piano, explores ballads with quiet intensity, and erupts with Caribbean exuberance on his own calypsos.

'Chattanooga Shoeshine Boy', it got to number five on the *Cash Box* country charts, earning him the nickname "Sugarfoot".

Garland began listening to Les Paul, and later to bop guitarists Barney Kessel, Tal Farlow and Barry Galbraith. His 1940s room-mate, bassist Bob Moore, recalled Garland starting practice at 5.30am and still going strong in late afternoon. Garland went on to play on Jim Reeves' RCA sessions, with Patsy Cline and Brenda Lee, and with legends of rock'n'roll including Elvis Presley and Jerry Lee Lewis. In 1955 Garland and Billy Byrd designed the Byrdland guitar for Gibson, a short-necked, thin-bodied instrument based on the L-5, intended for both country and jazz musicians. Garland loved new hardware: he uses an early echo chamber on the guitar intro to Patsy Cline's 1961 hit, 'I Fall To Pieces'.

Elvis Presley had turned the region's music toward a harder rock feel and away from fiddle players and pedal-steel specialists. Garland was able to adapt. In June 1958 he even replaced Elvis's regular guitarist Scotty Moore, and also played on one of The King's few live concerts of the 1960s, in Honolulu, where he was introduced as "one of the finest guitar players anywhere in the country today".

Though Garland cut few jazz records as a leader, he made them count. His first solo album (*Velvet Guitar*, for Columbia) was soft by his standards, but *Jazz Winds From A New Direction* quickly followed, and definitely wasn't. This was the set that was to be his crowning achievement in jazz. Energetic and conversational, the music teems with life (Dave Brubeck's drummer Joe Morello's urgent brushwork and crackling precision constantly stimulates it), the material is lively and varied, and Garland's clarity, originality of phrasing and long, loping improvisations on his Gibson Byrdland sweep through the music. The disc featured an unknown teenage vibraharpist, Gary Burton, and the collaboration followed the invention of a Nashville bop band called The Nashville All-Stars for the 1960 Newport Jazz Festival.

Garland's force as a jazz player was now evident to all, and the disc transformed the stature of country musicians in the sometimes elitist world of jazz. Hank Garland was 30, and seemed to be opening up a jazz career as illustrious as the one he had enjoyed on the country scene. But six months after the recording, Garland was involved in a road accident that left him brain-damaged. With characteristic dedication, Garland devoted himself to relearning his guitar skills, encouraged by his brother Bill. But it was 13 years before he again made a public performance, playing his old composition 'Sugarfoot Rag' at the 1976 Fan Fair Reunion Show in Nashville.

Lenny Breau was another jazz-playing country guitarist – and tragedy severed his growing bond with the jazz audience too. Though he was held in awe by many jazz guitarists, Breau was little known to jazz fans, and lived reclusively for much of his life, partly as a result of narcotics addiction. But in 1979 Chet Atkins said of him: "I think he knows more guitar than any guy that's ever walked the face of the earth, because he can play jazz, he can play a little classical, he can play great country, and he does it all with taste."

Born Leon Breau at Auburn, in Maine, on August 5th 1941, Lenny was raised on a farm, and began to play the guitar at seven. His parents were Hal "Lone Pine" Breau and Betty Cody, successful country artists, and his first teacher was Ray Couture, lead guitarist in his father's band and an admirer of Reinhardt. At 12, Lenny was working with the group professionally.

At about this time, Breau heard Chet Atkins on the radio, marvelled at a finger-style melodic approach he had not heard from guitarists around him, and began listening to jazz players, particularly Barney Kessel, Tal Farlow and Johnny Smith. But though Chet Atkins influenced Breau's development, so did the sophisticated harmonic vocabulary of the pianist, Bill Evans.

Breau moved to Winnipeg, Canada, in his late teens. His first jazz gigs were on bass guitar (he credited the experience with obliging him to learn the harmonies of many new tunes, and analysing their structures), but his skill on the regular guitar had advanced so fast that Canadian Broadcasting even gave him his own show. He was about 21 at the time, and listening to pianists almost exclusively for his ideas. He was also exploring other idioms, including flamenco and classical music (he always practised on a classical guitar), and growing increasingly interested in sitar music and Indian scales.

Breau's finger-style technique, expanded from Atkins', allowed him to walk basslines against piano-like "comping" of chords and add a single-line melody on top. He experimented with alternative methods of fingering and picking, sometimes using a thumbpick as if it were an ordinary plectrum for attack, sometimes sounding notes by plucking the string with the fingering hand ("pull-offs") and using slurring and percussive muted-strings techniques adapted from flamenco. Breau was also a superb player of harmonics, extending techniques that he acquired from Chet Atkins, and he loved the sound of the open strings to mirror that of a piano with the sustain pedal on.

When Chet Atkins caught up with Breau in Canada, he promptly arranged for the young guitarist to be signed to RCA. The deal immediately raised Breau's profile outside Canada, and seemed at first to offer solutions to his problems, revolving around the compromise between personal musical exploration and the demands of the studios. He moved to Los Angeles and quickly began to make an impact on the city's jazz scene, particularly in performances at drummer Shelly Manne's popular club, The Manne Hole.

By the late 1960s Breau was back in Canada. Problems with narcotics, exacerbated by performance nerves and his dissatisfaction with the music business and his own progress, stalled Breau's career just as it was taking off. For much of the following decade he rarely appeared, though he did play with George Benson at a convention in 1977. From that year, Breau began to record again, and the results confirmed his extraordinary gifts. *Legendary Lenny Breau... Now!* was an unaccompanied set (save a single drum overdub) recorded in Chet Atkins' house: the situation allowed the reticent Breau to imagine he was in one of his favourite tiny clubs. *Five O'Clock Bells* from 1979 followed a period in which Breau had been listening to John Coltrane and McCoy Tyner, another of the pianists who would so influence his work. Breau was now playing a seven-string instrument of his own design: the extra string was a high A rather than the usual additional bass string, and made of fishing line because no string-maker was producing a steel string robust enough.

Lenny Breau returned to Los Angeles in November 1983, teaching privately and writing a column for *Guitar Player* magazine. In August 1984 he was found dead in Los Angeles in what was originally thought to be a swimming pool accident, but was later believed to be murder. The music world was thus robbed of an astonishing talent. Breau had maintained that he wanted to paint with the guitar, like an Impressionist. He heard alternative inversions of chords as varying shades of a colour, and particular songs needed to have a spiritual resonance for him before he could explore them. These were tough standards to rise to, but they gave Lenny Breau's surviving music a

Jamaican guitarist Ernest Ranglin pictured at Ronnie Scott's Club, London, in May 1964. Also featured are Roy Burrowes (trumpet), Terry Shannon (piano), Freddie Logan (bass) and Allan Ganley (drums).

unique place in both guitar history and musical evolution. Breau conceived a unique hybrid sound of jazz and other contemporary musics that most of the world didn't hear, and his approach to playing was soloistic and private.

Ernest Ranglin, the Jamaican guitarist, has similarly forged something new from existing materials, but his approach has been open, popular and collective. Ranglin has been a pioneering spirit of ska and Jamaican popular music as well as a superb jazz guitarist.

Ernest Ranglin was born in 1932 and grew up in the small rural community of Robin's Hall in central Jamaica. Two uncles showed him the rudiments of the guitar when he was only two, but later he learned from guitar books and what he could pick up from the Jamaican dance bands. At 16, he was good enough to join a hotel band, and by the early 1950s he was working in some of the swing-based big-bands that toured the islands.

At the Half Moon Hotel in Montego Bay in 1958, Ranglin was playing with a band of his own when he was heard by Chris Blackwell, a young Englishman who dreamed of starting a label to record Caribbean music. Between them, Ranglin and Blackwell brought about the first release on Island Records, and the following year Ranglin started a big-band – but one that acknowledged the music of the wider world, including American R&B. Ranglin's 'Shuffling Bug' is regarded now as the first example of ska, a shuffle rhythm adding an exaggerated bounce to 1950s R&B "jump" accents. And from ska came the revolution of rock-steady, reggae and ragga.

Ranglin was a superb guitarist, but a skilled arranger too, talents he had honed in the big-bands. When Chris Blackwell launched Island in Britain in 1962 he was looking for a Caribbean pop hit. Ranglin knew a young Jamaican singer called Millie, and a ska song he thought would suit. Both came to London to record it and in the spring of 1964 'My Boy Lollipop' went to number two in the UK chart, before becoming the first international ska hit.

But if Ernest Ranglin could be a hitmaker, he also liked to keep his hand in as a jazz guitarist. He made a series of albums for Island, including *Guitar In Ernest*, the immaculate *Wranglin* and *Reflections*. He sat in with the house band at Ronnie Scott's club one night in 1964. They called tunes they thought a Jamaican pop guitarist would not be able to handle, but he overcame their scepticism with some dazzling improvisation which kept him in the band for the rest of the year. The light and shade in his playing, and his dance-influenced rhythmic feel, made his sound quite distinct from purely bop-inspired jazz guitarists, and there was a sparkling vibrato colouring his intonation that marked it out from the drier sound of the boppers.

Back in Kingston, Ranglin began working with Bob Marley, reggae-influenced American pop star Johnny Nash, and with Jimmy Cliff's group on tours of Europe, the States and the Far East. But Ranglin could not abandon jazz for long, and in 1973 and 1974 he played the Bill Harris Guitar Festival to great acclaim, and the Newport Jazz Festival with the Randy Weston Orchestra. *Ranglin Roots* was released in 1977.

The following year, on moving to New York, Ranglin played international festivals with the distinctive, Oscar Peterson-influenced Jamaican jazz pianist Monty Alexander. In 1982, the guitarist released his *From Kingston JA to Miami USA* album. Jamaica is where Ranglin's heart is, however, and with his album *Below The Bassline*, he both confirmed that and indicated how fruitful his relationships with contemporary jazz musicians remain. Guitarists including Kenny Burrell, Stanley Jordan, Charlie Byrd, Barney Kessel and Tal Farlow have all paid tribute to him.

For many years the most powerful and original jazz musician to have been born outside the US was Django Reinhardt, a European with Gypsy roots. Reinhardt's story had echoes in the life of the Hungarian guitarist Attila Zoller. Zoller was one of the few guitarists of his era to have been influenced as much by free improvisation as conventional playing. With his 1965 recording *The Horizon Beyond* (his own favourite, alongside the recordings he made with guitarist Jimmy Raney) Zoller revealed the blend of exploratory boldness and street-cafe romanticism that made his music so distinctive.

He was born Attila Cornelius Zoller, at Visegrad, in Hungary, on June 13th 1927. His father was a music teacher and conductor who taught his son to play the violin from the age of four, though the boy switched to trumpet at nine and played brass in his school orchestra for the next seven years. At the end of World War II, when he was 18, Attila Zoller decided to become a professional musician in the capital, Budapest. Competition from rival brass players led Zoller to switch to guitar, an instrument on which he made remarkable progress, and this quickly led to work with dance bands.

Zoller listened eagerly to American jazz on the Voice of America radio station, encouraging him to move to Austria in search of wider musical stimulation. It was there that he met a variety of like-minded musicians, including Joe Zawinul, later of Weather Report. He also came across accordionist Vera Auer, an encounter that turned into a five-year regular job. Auer's quartet was a cabaret band, but it won prizes for its jazz skills, and by the mid 1950s the guitarist was convinced that his real fulfilment lay in jazz. He moved again, this time to West Germany, working first with pianist Jutta Hipp and then, from 1956 to 1959, with saxophonist Hans Koller.

There Zoller worked with visiting Americans, including Bud Shank, Oscar Pettiford and Lee Konitz. These experiences, frustration with his playing circumstances, and a trip to New York that refreshed his acquaintance with Konitz, led Zoller to emigrate to the US in 1959. Framus, the guitar makers, sponsored him initially, and on the recommendation of Jim Hall and pianist John Lewis, Zoller received a scholarship to the Lenox School of Jazz in Massachusetts, where he roomed with Ornette Coleman and Don Cherry.

When Zoller arrived, Lenox was a significant force for change and evolution in jazz. Proximity to Ornette Coleman and Don Cherry, who did much to reshape bebop on a different harmonic basis, may have influenced Zoller, as may familiarity with Lee Konitz, who had developed a style under the influence of pianist Lennie Tristano that exposed Charlie Parker's methods to looser structures and a more purist dynamic discipline. Early experience of

Ernest Ranglin at The Jazz Cafe, London, in January 1997. A superb jazz guitarist, Ranglin has also been a pivotal figure in Jamaican music, from ska to reggae. His 1998 album In Search Of The Lost Riddims *is a collaboration with Senegalese musicians and features Baaba Maal.*

classical music, with its extended forms, openness to impressionism and broad melodic and harmonic palette, was also undoubtedly a powerful factor

But the guitarist also had the knack of being in the right place at the right time and playing the right thing, as when he joined drummer Chico Hamilton's band at the end of the 1950s. This led him, in 1962, to another group in which the prevailing vibe was as strong as what anyone played, the nucleus of the proto-fusion band led by flautist Herbie Mann.

Zoller worked with Mann into the mid 1960s, freelanced for bandleaders including Red Norvo and Benny Goodman, and then co-led a group with Don Friedman. He was too alert and intelligent, too well-informed, and too musical to be easily drawn into the tightening agenda of fusion, despite its increasing fashionability and his suitability for it. In 1968 he regularly worked with Lee Konitz and German trombonist Albert Mangelsdorff, two of the most inquisitive and unwillingly-categorised performers in developing jazz. Like Zoller, they relished the best of conventional melody but were happy to proceed by an unwritten rulebook. In 1970 Zoller accompanied singer Astrud Gilberto on a tour of Japan, and in 1972 he returned to that country as part of a guitar festival with Jim Hall and Kenny Burrell. In later life Attila Zoller became intensely interested in musical education, and also in music technology, inventing pickups for guitar, bass and vibraphone.

On April 14th 1997, the American jazz world celebrated the ailing musician's 50th year in the music business at the American Guitar Museum in New York. Jazz guitar celebrities including Jim Hall, Howard Alden, John Scofield and John Abercrombie attended. The Hungarian government gave Zoller a statue of his fellow-Hungarian Bela Bartok. Letters and telegrams of thanks arrived from stars including Sonny Rollins and Joe Zawinul. Zoller died on January 25th the following year, in Townsend, Vermont, where he ran a jazz tuition centre.

The lives of few jazz guitarists are comparable to Zoller's, but that of fellow Hungarian Gabor Szabo runs close. Szabo was born in Budapest in 1936, and like Zoller acquired his early jazz experiences from the Voice of America. He had taken up guitar at 15, but his familiarity with East European folk musics gave him a different starting point for his jazz evolution, involving finger-style technique and a method that could be expanded into something closer to jazz piano than orthodox jazz guitar.

In his teens, Szabo played with Hungarian folk bands and accompanied vocalists. He was good enough to get studio and radio work, and sent a tape of his own playing to Voice of America. The station broadcast it the night Szabo left his native country, immediately before the 1956 Soviet invasion. Interned on arrival in the US, Szabo eventually settled in Boston, Massachusetts, and was an early student at the Berklee School, from 1957 to 1959. His stock on the American scene quickly grew. He appeared at the 1958 Newport Jazz Festival, and joined Chico Hamilton three years later, remaining with him until the mid 1960s, making a significant contribution to the ensemble's sound. His tone was exquisite and evocative, a throwback to the singing intonation of the string players of his childhood. But Szabo was also secure yet surprising in phrasing at any tempo, and was capable of great emotional eloquence: such pieces as 'Who Can I Turn To?' and 'Evil Eyes' testify to that. Later Szabo joined another Hamilton sideman, saxophonist Charles Lloyd, but also formed his own group in the late 1960s.

Szabo was interested in approaching dance and pop sounds from

Lasting Love was recorded in 1997 towards the end of Attila Zoller's life, and captures the essence of the guitarist's creativity in a collection of his own compositions, recorded entirely unaccompanied.

unexpected angles, but he was also influenced by John Coltrane's search for spiritual fulfilment within a wider musical culture, and he sought both to adapt some of Coltrane's techniques for guitar and bring Indian influences into his own work. Blues and funk became significant preoccupations for Szabo, but at the same time he was also evolving as a composer and orthodox accompanist, writing the *Repulsion* theme music for Roman Polanski and working on the Lena Horne album *Something In The Way She Sings*. He formed the band Perfect Circle, to explore both fusion and acoustic jazz simultaneously, scored Gabor Kalman's film *Farm Boy Of Hungary*, made a television special of his own work and filmed the documentary *Jazz Podium* in Budapest. He died unexpectedly on another visit there in 1982.

Finger-style playing has played a far more active part in the creative evolution of the guitar's role in jazz than has been widely acknowledged: the plectrum guitarists who mimicked single-note horn lines in the wake of Charlie Christian represented the bebop method, and bebop was the dominant jazz of the postwar years. But there was a tributary of bebop, played by a coterie of dedicated specialists, which explored some of the fundamental tenets of what came to be known as the "cool school". Pianist Lennie Tristano was the principal architect of this style's quiet and oblique melodic approach, full of collective counter-melody, and so fluid and seamless in its improvisations that Tristano hoped to abolish bar-lines from his music altogether. Tristano had a number of sympathetic partners, notably the saxophonists Lee Konitz and Warne Marsh and the guitarist Billy Bauer. Bauer improvised hushed, tiptoeing melodies of considerable originality and invention around Tristano's piano on some of the classics of early cool – notably the 1949 album *Crosscurrents*. And on 'Intuition' from that session, which had no formal harmonic base, some observers maintain that free-improvised jazz was born.

Billy Bauer was born William Henry Bauer in New York on November 14th 1915. He was originally a banjo player, who shifted to guitar in the 1930s as the general rhythm-section emphasis changed. He joined the Jerry Wald Orchestra, and then a variety of bands led by Carl Hoff, Dick Stabile and Abe Lyman, but his real opportunity came with the Woody Herman band in 1944. Herman's 'Herds' were sophisticated and highly popular outfits and working in them was an invaluable education. There was an inclination among some of the Herman performers toward the cooler articulation of jazz that was to follow the big-band era and the first frantic wave of bebop.

The Herman band broke up in 1946 and Bauer freelanced in New York with leaders including Benny Goodman and Chubby Jackson. But a meeting with Lenny Tristano brought about the guitarist's most lasting and significant contribution to the development of the jazz guitar. Bauer's style suited Tristano's method, which was linear, full of melodic subtleties and unexpected turns of phrasing, but avoided emotional extremes and wide dynamic changes. The recordings they made together proved to be milestones in jazz history. In 1949 and 1950 Bauer won *Downbeat*'s jazz guitar poll, and the same accolade in *Metronome* magazine for five years running from 1949.

Starting in 1950 Bauer taught at the New York Conservatory of Music for three and a half years. From the early 1960s to the 1970s he was mainly involved in studio and session work. He appeared at the jazz club in McGurl's Sherwood Inn, Long Island, with his own group from 1961 to 1963, but much of his time since those days has been devoted to freelance work, teaching at his guitar school in Roslyn Heights, and with his own publishing company.

Hungarian-born guitarist Attila Zoller performing in the 1990s with saxophonist Lee Konitz at The Jazz Cafe in London. Zoller's enquiring mind constantly sought fresh creative challenges. He enjoyed the possibilities of freely improvised music as well as the discipline of chord progressions.

KENNY MATHIESON

WES MONTGOMERY

HE STARTED USING HIS THUMB BECAUSE HE DIDN'T WANT TO DISTURB THE NEIGHBOURS. HE STUMBLED ON HIS FAMOUS OCTAVES WHILE TUNING UP. HE COULDN'T READ CHORD SYMBOLS. BUT WES MONTGOMERY'S INNATE GENIUS ENSURED HIS PLACE AMONG THE GREATS.

In any jazz version of a word-association test, it is a safe bet that the prompt "Wes Montgomery" would automatically produce one of two responses – either "thumb" or "octaves". The modest Indianapolis-born guitarist effected a quiet revolution in jazz guitar, and those two things played a disproportionate part in that achievement.

Montgomery, though, had an even more crucial asset to draw upon, and it held the key to his development as one of the most important guitar stylists of the century. What really marked him out was his incredible ear, and a refined musical intelligence which belied his self-effacing manner. Put simply, Wes was a consummate natural musician, and everything else – the touch, the stylistic innovations, the famous octaves – flowed from that foundation.

While attitudes to education in jazz have changed radically, many people still cling to the idea of the jazz musician as a natural, untutored genius. The romanticisation of great performers who could not read music, like pianist Errol Garner, means that that has been paraded as a badge of distinction rather than a failing. In fact, even early jazz musicians were much more tutored than is often allowed, while the swing era ushered in a great emphasis on reading, and bop required a fairly refined understanding of harmony.

Wes Montgomery, however, seems to have been a genuine example of a self-taught musical genius whose understanding of complex theory was derived directly from his remarkable ear, with some assistance from fellow musicians in Indianapolis. He never learned to read even chord symbols, far less notation (although he was sometimes embarrassed about that fact, notably in the studio), and claimed his understanding of harmony and harmonic movement came from puzzling out the relationships of the constituent sounds which made up chords, rather than a theoretical knowledge of their parts. To describe him as a natural musical genius, then, entails no real overstatement.

Montgomery was born in Indianapolis on March 6th 1923. His parents split up when he was very young, and he lived with his father in Colombus, Ohio, until he was 17. His older brother, Monk, bought him his first instrument, a four-string tenor guitar, in 1935. But his musical horizons opened up in 1943, when he first heard records featuring Charlie Christian at a dance in Indianapolis. He went out and spent a small fortune (one the newly married guitarist could ill afford) on a guitar and amplifier. He told several interviewers the story of how he began to use his right thumb to pluck the strings in preference to either conventional finger-picking or a plectrum (or pick), in part to keep down the noise for his neighbours, and in part because he found the pick awkward, although he acknowledged its advantages in phrasing smoothly at fast speeds. Not, it has to be said, that he ever sounded

Wes Montgomery was one of the most popular jazz artists of the 1960s, not least because of his thumb-driven guitar sound, his unceasing flow of ideas, his use of octaves and extended chordal passages, and his ability to build a solo that would sustain interest chorus after chorus.

unduly encumbered at even the most rattling of tempos. The use of the thumb became one of the great defining elements of his mature style, and the softer, deeper tone it gave him was an instantly recognisable trademark.

If his account is to be believed, his other major stylistic characteristic, the use of octaves, was something of an accidental discovery, but one he took to previously unanticipated lengths. He told Ralph Gleason that "playing octaves was just a coincidence", and later claimed (in a recorded interview included on a posthumously released album, *Live At Jorgie's And More*) to have discovered the possibilities when he "ran a scale accidently" in octaves while tuning up. Although doubtless true, both accounts sound a little disingenuous in the light of his subsequent adventures with the style.

Earlier guitarists, notably Django Reinhardt, had played in unison octaves – simultaneously sounding two identical notes an octave apart – as an occasional enriching or emphasising device, but Montgomery developed it as a central element in his solo style in an entirely new fashion. In the process, he evolved a singularly individual and technically awesome system of left-hand finger positions on the fretboard, which enabled him to limit the number of intermediate strings which had to be dampened between the required notes.

Indianapolis had an active music scene in the clubs and after-hours joints in the 1940s and 1950s, and the guitarist was able to put in a lot of bandstand time – initially playing Charlie Christian solos he had memorised from the records – while holding down a full time day job. He had his first taste of touring when he was recruited by Lionel Hampton in 1948-50, and was included in his first recordings during that period as well, but he already had a large family, which eventually grew to seven children, and he never really took to the touring life. He spent the 1950s in Indianapolis, working in factories by day and gigging most of the night at places like the Tropics Club, The Turf Bar, and the Missile Club, a routine which some writers have seen as contributing to the heart attack which brought a premature end to his life.

Whatever the truth of that, it allowed him ample opportunity to develop as a musician, and there was no lack of encouragement from those around him. Two of his brothers, Monk and Buddy, were professional musicians, and Wes cut his first significant records with them for the Los Angeles-based Pacific Jazz label. Recording both as The Montgomery Brothers and The Mastersounds, the discs they cut in 1957-8 reveal Wes as an almost completely formed stylist by that stage. If his fiery solo on 'Billie's Bounce' has a rougher tone than we generally associate with him, a tune like 'Old Folks' is already quintessential Montgomery. His beautiful, almost unadorned statement of the theme underlies his love of melody, while his solo employs the explosive switch from single-line to octaves which would become so familiar in his work.

Although he had joined his brothers on the West Coast for a time, and also recorded with singer Jon Hendricks while out there, Wes was still living in Indianapolis in 1959, when Cannonball Adderley arrived in town, heard him at the Missile Club and was blown away. On his return to New York, the saxophonist lost no time in convincing Orrin Keepnews that his Riverside label had to record this phenomenon. An article by Gunther Schüller in *The Jazz Review*, bestowing lavish praise on the guitarist, clinched matters.

In October 1959, Keepnews brought Montgomery's trio with organist Melvin Rhyne and drummer Paul Parker to New York to cut his debut album, *Introducing Wes Montgomery*, which provided a solid start to the Riverside phase of his career. In purely jazz terms, he did his most important work for that label, and this album provided pointers to the jewels to come, notably in ballads like 'Round Midnight' and 'Yesterdays', but also in his tougher treatment of 'Missile Blues', a tribute to the after-hours joint in Indianapolis which had become a second home for him.

For many listeners, his next venture into the studio, in January 1960, produced the single finest record of his career. *The Incredible Jazz Guitar Of Wes Montgomery* is a repository of the riches of Montgomery's style, and provides several text book examples of his approach to jazz's central genres – the ballad ('Polka Dots And Moonbeams'), the blues ('D Natural Blues' and his own 'West Coast Blues'), driving uptempo material reflecting Charlie Christian's rhythmic drive (Sonny Rollins's 'Airegin'), and his own capabilities as a composer on 'West Coast Blues', 'Four On One' and 'Mister Walker' (Adrian Ingram's biography of the guitarist lists 45 such compositions).

Anyone seeking a single defining sample of his style, however, need look only as far as his version of 'Gone With The Wind', which not only demonstrates his ability to build an extended solo in logical but never predictable musical fashion (what jazz players often call "telling a story"), but also lays out his most characteristic technical means of achieving that end. The classic Montgomery solo pattern began in improvised single-line runs, then upped the tension with an explosive shift into unison octaves, and topped that with an even more intense leap into running an outline of the melody in block chords, a method he probably derived from the "comping" style favoured by bebop pianists, and from guitarists like Barney Kessel.

If that sounds a little formulaic on paper, Montgomery consistently brought fresh and subtle melodic and harmonic ideas to the process, and did so in spontaneous and highly organic fashion, making effective use of a

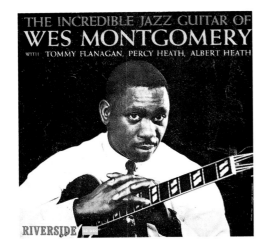

For his 1960 album The Incredible Jazz Guitar of Wes Montgomery, the guitarist was separated from his Indianapolis colleagues and teamed with a top-flight New York rhythm section. The results justified the album title and confirmed the arrival of a major new jazz-guitar voice. Many sides of his talent were on display here: his delicate treatment of a ballad, his breathtaking up-tempo soloing, his mastery of the blues form, the famed octave passages, and his ability to write memorable tunes, such as 'West Coast Blues', 'Four On Six' and 'Mister Walker'.

battery of expressive embellishments. Those qualities are all clearly evident in the 6 minutes and 20 seconds of 'Gone With The Wind'. The guitarist is accompanied by an ace rhythm section of Tommy Flanagan (piano), Percy Heath (bass) and Albert Heath (drums), and their highly supportive playing allows the guitarist to stretch out in the relaxed but springy tempo they have chosen. He is the only soloist, and that solo, sweetly executed and brimming with intuitive invention, is a perfect microcosm of his single-line/unison-octaves/block-chords style.

That same week, Wes was also featured as a sideman on trumpeter Nat Adderley's solid hard-bop album *Work Song*, and in May recorded with tenor saxophonist Harold Land – who had participated in some of the earlier Pacific Jazz sessions – on a robust blowing session named for the guitarist's composition 'West Coast Blues', and with Cannonball Adderley in a Pollwinners set. On *Movin' Along*, his next Riverside album, Wes chose to play a six-string bass guitar to get the exact sound he wanted on 'Tune Up', long ascribed to Miles Davis but now thought to have been written by Eddie Vinson (jazz authorship has often been an elastic business).

That is indicative of the importance he placed on the issue of sound and

Success came to Montgomery quite late in his career, but it was to prove a double-edged sword. Many critics rejected his later recordings with orchestras and string sections as light music lacking in artistic depth, but the guitarist may genuinely have enjoyed these projects, seeing them as a fresh and interesting challenge.

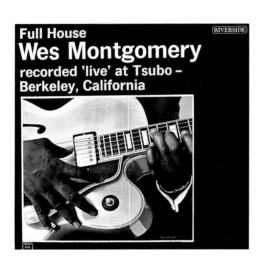

Full House was recorded live in June 1962 at Tsubo, a coffee-house in Berkeley, California. Montgomery is featured alongside tenor saxophonist Johnny Griffin and Miles Davis's rhythm section in a sparkling set. Up-tempo interchanges between Griffin and Montgomery raise the temperature, while the guitarist's quietly passionate solo interpretation of 'I've Grown Accustomed To Her Face' is a gem.

tone, going back to his initial momentous decision to opt for thumb rather than pick, a choice ultimately determined by his preference for the warm, softer tonal qualities which the thumb produced. The record was cut in October, and that same autumn also saw him reunited with Monk and Buddy as The Montgomery Brothers. They recorded an album under that name in San Francisco, where Wes had relocated to join them, and another in January, released as *Groveyard*, both featuring Buddy on piano rather than the vibes he had used in the first Montgomery Brothers records.

While in San Francisco, the guitarist formed a fascinating but short-lived association with John Coltrane, and played some live dates as an addition to Trane's quintet with Eric Dolphy. They never officially recorded, nor was the relationship developed from there, and given their respective paths – Wes into more commercial areas, 'Trane to interstellar space – it is hard (although fascinating) to see where it might have gone. He cut another powerful album, *So Much Guitar!*, in New York in August 1961, with a quintet featuring pianist Hank Jones and the conga drums of Ray Barretto. In addition to his usual immaculate single-line/octave/chord stylings, the album featured an unaccompanied ballad, 'While We're Young', unusually (for Wes) played entirely in chordal form, as well as his nod to Milt Jackson's 'Bags Groove' on 'Somethin' Like Bags', and a rip-roaring version of Ellington's 'Cotton Tail'.

A disappointing collaboration with George Shearing on the overly diffident *Love Walked In* and a better one with Milt Jackson on *Bags Meets Wes* rounded out his year in the studio, but his next Riverside release would capture him live, something already accomplished in a Montgomery Brothers live set, cut in Canada in December 1961. *Full House* was recorded at the Tsubo Club, Berkeley, in June 1962, with a high-power quintet featuring tenor saxophonist Johnny Griffin and a stellar rhythm section of Wynton Kelly (piano), Paul Chambers (bass) and Jimmy Cobb (drums), in town for a club engagement with Miles Davis, their employer at that point. It was the first in a string of sensational live recordings which revealed Montgomery's most essential qualities as a pure jazz performer, and acted as an antidote to the more commercial leanings of his studio work in the final years of his career.

Neatly, if perhaps ironically, his next Riverside album pointed the way to that more commercial future. *Fusion! – Wes Montgomery With Strings*, recorded in April 1963 featured the guitarist set amid very good string arrangements by Jimmy Jones, which succeeded in retaining more of a genuine jazz flavour than much of his subsequent work in that crossover mode. In the shape of things to come in the studio, Montgomery's own contributions, while unfailingly melodic and musical, were restricted by comparison with his usual flair. The Riverside phase of his career was now drawing to a close, as the company began to run into financial difficulties.

He cut three more albums for Keepnews in 1963, *Boss Guitar*, *Guitar On The Go* and *Portrait Of Wes*, all in the organ trio format of his first album (and each featuring his Indianapolis homeboy Melvin Rhyne on organ) before the label folded. Norman Granz, the famous jazz impresario, who had made his name with his Jazz At The Philharmonic concerts and a string of successful record labels, signed the guitarist to his Verve label in 1964. He made his debut with *Movin' Wes*, a set recorded in November which featured an expanded horn section and the Latin percussionist Willie Bobo. What came next began a controversy that has never really faded away.

In the course of 1965, Montgomery cut two albums under the direction of producer Creed Taylor, featuring a string orchestra. *Bumpin'*, with its infectious title track (arguably the best of his crossover albums), and *Goin' Out Of My Head* mark a clear move away from hard jazz and into a more accessible, radio-friendly format designed to appeal to a much broader audience than the one which lapped up his contemporaneous live sets.

The difference in approach can be heard quite clearly on the club dates preserved from the Half Note in New York in June of that year, released as the classic *Smokin' At The Half Note* and *Willow Weep For Me*, albeit with added-on string arrangements by Claus Ogerman on three cuts of the latter album. The slightly earlier live recordings from a Paris concert in March, released as *Impressions* and *Solitude*, did not become available until 1978, but provide an equally scintillating snapshot of the growing gulf between his live and studio directions. The rich flow of unfettered but always finely controlled invention which the guitarist pours out on these small group dates remains the authentic voice of Wes Montgomery as a creative jazz musician.

Smokin' At The Half Note in particular stands alongside *The Incredible Jazz Guitar* as the indispensible example of his art on record, but his career was now moving to a different groove. The single release of 'Goin' Out Of My Head' was a huge success, and won the guitarist a Grammy award as well as unprecedentedly large sales. It also meant the die was cast in terms of his subsequent direction, especially in the studio. Faced with the chance to make some serious income for his family for the first time, Montgomery turned out more albums in a similar orchestral format in the shape of *Tequila* and *California Dreaming* in 1966, drawing on pop and featuring an increasing reliance on simple melody and the smooth, lush sonority of the octave style.

That process went even further when he joined Taylor at Herb Alpert's newly launched A&M label, where the commercial approach was even more marked. Montgomery played beautifully on the three albums he cut for the label, but he could almost have done so in his sleep, such was the limitation which the sophisticated pop-inspired format imposed on his contribution. He made the best of it, and if his jazz admirers – both critics and fans – cried foul, the sales figures proved the commercial wisdom of the choice. There has been much conjecture over Montgomery's feelings on the matter, and various musicians and critics have reported his disquiet over the material, especially when his live audiences increasingly demanded only a note for note re-hash of the recorded version, thereby denying him the compensation of cutting loose on live dates which had marked his Verve period.

Fate conspired to rob us of the chance to discover whether or not he would have returned to jazz fundamentals in due course. The guitarist died prematurely after suffering a heart attack on June 15th 1968. He left a remarkable legacy, both in great records (the 12-CD box set of his complete work for the Riverside label is a fitting monument in itself) and in the stylistic influence he bequeathed to the generation of guitarists who followed him, including such figures as George Benson, Pat Martino and Pat Metheny (who has described *Smokin' At The Half Note* as "the greatest jazz guitar album ever made"), as well as Jim Mullen – a devout thumb-picker – in the UK. More broadly, his style became a pervasive staple of the jazz guitar vocabulary. His legacy is rich enough for even the most avid jazz fanatic to forgive his more commercial transgressions. Wes himself always maintained that his late studio work was pop rather than jazz, and by then he had done more than enough to ensure his ineradicable place in the jazz guitar pantheon.

THE HARDBOPPERS

THE STUDIED ELEGANCE OF COOL WAS NOT FOR EVERYONE. THE HARDBOPPERS WERE CONVINCED THAT JAZZ SHOULD REDISCOVER ITS CONNECTIONS WITH BLUES AND GOSPEL, AND GUITARISTS HAD TO LIVE ALONGSIDE THEIR INSTRUMENT OF CHOICE: THE HAMMOND ORGAN.

The "cool school" jazz of the early 1950s was popular, often innovative, and influential – but some jazz-lovers missed the earthy wail of the blues, the fire and rootsiness that had been heard in the jazz of an earlier period. Hard bop and funk emerged in the mid 1950s, to throw fuel on these embers – a return to shouting, gospelly melodies, percussive, repeating chord-patterns and driving drumming.

If ever there was an instrument tailor-made for turning up the temperature in this period, it was the Hammond organ, with its thunderous, holy-rolling climaxes and churchy chords. The Hammond became a popular vehicle for the rootsier varieties of hard bop, and the idiom's musicians often came from areas where the blues had never receded – industrial cities like Pittsburgh, Philadelphia and Detroit in particular. Jimmy Smith emerged as the kingpin of a virtuoso organ style that combined fast bebop lines and the roughest of R&B.

The ideal foil for the Hammond organ – the gospel choir of these instrumental ensembles – was the electric guitar. But this presented a dilemma. Most younger jazz guitarists of the 1950s were beboppers, keen to unfurl long, horn-like lines over the tickety-tick of a straight-ahead cymbal beat. Or else they were blues guitarists: but most of the musicians of that background had trouble improvising in the tricky harmonic frameworks of a music as much shaped by bop as R&B. A new kind of guitar player was needed, able to play with simplicity and an unambiguous beat, but with technique and vision in reserve to handle double-time bop runs and the unexpected swerves and turnbacks of modern jazz.

Two guitarists, both born in 1931, were among the pioneers of this way of playing. Perhaps the most admired, for his versatility and fluency in many styles as much as for his funkiness and blues feel, is Kenny Burrell. He gained his experience in the late 1940s with leaders of the calibre of Dizzy Gillespie, Oscar Peterson and Benny Goodman before his solo emergence as a Blue Note recording star and long-standing partner for Jimmy Smith in the 1960s. The other was Grant Green, a player who – in George Benson's opinion – could have performed as readily with Muddy Waters as Charlie Parker, and whose career was cut short at 47 by drug-related illness.

Kenny Burrell remains the guitarist's guitarist. His approach still astonishes his fellow musicians, even though guitar technique and the technology of reproducing the instrument's sounds have changed immeasurably since he first appeared. His tone sings, his phrasing avoids cliché no matter how well-travelled the idiom, his articulation is both precise and relaxed, and his solos glow with a sense of freedom and spontaneity that

makes the reshuffling of even the most familiar blues-bop phrases sound fresh and urgent. Though a highly erudite performer, who majored in music at college, Burrell never lost his feel for the blues, which he plays with understanding and warmth. Yet his ballad playing on standard songs also remains an object lesson, not just for guitarists, but for jazz musicians on any instrument.

Burrell's recordings with Jimmy Smith, and with legendary saxophonists Coleman Hawkins, Stanley Turrentine and Gene Ammons, testify to his power as a blues musician. His own recordings of 'Everyday I Have the Blues', 'Asphalt Canyon Blues' and 'Wild Man' confirm it. But his ballad versions of 'Angel Eyes' and 'God Bless the Child' are comparable to the most exceptional jazz ballad improvisations on any instrument, and he proved as expressive on the acoustic guitar on such classics as Harold Arlen's 'Last Night When We Were Young'. But Burrell could also be a peerless uptempo bop player, as he proved on hard-driving pieces like 'Mambo Twist' and 'Tin Tin Deo'.

He was born Kenneth Earl Burrell in Detroit, Michigan, in 1931. His mother was a pianist and his father played banjo; and of three brothers who all became musicians, two were guitarists. Kenny Burrell taught himself guitar from the age of 12. It was his second choice after the saxophone, which had been too expensive for the family to buy. His older brother Billy was a significant early influence, but so was the Miller High School in Detroit. Budding musicians abounded there, including pianist Tommy Flanagan, and vibraharpist Milt Jackson's brother Calvin, a bassist. Burrell liked the sound of Charlie Christian – almost inevitably for an emerging jazz guitarist in this period – and also Oscar Moore, guitarist with the massively popular Nat King Cole trio. Moore had been extensively influenced by Christian, and adapted the guitar pioneer's methods to the cooler, more restrained and romantic setting of the Cole trio. The group's succession of hits in the 1940s widened public awareness of the electric guitar, and for a brief period Oscar Moore's relaxed and elegant style was one of the most prominent guitar sounds in jazz. Its effect on the young Kenny Burrell was to become clear in his

Kenny Burrell on stage at the Hammersmith Odeon, London, during the "Jazz Expo" of 1969. The consummate jazz guitarist with roots in the blues, Burrell has recorded with a host of leading jazz artists, from John Coltrane to Jimmy Smith, Coleman Hawkins to Gil Evans.

Grant Green in performance at the Hammersmith Odeon, London, during the "Jazz Expo" of 1969. Staff guitarist at Blue Note for many years, Green offered clear, uncluttered, soul-inflected lines that made him ideal for tenor players such as Stanley Turrentine and Hank Mobley.

characteristic mixture of yielding tone and crisp, economical phrasing.

Burrell began to play professionally from 1948, initially with saxophonist Candy Johnson's Sextet, but his breakthrough, when he was still only 20, came through work with Dizzy Gillespie. Gillespie had been forced to wind up his revolutionary four-year-old big-band under the pressures of both postwar economics and public unpreparedness for an orchestra so audaciously splicing swing, Latin music and bebop. Kenny Burrell was an early part of what turned out to be the trumpeter's lasting move toward a smaller format. Early recordings by these small groups, on Gillespie's own Dee Gee label, were mixed in quality, but Burrell's taste and early composure testify to why he was to become such a popular addition to jazz recordings even in the 1950s. Burrell made his recording debut for Gillespie, and then spent the 1950s developing both as a popular sideman and as a bandleader, whilst still managing to complete his formal studies.

He graduated from Wayne University, Detroit, with a Bachelor of Music degree in 1955, and shortly afterwards moved to New York. Working for the Prestige label in the latter part of the decade, Burrell then recorded with some of the most exciting and fast-developing exponents of the hard-bop style, including John Coltrane, Tommy Flanagan and Elvin Jones. Burrell was proving that he could be smooth and graceful on ballads and punchy, succinct and swinging on the kind of mid-tempo bop blues he seemed to have been born to play, and at least one intimate collaboration with John Coltrane ('Why Was I Born?' from 1957's *The Cats*) also indicated that he was already a young master of subtle textures.

Burrell worked briefly with Benny Goodman in 1957, and through the following decade regularly topped the guitarists' polls in jazz magazines all over the world. Recording for Blue Note (with Tina Brooks, Art Blakey and others) in 1958, Burrell took part in some memorably forthright and exciting sessions including the freewheeling *Blue Lights*, and the guitarist's collaboration with an ageing but still imperious Coleman Hawkins on 1962's *Bluesy Burrell* was a memorable example of Burrell's adaptability and empathy. Then came one of his finest albums, *Guitar Forms* in the mid 1960s. On five of the tracks the guitarist is accompanied by an illustrious big-band including saxophonists Lee Konitz and Steve Lacy and drummer Elvin Jones, and the balance between some eloquent soloing and atmospheric Spanish-flavoured orchestral dynamics is typical of the sorcerer Gil Evans, who wrote the arrangements. Evans' soft and delicate chording and insistent swing was beautifully complemented by Burrell's subtlety.

Burrell came to Europe for the first time in 1969 and explored other ventures, such as opening his own nightclub and teaching clinics and seminars in guitar, worked lucratively in the studios and toured extensively. But it was in 1975, a year after Duke Ellington's death, that Kenny Burrell led what was almost certainly his most imaginative, freewheeling and substantial session. *Ellington Is Forever, Vol 1* was a brilliant tribute to the departed maestro, which captured much of the colour and clamour of idiosyncratic voices in the Duke's own music. Tenorist Joe Henderson and trumpeters Thad Jones and Jon Faddis made memorable contributions and Burrell was as thoughtful and full of understated surprises as ever.

Burrell has continued to record with fine musicians, mostly on blues and standards, and his earlier work has been extensively reissued. He remains one of the most swinging lucid, and personal of jazz guitarists.

If Kenny Burrell's career has described a long and graceful curve, Grant Green's started similarly, but spiralled off into the personal traumas that have removed too many jazz musicians from the stage before their time. Green, who was born in St Louis, Missouri, in 1931, studied guitar in grade school, and began making a professional impact by the time he was in his early teens. He was a gifted instrumentalist whose posthumous career through the fashionable 1980s acid-jazz resurgence was almost as successful as the one he enjoyed in his prime. Like Kenny Burrell, he was a superb blues guitarist, but similarly endowed with a sense of form and solo shape that enabled his improvisations to be models of clarity and emotional directness. In other forms, Green seemed both to challenge and to accommodate his partners and surroundings, at times delicate and reserved, at times slanting across the prevailing tempo or mood with controlled abandon.

Like a folk musician, Grant Green tended to choose whole-note intervals over more typically boppish and intricate melodic lines involving half-steps, and the preference – coupled with his warm, embracing tone and supple delivery gave his music its engaging and communicative forthrightness. Green had begun working professionally with St Louis bands in both jazz and R&B,

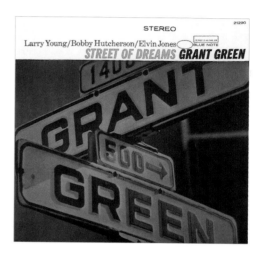

Grant Green recorded several albums as a leader during his association with Blue Note. On this 1964 album (above) were Bobby Hutcherson (vibes), Larry Young (organ) and Elvin Jones (drums), with Green in typically melodic form.

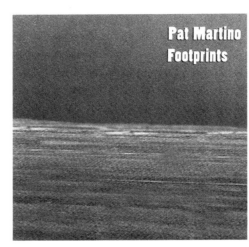

On the 1963 album Midnight Blue (above) Kenny Burrell displays an early interest in blues as well as his appreciation of artists such as T-Bone Walker. As always, Burrell's mastery of dynamics and careful, economical phrasing ensure that every statement carries its full weight. Pat Martino recorded Footprints (centre) in 1972 with Bobby Rose on second guitar, Richard Davis on bass and Billy Higgins (drums). This is Martino in total control, technically and artistically, paying homage to Wes on 'Road Song' and delving deep into Jobim's 'How Insensitive'. On his 1966 debut album (right) for Columbia as a leader, George Benson revealed his vocal talents on 'Summertime' and two other tracks, but it is his restless, bluesy guitar playing that cuts through.

most notably in the band local saxophonist Jimmy Forrest (of 'Night Train' fame) ran in the 1950s following his departure from a short stint with Duke Ellington. Green made his recording debut in Chicago with Forrest (with Elvin Jones on drums) and proved on that occasion how effective he could be in a context leaning heavily toward the blues. He was hired shortly afterwards by organist Brother Jack McDuff and moved to New York in 1960, beginning a successful, and briefly lucrative, recording career. It was with McDuff and the dry-toned, imaginative, world-music saxophonist Yusef Lateef that Green cut *Grantstand* for Blue Note in 1961, the set that kicked in his solo career. *Born To Be Blue*, the follow-up, brought in the rugged saxophonist Ike Quebec and the fluent and compositionally-gifted pianist Sonny Clark, and Green's characteristic mix of clean, uncluttered lines and expressive earthiness enhanced the reputation he was already winning among musicians and critics. *Downbeat* gave him its "Talent Deserving Wider Recognition" award in 1962.

Once associated with Blue Note, Green worked extensively as a sideman as well as a leader, on projects led by Stanley Turrentine, Hank Mobley, Lou Donaldson and Horace Parlan among others, and he also repeatedly confirmed how suited his guitar sound was to organ-led bands, appearing with John Patton and Don Wilkerson as well as Brother Jack McDuff. He also collaborated infectiously with Herbie Hancock on the gospel-flavoured session *Feelin' The Spirit*. 1964's *Matador* was a brilliant investigation of the possibilities of working with part of the then John Coltrane band, McCoy Tyner and Elvin Jones joining bassist Bob Cranshaw, and the repertoire including the Coltrane staple 'My Favorite Things.'

A succession of mostly punchy Blue Note albums featuring organists (Larry Young and Ronnie Foster) followed, and the group sound virtually became Grant Green's trademark. But the label's understandable tendency to over-record their bankable star had its price in occasional transgressions into the routine and the clichéd. This was the beginning of Grant Green's down period, and between 1967 and 1969 he was mostly off the scene with narcotics problems. He did return for some striking sessions (Blue Note's *Live At The Lighthouse* had its moments) and he performed music for the soundtrack of the film *The Final Comedown*.

George Benson, nearly 12 years younger than Grant Green and Kenny Burrell, developed along much the same paths as the older men (adept at the blues, accommodating of music outside bop alone, regularly working with organ bands) but eventually took a career turn that made him a much bigger

George Benson plays for the people of
Harlem, New York, in 1967 (above left).
Commercially, Benson is now the most
successful jazz guitarist of all time, but this
is attributable more to his vocal talents
than to public recognition of his guitar
artistry. With superb arrangements and
grooves from Marcus Miller, Greg
Phillinganes and James Newton Howard,
Collaboration (above) was a 1987 reunion
of Earl Klugh with his mentor George
Benson that found both men on top form.

commercial proposition than either. This Pittsburgh-born guitarist became one of the most successful and respected singer-instrumentalists in soul music, although he has never lost his appetite for the most demanding improvising settings, and will still enthusiastically jam afterhours in clubs whenever he can gets the opportunity.

Like Nat "King" Cole in the generation before him, George Benson is an artist whose instrumental skills would have been quite enough to secure him a place in jazz history, but whose audience was immensely expanded through the appeal of a light, romantic singing voice. In 1976, Benson's recording of 'Breezin'' made him a pop star, but in the decade previously he seemed perfectly cut out to fill the gap left by the premature departure of the great Wes Montgomery. Like Montgomery, Benson swung hard but with infectious relaxation, his phrasing was inventive, and like Grant Green he had a voluptuously glowing sound.

But Benson's career as a singer/guitarist was not such an abrupt shift from the musical experiences of his childhood as it might have seemed to guitar buffs. He was singing and playing ukulele on street-corners for change by the time he was eight, having been taught the instrument by his stepfather, also a guitarist, who introduced him to the work of Charlie Christian. The young Benson immediately recognised the bite and originality of Christian, and once remarked that most of the guitarists he heard over the next decade didn't match up to the impact Christian had made. He had to wait to hear Wes Montgomery, Kenny Burrell, Grant Green, Jimmy Raney, Tal Farlow and Barney Kessel before the magic was rekindled. The boy began to play with his stepfather at local clubs as Little Georgie Benson, singing and dancing as well as playing. In 1954, when he was 11, he took up formal guitar studies, but made his first recording – as a singer – in the same year. Coming from Pittsburgh, R&B and soulful ballads were his natural metier. Walking the streets as a child, George Benson heard Jimmy Reed and BB King on the jukeboxes: blues was the music all around him.

Benson's stepfather, a substantial influence on the boy's talents, made George a guitar during his high school years, and he played in rock bands as a teenager. But listening to Charlie Parker and to Wes Montgomery – who was to become the model for his mature technique – inspired in Benson a devotion to jazz that he has never lost.

Benson was encouraged by many of his contemporaries to leave Pittsburgh and look for work in a wider musical world where his natural ear and fluency might be better rewarded. But he liked his home town and had married young. Maybe he would never have left but for the winter of 1961-62 when his car was damaged and he couldn't travel to his usual jobs. To make a living, he needed to be hired by someone who could provide the transportation.

Hammond organist Brother Jack McDuff ran the kind of R&B-flavoured jazz group in which funky, communicative guitar players were obligatory, and Grant Green was holding down the post when Benson encountered him. Organ bands had long been popular in Pittsburgh too – so although the young Benson's theoretical knowledge was slight, he could mimic almost any guitarist he heard and knew what guitar accompaniment was supposed to sound like in an organ band.

Grant Green left McDuff in 1962 as his career blossomed, so when George Benson was 19 he stepped in. The job was to last until 1965, when Benson returned to Pittsburgh to lead his own group. His playing in this period sounded promising though derivative, and his sound was yet to acquire the rounded, luxurious quality it would have a couple of years later. The early stages with McDuff had been shaky because of Benson's inexperience – he admitted that the organist had tried to fire him when he found he couldn't solo – but he found jazz, and a mixture of blues and R&B belonged together, a perception not that common among bop guitarists of the time. And, as his ear guided him, Benson began to develop a solo style. If it was hot, urgent and packed with incident, that might be because McDuff used to give him only one break a night in the early days, and he had to say everything he wanted to within it.

Though he was to return to McDuff briefly, it was as a group leader that George Benson was now finding his feet – in much the same kind of setting as McDuff's, with Lonnie Smith on organ. He began to apply stringent criticism to his own playing, disliking his tone on record and working to improve it.

Benson began to record for Columbia under his own name during 1966 and 1967, and on albums such as *Stormy Weather* the guitarist began to show his real colours. 'Big Fat Lady' from *Stormy Weather* shows Benson's sophisticated handling of the technicalities of fast bop. He demonstrates a blues feeling not so affectingly apparent in his earlier work, and the drive of his funky playing is magnetic. *Blue Benson*, which followed, was also a standout disc from the period, with the headlong bebop of 'Billie's Bounce', the earthiness of 'Low-Down & Dirty' and 'Doobie Doobie Blues', and the lyrical Montgomery tribute 'I Remember Wes'.

Given his background, George Benson remained inevitably fascinated by the ways in which the intricacies and ambiguities of jazz improvisation could be squared with the directness and physicality of rock music and funk. He hinted at some answers to those questions in his spare, brooding solo as a guest artist on Miles Davis's groundbreaking mid-1960s album *Miles in the Sky*. But in the 1970s, Benson's career was to take a quite different turn. As with Wes Montgomery and Grant Green, the record companies heard in Benson's deceptively lazy development of a solo, and the voluptuousness of his tone, the potential for a wider market.

Shifting labels to Warner Brothers, Benson released an album simply called *Breezin'* in 1976 – mostly funky instrumentals, but featuring one vocal track, 'This Masquerade', in which the guitarist revealed that as a singer he had learned almost as much from Stevie Wonder as he had from Wes Montgomery's guitar. The public loved Benson's sensuous, bouyant sound,

Brother Jack McDuff (above) fronted a succession of organ-propelled groups that have been the training ground for many great guitarists, including Grant Green, George Benson and Pat Martino.

and the the way in which he would often scat to improvised guitar solos. Songs like 'Nature Boy', 'On Broadway', 'Give Me The Night' and 'Turn Your Love Around' brought superstar status for Benson.

Some jazz lovers have taken this turn in Benson's career as a sign of decline in every other respect but financially, much as happened to Wes Montgomery. But Benson has constantly reaffirmed (as Montgomery did in jazz club appearances long after his pop discs began to emerge) that his improviser's talents have not been blunted by the reduction in opportunities to play jazz – and neither has the remarkable resonance and expressiveness of his tone. It seems likely, as his brand of 1970s soul is perhaps eclipsed by changing fashions, that he will increasingly return to the jazz guitar.

Kenny Burrell, Grant Green and George Benson are the best-known of the jazz guitarists to have been closely associated with organ-combo funk, but Philadelphia-born Pat Martino is close behind. Like the others, Martino (who was born Pat Azzara in 1944), came from the industrial heartland of the States, and from its soul and R&B traditions. His most acclaimed work other than under his own direction was with Texas saxophonist John Handy's band in the late 1960s, and in a variety of organ/guitar groups.

He was originally inspired by his singer/guitarist father's enthusiasm for Django Reinhardt and Eddie Lang, early assistance from a guitar-playing cousin and lessons from Dennis Sandole, a local guitarist. After four years of learning the instrument as a teenager, Pat Martino was working professionally, in both jazz and R&B bands, and spent the first nine years of his career on the road with outfits led by Lloyd Price, Willis Jackson, Red Holloway and Sonny Stitt, and in Hammond bands led by Brother Jack McDuff, Richard "Groove" Holmes and Jimmy McGriff.

Martino's most audible inspirations are Grant Green and Wes Montgomery, and for sheer technique he sometimes even outstrips them, with furious speed hitched to clear, articulate improvisation. His lines are thoughtful and free of repetition or cliché even at high tempo, he can sound fluent in bebop, fusion, Latin music or even the most ambitious outer reaches of postbop. He usually enhances the work of fellow-musicians, and is sometimes the most memorable attribute of otherwise humdrum recordings. Martino's achievements testify to the seriousness and dedication with which he has approached his work. After long years on the road in the early part of his career, Martino withdrew at the end of the 1960s, returning to Philadelphia and devoting himself to an intense period of study and exploration. He also became increasingly involved in teaching the instrument and in composition.

Pat Martino became closely associated with the Muse record label in the 1970s, and cut a succession of powerful recordings for the company, usually with small groups exploring bebop, Latin music and ballads. In the 1990s, his earlier achievements have been more widely celebrated, and he has joined Blue Note records and confirmed that his inventiveness, technical adroitness and distinctiveness of sound have lost little during the more subdued periods of his career. *All Sides Now*, his Blue Note debut, coupled him with a number of other guitarists (including Charlie Hunter, the veteran Les Paul, Mike Stern and Tuck Andress) and with singer Cassandra Wilson – and if the session itself seemed more absorbed in its celebrity roll-call than the resulting music, Martino's own contributions were consistently sharp and fresh. He remains one of the most eloquent and well-equipped of all contemporary guitarists.

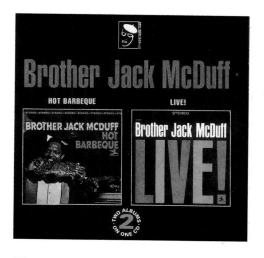

The young George Benson at the university of McDuff, this 1993 CD reissue (above) demonstrates the lessons Benson learnt on the club and concert circuit: how to groove, how to begin a solo with a clear statement, and how to build that solo to a crowd-satisfying climax.

JOHN FORDHAM ## JOE PASS

THE SON OF AN ITALIAN-AMERICAN STEEL-WORKER, JOE PASS STRUGGLED THROUGH DRUG ADDICTION AND PETTY CRIME BEFORE ACHIEVING IMMORTALITY AS THE UNDISPUTED MASTER OF THE UNACCOMPANIED JAZZ GUITAR PERFORMANCE.

John Surman, the British saxophonist who, among other activities, has been known to play unaccompanied concerts, once quoted Joe Pass on the challenge of playing jazz with nowhere to hide. Surman recalled Pass describing the awesome responsibility of going alone into the footlights, getting comfortable, playing some tunes, and then looking unobtrusively at the strategically placed watch. "Sometimes I'd think I'd played for a half hour or so," Pass would wryly reflect, "and the watch would say I'd only been on five minutes."

Few guitarists in the history of jazz, even among the most technically accomplished, have risked unaccompanied performance – or pulled it off with such breathtaking elegance and conviction. Classical guitarists, equipped with finger-style plucking techniques that permit countermelodic playing, have made a speciality of such performances. But the prevailing techniques among the jazz guitarists who developed after the rise of bebop were those that mimicked the style's beloved horn players. The lines these guitarists played were taut, linear, economical improvisations, often coloured with the intonations of the blues, executed with the plectrum or the thumb acting as a plectrum (Wes Montgomery's revolutionary introduction). They were thus flowing single-line figures that generally needed a rhythm section, usually augmented with a keyboard, on which to stay afloat.

Joe Pass proved that wasn't necessary, and he proved it so successfully that many younger jazz guitarists (such as Stanley Jordan or the 1990s hip-bop virtuoso Charlie Hunter) have come to develop multi-line techniques as if they were the most natural thing in the world. They use them both unaccompanied and as sound-sources of greatly expanded potential within groups. But it was Pass who broke the mould.

Joe Pass was a self-taught guitarist who went on to develop a style that permitted melody, harmonies and basslines to be played simultaneously. A Pass recital would be a tapestry of rich chords often dissolving into trickling arpeggios; light, dancing melody lines over sonorous backing figures that could suggest, if you closed your eyes, that a bassist on a walking four-four was in the room; sumptuous ballads as affecting as if they were being sung; and uptempo bebop that seemed to have its own built-in rhythm section. Pass was the complete jazz guitarist, and so musical (rather than simply technically awesome) that some of the biggest stars in jazz wanted him behind them. He accompanied George Shearing, Ella Fitzgerald, Sarah Vaughan, Oscar Peterson and many others in the course of his career, assignments requiring virtues as different as sympathetic harmonic embroidery behind the singers and breakneck virtuosity to keep up with the express train of a Peterson

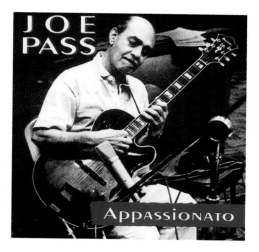

Before Joe Pass (left) developed his individual approach, few other jazz guitarists had considered performing for a complete concert without any accompaniment. Pass would weave melodies, chord accompaniment, bass lines and improvised single-line solos into a total performance. Twenty-six years after recording his acclaimed album For Django, Pass re-entered the studio in 1990 for Appassionato (above) with the same rhythm team: John Pisano (second guitar), Jim Hughart (bass) and Colin Bailey (drums). The focus is on Pass's single-string soloing, which excels on 'Body & Soul' and 'Relaxin' at Camarillo'.

performance. Yet all this was done without the usual guitar-players' rulebook. "I made a point of avoiding any guitaristic playing," Pass once declared. "There are certain things that are peculiar to a guitar – certain bending of notes, interval sounds and rhythmic playing. And I didn't do any of them." This independence of spirit and technique, born of a desire to blend the melodic impact of saxophones – the bebopper's impulse – with the harmonic possibilities of the piano and a cultivation of the ability to pull it off, gave Joe Pass's playing its unique signature.

Joe Pass was born Joseph Anthony Jacobi Passalaqua, on January 13th 1929, in New Brunswick, New Jersey, the oldest of four children. He grew up in the Italian area of Johnstown, Pennsylvania, where his father Mariano Passalaqua worked in the steel mills. He was given a guitar for his ninth birthday, having been attracted to the instrument by seeing the cowboy singer/actor Gene Autry play in the western *Ride, Tenderfoot, Ride*. Mariano Passalaqua gave the boy his first lessons, and guitar-playing friends of the family chipped in with help and advice. Soon he was taking weekly lessons, and spending much of his spare time practising and playing the guitar.

His single-mindedness and enthusiasm quickly paid off. He was to recall later that his ear was always good, and that he picked up melodies quickly, and intuitively understood their harmonies well enough to use them as a basis for improvising. By the time he was 14, Pass's guitar was already pointing him towards a life potentially less arduous than the Pennsylvania steelworks. He began working with local bands for clubs, weddings and parties, mostly with a string band called The Gentlemen of Rhythm, which had adopted a style drawn from Django Reinhardt's Quintet. Pass listened closely to Reinhardt's records, and to Charlie Christian's – but in Johnstown, Pennsylvania, they were hard to come by. A sympathetic shop assistant in the local store used to add Joseph Passalaqua's surreptitious requests for discs to the stock orders, but it was easier to obtain jazz discs featuring popular horn players like Dizzy Gillespie, Charlie Parker and Stan Getz. The boy took to listening to these musicians as much as to guitarists, and their influence made a profound impact on the way he heard and executed melody. But so did the improvising inclinations of the musicians in his neighbourhood.

"I can't say how or why I started, or even why I played guitar," Pass once told *Guitar* magazine. "There were guitar players around the neighbourhood, but they were really amateurs. I think it was simply that, for some reason, I had the gift of being able to pick up melodies and improvise on them. I always liked that, and I was always interested in harmonies. I could hear different harmonies on any tune, even pop tunes. And then I started hearing the jazz records, of course, and as a young man I found myself playing a lot with guys who would improvise – in fact, that's all they did. So I'd play at dances and they'd teach me what they knew, and that was my introduction to it all."

But if he was learning from his contemporaries, the young guitarist's skills and musical ear quickly proved to be in a class of their own, and the jazz performance bug had such a hold on him that it was inevitable that he would not remain in a Pennsylvania small town for long. When he was 20 he left home and began playing with former Artie Shaw saxophonist and singer Tony Pastor and then touring with the popular and exciting orchestra of Charlie Barnet in 1947. But it was bebop that fired him the most, and in the late 1940s playing bebop meant playing in New York. Joseph Passalqua moved there in 1949, initially to work with cool school saxophonist Brew Moore. But if young bebop players of the time were under Charlie Parker's spell musically, they often also fell under the influence of his lifestyle. The boy from Johnstown fell into heroin addiction like others of his jazz generation.

Throughout the 1950s, drugs hampered what should have been an illustrious career, with much of the decade spent in bad shape and clinging to jobs around Las Vegas, or in institutions. Passalaqua was eventually sent for a four year stretch of rehabilitation at the US Public Health Service Hospital in Fort Worth in 1954. When he returned to Las Vegas, he accompanied accordion player Dick Contino: at this time he still appeared as Joe Passalaqua on the liner notes to Contino's records. But the stay in Fort Worth hadn't solved the guitarist's problem. Contino recalled he once had to search the Vegas taxi-cab offices to locate his sideman's guitar, which he had hocked to a cabbie for drugs money. But he valued his troubled partner's friendship as well as his musicianship, and felt that for all his difficulties, Pass was a creative musician first and foremost who pushed the other band-members to play above themselves.

If Joe Pass's life was a mess at this time, a turning point was close. He was eventually arrested for selling pawn tickets on musical instruments he'd stolen and then hocked, and in 1960 he went to the Synanon Foundation's rehabilation centre in Santa Monica, California. At first Pass thought of it as a brief interlude, but the staff understood his problem and had better ways of stopping him returning to the old life than anyone had revealed to him before. At first he was hardly allowed to play, because his carers believed the connection between the music world and drugs was part of his problem. But when they thought he was ready, they let him join the institution's band.

Pacific Records producer Richard Bock was persuaded to release a disc featuring the patients' music. Called *Sounds Of Synanon*, it allowed Pass's talents to become more widely known. Through Bock and Pacific, Pass began to play with organist Richard "Groove" Holmes, and with Les McCann, Bud Shank, Johnny Griffin and many others. The year he left Synanon, 1963, he was given a Gibson guitar to replace the house Fender Jazzmaster he'd been borrowing, and quickly made his first recording as a leader. *Catch Me* was a quartet disc, but Pass and pianist Clare Fischer differed over the choice of material, possibly because the guitarist, his concentration still variable, was reluctant to rehearse and Fischer's choices needed work. *For Django* followed in 1964, its material almost entirely dedicated to the Belgian guitar genius. Pass made several recordings for Bock's World Pacific Jazz label, and went on to join George Shearing between 1965 and 1967. During the Shearing period, Pass cut the album *Simplicity* (1966), a Latin-angled disc that the great Wes Montgomery cited as a special event in an interview in *Downbeat* in the year of its release. It represented the zenith of the first phase of Joe Pass's re-emergence. He made a number of more commercial discs for Pacific in this period (featuring backing vocals, or covers of pop hits), but though the guitarist's style was already fully formed and his tasteful musicality evident in everything he touched, they were not really in the same class.

Featuring Joe Pass redefining a series of familiar jazz standards solo, without accompaniment, Virtuoso from 1994 was a breathtaking display of technical skill, harmonic dexterity and creative stamina, elevating Pass to star status within the jazz world and enabling him to tour as a soloist.

Pass began to record extensively, as if making up for lost time. He was a fine accompanist for singers, and cut sessions with Julie London, Carmen McRae and Johnny Mathis among others, but also with instrumentalists including Eddie "Cleanhead" Vinson and Chet Baker. In 1971, he also began to hook up regularly with bop guitarist Herb Ellis, whom he had met whilst deputising for him on a TV show. These duo sessions fascinated both listeners and guitarists of all persuasions for their variety, bouyancy, contrast of musical personalities, intricate counterpoint and sheer mind-boggling speed.

Guitar enthusiasts flocked to the clubs where Pass and Ellis played. Ellis was a powerful blues player, and his directness meshed effectively with Pass's complex bop lines. "I never found another guitarist who was that musical and easy to play with," Ellis said. They never practised together, but their techniques and alertness were so sharp they picked up each other's ideas without dropping a stitch. The two appeared at the 1972 Concord Jazz Festival, and then on the debut album of the festival's own label with bass giant Ray Brown and drummer Jake Hanna. 'Seven Come Eleven', a popular jazz guitarists' staple, was one of the duo's most remarkable collaborations, and was recorded at the Concord Festival the following year.

Concord's Carl Jefferson recommended Pass to that most demanding of bandleaders, Benny Goodman, for a gig in 1973. If anyone was likely to be a critical judge of a guitarist it was Goodman, whose featured guitarist in the late 1930s had been none other than Charlie Christian, the man who had started the entire bop guitar avalanche. Goodman didn't say much to Pass at the rehearsals, nor give him much to do, but those who knew the veteran bandleader realised that he had appreciated that here was a guitarist a cut

Ella Fitzgerald at the Montreux Jazz Festival, Switzerland, in 1979. Ella's association with Joe Pass benefited both parties. It drew Pass to the attention of an audience much wider than that usually afforded to jazz guitarists and demonstrated his unique talent for accompaniment. It also gave the already world-famous Fitzgerald a fresh and intimate context for both performance and recording.

above the average. In the concert, Pass played superbly, and Goodman promptly booked him for an upcoming Australian tour.

Joe Pass's career path turned even more sharply upward during 1973. He joined the whirlwind pianist Oscar Peterson and the bassist Niels-Henning Orsted Pedersen in what became one of the pianist's most celebrated trios. Pass once said that in order to keep up with Peterson's exceptional speed and dexterity he had to play and dance at the same time. Through his connection with Peterson, Pass joined the group of artists managed and recorded by the impresario Norman Granz, architect of the Jazz At The Philharmonic touring packages and the high priest of commercial jazz promotion. Granz had set up Pablo Records to feature the Jazz At The Philharmonic artists, and he signed Pass to the label as soon as Peterson hauled him down to Donte's Club in Los Angeles, where Pass often played on the Monday guitarists' nights. The deal meant another step up for Joe Pass, recording with Duke Ellington on *Duke's Big Four* and a series of duets with Ella Fitzgerald on *Take Love Easy*. *The Trio*, with Pass, Peterson and Ray Brown, also won a Grammy Award.

Pass cut a milestone in his career, and a harbinger of things to come, with *Virtuoso*, a set of unaccompanied pieces on standards including 'All The Things You Are', 'Night And Day' and 'Stella By Starlight'. He had been attempting this new way of working for some time, having been obliged to begin a show on his own on an earlier occasion, when his rhythm section was delayed. The guitarist's memory of the experience was mixed, but promoters liked the sound (and, probably, the impact on their profit margins of hiring one player rather than three) and solo guitar bookings had begun to come.

The opportunity shifted Pass's technique from a bop guitarist's usual dependence on a pick to a fingerstyle method that would permit an independent bassline, and though he complained that the approach hampered his ability to play uptempo, it wasn't a shortcoming that was apparent to his admirers. With the *Virtuoso* album, Pass was suddenly selling more records than his better-known stablemates on the Pablo label, Ella Fitzgerald and Oscar Peterson, almost certainly the result of his appeal to lovers of guitar music of all kinds, whether classical, jazz or rock.

Pass began to develop as a composer with subsequent discs, though the standards format was the closest to his heart, and he recorded a furiously inventive two-guitar conversation with Herb Ellis under the title *Two For The Road* in 1974, followed by *Portraits Of Duke Ellington* with bassist Ray Brown, *Kansas City* with the Count Basie Sextet, *Blues For Two* with Zoot Sims, and a raft of others, showing that he could be comfortable in idioms from bop to blues or Latin, and as a sensational soloist or a sympathetic accompanist.

He recorded extensively, on his own account and others', though his second wife confirmed that he disliked hearing himself on disc and only began to listen to his own recordings in his declining years, particularly those accompanying Ella Fitzgerald. These had been encounters of particular resonance for him, and his meticulous musicianship coupled with a relaxed spontaneity had made him an ideal foil for the vocalist, allowing her to soar and glide on the gentle breezes of his music. Joe Pass's brother Tony once recalled that he had heard Joe knock on Ella Fitzgerald's dressing-room door before a Carnegie Hall concert to ask her what she planned to sing. She told him, and he wrote the titles and the keys inside the flap of a matchbook. He admitted to Tony Passalaqua later that he had no idea where it was, and had never looked at it during the show.

Joe Pass's music made friends for him all over the world because it did not appeal to a specialised jazz audience alone. Though he could play the daylights out of the demanding form of bebop, Pass did it with such elegance that the frantic, even manic qualities the idiom could exhibit evaporated entirely. On the other hand standard song-forms and straightahead swing were invested with new subtleties and intricacies that intrigued listeners with the prospect of hearing the reassuringly familiar made over.

In 1989 Pass recorded again with a rhythm section from his early days – fellow guitarist John Pisano, Jim Hughart on bass and Colin Bailey on drums. *Summer Night* was the result, an understated homage to Django Reinhardt that found Pass in typically relaxed and reflective mood, and the same year's *Appassionato* (also with Pisano) featured some 1940s bebop anthems delivered with a businesslike crispness that was not always true of Pass's more romantic outings. For *Summer Night*, the two guitarists decided to play acoustic to give the music a more intimate shimmer appropriate to the title and the Reinhardt connection, Pass using an old Epiphone Deluxe that had belonged to John Pisano's father, while Pisano used a nylon-stringed instrument.

In duet with Pisano (on the *Duets* disc in 1991) Joe Pass could often sound more urgent and forceful than he customarily would, and this constantly productive partnership only ended with the maestro's death. The guitarist also worked in Europe with radio station big-bands at the end of 1991 and beginning of 1992, at which point he learned that he was suffering from liver cancer. Continuing to play while he received treatment however, Pass continued to perform into 1994, when he had to withdraw from a showcase gig featuring Paco Peña among others. On May 7th 1994, a failing Joe Pass sat in with John Pisano on a club gig in Los Angeles. "He sounded better than most guitarists," Pisano told *Guitar Player* magazine. "But afterwards he looked at me with a tear in his eye and said 'I can't play any more'." He died in Los Angeles a little over two weeks later.

Joe Pass was a complex man, whose moods were unpredictable but whose most awkward and unaccomodating side was usually warmed by an irrepressible sense of humour. He could be sympathetic and attentive, or unpredictable and impatient. Shortcomings in hotel facilities would particularly get to him, and he was alleged to have returned immediately to LA after the long flight to Paris because he hadn't liked his rooms when he got there. He liked practical jokes and put-ons, often carrying them close to the point of inviting hostile reactions, but he could be moved to considerable human warmth, particularly when he encountered young people getting into difficulties with drugs. He also taught, wrote guitar tutors and made instructional videos – though he could be a teacher with a short fuse, sometimes instilling a sense of purposeful wonderment into pupils, sometimes the sense that the best thing they could do was quit.

But he never wavered from his innermost convictions, the fundamental one being that a guitar was a guitar and not a keyboard or a trumpet. Pass believed that everything a jazz guitarist needed was available on the conventional instrument. He disliked the electronic and synthesised effects of rock guitarists, and believed that technique and imagination could achieve most, if not all, of the emotional impact possible by pushing a button. Pass's technique extended the jazz guitar's potential more ambitiously than almost any of his fellow practitioners on the instrument, and it was no exaggeration when he was described as "Art Tatum with a piano in his lap".

The combination of Fitzgerald's interpretative skills, Pass's sensitive musicianship and the beautiful sound of his guitar could be a recipe for a pleasant laidback set, but this 1974 album (above) is more than just that. There are moments of tender regret and of exuberant joy, of deep passion and light fun, but underpinning it all is the responsive accompaniment of Pass. No other guitarist could have done it so well.

STUART NICHOLSON

FUSION: THE FIRST WAVE

WHEN THE BEATLES STORMED THE US POP CHARTS IN 1964, TO BE FOLLOWED BY THE BEGINNINGS OF THE ROCK REVOLUTION, JAZZ SUDDENLY LOOKED OLD-FASHIONED. BUT YOUNG JAZZ GUITARISTS FELT THEY COULD BUILD A BRIDGE BETWEEN THE MUSICAL WORLDS.

Miles Davis's Bitches Brew album of 1970 was constructed by producer Teo Macero from music taped over several days by Davis with a variety of musicians including John McLaughlin on guitar. Bitches Brew's insistent rhythms and swirling electronic sounds exerted a profound impact on young musicians.

The 1960s were the 20th century's most celebrated decade, and if you were young then, the pop star was even more seductive than the film star had been to previous generations. By 1964, 40 per cent of the population of the United States were under 20 and enjoying an unprecedented level of affluence, making them desirable targets for cultural industries.

When, on February 7th 1964, the Beatles touched down at Kennedy Airport, it marked the beginning of the "British Invasion". Almost overnight, American performers were knocked off radio and out of the Top Ten by British acts. It triggered the rock explosion, and by 1966 the music industry was looking at its first ever billion-dollar gross. In June 1967, 1,100 members of the world's media were flown to a field near Monterey, California, where some of the biggest rock acts of the day roared the new sound through banks of speakers that echoed around the world. "All of a sudden," reflected Miles Davis, "jazz had become passé."

The sudden and unexpected rise of rock captured the imagination of a whole generation, who looked down with disdain at the perceived shortcomings of the hopelessly square generation that preceded them. "Hey, you hepcats, dig that craaazy beat!" cried one rock fan as he passed a jazz club. His friends collapsed to the pavement, crippled by mirth. "During the heavy rock years from 1966 to 1969," wrote music journalist Albert Goodman in 1971, "we heard the same old stuff the guys had been playing for years. It was an embarrassment. Jazz had lost its audience and was talking to itself."

As the end of the 1960s approached, the music was in crisis. Clubs were either closing down or turning themselves into things called "Discotheques", several leading American jazz musicians had emigrated to Europe, and the major recording companies were no longer interested in recording a music that offered a poor return compared to the massive potential offered by rock. In such a climate the music press was beginning to predict that the end of jazz was in sight. *Melody Maker* contained a "Requiem for a jazz we loved and knew so well", *Rouge* magazine headlined "Jazz is Dead... Folk is Dead... Long Live Rock!" while *Downbeat* pronounced "Jazz As We Know It Is Dead" on its front cover.

Yet for aspiring young jazz musicians growing up in the 1960s, a social revolution was happening all around them. Acid was making the unthinkable commonplace, as popular culture was swept by unusual connections and new ideas, leading to a greater sensibility towards colour and design that certainly had an important influence on pop culture, media style and advertising. In this new climate, integrating jazz and rock seemed like the most logical connection in the world. Here was a way for young jazz musicians to find a

voice in jazz that did not cut them off from the culture of their own generation. "Everybody was dropping acid and the prevailing attitude was 'Let's do something different'," said guitarist Larry Coryell, who was 22 in 1965. "We were saying, 'We love Wes [Montgomery], but we also love Bob Dylan. We love Coltrane but we also love the Beatles. We love Miles but we also love the Rolling Stones.' We wanted people to know we are very much part of the contemporary scene, but at the same time we had worked our butts off to learn this other music [called jazz]. It was a very sincere thing."

Coryell moved to New York in September 1965 and quickly established a reputation as fleet-fingered guitarist in the Wes Montgomery mould, sitting in at jam sessions with young musicians such as Randy Brecker, Mike Mainieri and Warren Bernhardt. These were jam sessions with a difference, however, since the new rock rhythms were being used instead of jazz's straight-ahead time keeping.

"This went on for about a year," said Bernhardt. "Certainly well into 1966. To me that was the beginning of jazz-rock; to my knowledge there was no one else combining rock and jazz improvisation at that time, combining styles like that." Around this time, Coryell formed a group, Free Spirits, with

From his early career with Charlie Parker until his death in 1991, trumpeter Miles Davis never stopped to look over his shoulder on his journey through music. By the late 1960s he had discarded the swing basis of jazz rhythm in favour of the even eighth notes of rock. Ostinato bass grooves and electric keyboards featured on his 1969 release In A Silent Way and this direction was confirmed by the powerful Bitches Brew album of the following year, both albums featuring guitarist John McLaughlin. Davis is pictured above on-stage in 1989.

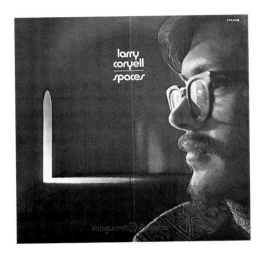

The guitar work of Larry Coryell (right) featured on the Gary Burton Quartet's 1967 album Lofty Fake Anagram, which blended influences as diverse as country music and rock with jazz. Coryell went on to form Eleventh House in the 1970s but eventually moved away from fusion. One of Coryell's best recordings was Spaces (above) from 1970, featuring four of fusion's founding figures: Chick Corea (electric piano), Miroslav Vitous (bass), Billy Cobham (drums) and John McLaughlin (guitar). It includes an impressive Coryell-McLaughlin guitar duet, 'Rene's Theme'.

saxophonist Jim Pepper, guitarist Columbus "Chip" Baker, bassist Chris Hills and drummer Bobby Moses. Their rather self-conscious mix of rock rhythms and jazz improvisation was featured on *Free Spirits*, recorded in 1966 and considered among the very first jazz-rock albums.

Free Spirits enjoyed sporadic work until it finally broke up in 1967, but in January that year Coryell was invited to join the Gary Burton Trio for an engagement at Lennie's-on-the-Turnpike. It proved to be a mutually stimulating meeting of minds and after three months of gigs, Burton invited Coryell to join his group. In April the Gary Burton Quartet recorded *Duster* and here, perhaps more than on *Free Spirits*, was the clearest indication that an artistically and aesthetically satisfying synthesis of jazz and rock was possible. Coryell's acid-tone guitar was a sound associated with rock rather than jazz, but his technical facility, melodic construction and harmonic ingenuity set him apart from most rock guitarists of the time. Four months later the group recorded *Lofty Fake Anagram*: "The musicianship is of a very high level – as one would expect," opined *Rolling Stone*.

A measure of how the group's progress was being followed by other young jazz musicians is revealed in a private recording made in early 1968 at the home of London pianist and composer Bob Cornford.

In a rehearsal duet with young British guitarist John McLaughlin they recreate the final track from *Lofty Fake Anagram*, 'Good Citizen Swallow', with McLaughlin consciously emulating Coryell's style.

Born in Yorkshire in 1942, McLaughlin moved to the busy London music scene in 1961, where he worked with a variety of groups, including those led by Georgie Fame, Tony Meehan, Brian Auger, Herbie Goins and Alexis Korner. London at the time was swept with a blues revival and Korner was a central figure. As early as 1962 he was mixing jazz musicians with blues musicians in his band Blues Incorporated, producing music that many believe pointed very strongly to a confluence of jazz and rock. McLaughlin worked in Korner's band alongside organist/saxophonist Graham Bond, who went out on his own with his Organ-isation, including bassist Jack Bruce and drummer Ginger Baker. McLaughlin was briefly with this group in 1963, appearing on the album *Solid Bond*, which revealed a capable jazz group playing with the

Larry Coryell, himself a competitive personality, once said of John McLaughlin (left): "He even has to win at ping-pong." This single-minded determination may account for McLaughlin's outstanding skills as a guitarist. Pianist Leon Cohen, who played with McLaughlin in the mid 1960s, recalls sharing a room with the guitarist after a gig in England. While Cohen was preparing to sleep, McLaughlin had got out his guitar and started to practise. When Cohen awoke several hours later, there was McLaughlin still dressed in his tuxedo and still practising. His explanation? "There's not a lot of time."

intensity and fire of a Charles Mingus ensemble on jazz numbers but including a strong improvisatory element on pop numbers that marked a stepping stone on the way to a jazz-rock fusion. A larger-than-life figure, Bond caused Baker to leave the group in 1966. Teaming up with Bruce and guitarist Eric Clapton, he formed the group Cream. With Clapton breaking open the temporal limits of the blues form with long, extended improvisations, backed by a bassist and a drummer who had learnt their craft within jazz, Cream suggested, more than any other group of the day, just what a successful jazz-rock synthesis might sound like.

Meanwhile McLaughlin continued to work in a variety of musical situations after leaving Bond, including an increasing involvement in session work, where he appeared on albums by the Rolling Stones, Tom Jones, Petula Clark and David Bowie. It was a career path that was taking him further and further from jazz, causing him great frustration. In 1967 he abruptly gave it all up and moved to Germany to immerse himself in free jazz with Gunter Hampel's group. He also formed a band with John Surman on baritone, Dave Holland on bass and Tony Oxley on drums that experimented with open form and "time, no changes" as a basis for improvisation. In July 1968, Holland left London to join Miles Davis, and Brian Odgers took over the bass chair. On January 16th 1969, the group recorded *Extrapolation*, and it is clear that here was a major talent poised to move to centre stage. What is immediately apparent is McLaughlin's technical facility and a tone that was hard and cutting in the manner of rock guitarists. Breaking with the "jazz swing" feel by accenting his notes evenly using little or no syncopation in the construction of his phrases, he had devised an approach to the jazz guitar that broke with the claustrophobic role-model hierarchy of the Charlie Christian/ Barney Kessel/Mundell Lowe/Jimmy Raney/Herb Ellis/Grant Green/Tal Farlow/Kenny Burrell/Wes Montgomey axis that was based on the single-note lines of horn players.

It was not long before Dave Holland had played some of McLaughlin's work to colleagues in the Miles Davis group. Tony Williams, in particular, was impressed. About to leave Davis and form his own band, he called McLaughlin, who left London for New York to join Williams in February 1969. On his arrival he was taken up to Harlem to jam. "I first heard John at Count Basie's," said Larry Coryell. "After 30 seconds of his first solo I turned to my wife and said, 'This is the best guitar player I've ever heard in my life'." Miles Davis immediately invited McLaughlin to participate on his upcoming record session. When McLaughlin turned up, Davis said, "Just relax and play like you did at Count Basie's and everything will be all right." McLaughlin did, and *In A Silent Way* announced to the world that the jazz landscape was about to change radically.

Davis was greatly impressed with McLaughlin's playing and tried to get him to join his band, but although McLaughlin refused, he did play on several live gigs with Davis and became a regular presence on Davis albums for the next two years, including *Bitches Brew, Circle In The Round, Directions, Jack Johnson, Get Up With It, On The Corner* and *Live Evil*. Yet it was perhaps less in his role in helping to define and shape Davis's music, more as the catalyst in Tony Williams' new band Lifetime, that McLaughlin's vast potential was first realised.

With Larry Young on organ, the trio revealed their apocalyptic vision of what jazz could be on *Emergency!* from 1969, one of the most underrated albums in jazz history. Lifetime appeared to have glimpsed the future and for a moment at least it seemed as if it belonged to them and not to Davis. Here was an extension of the ideas first revealed in *Extrapolation* but reinforced with the energy and vigour of rock. It was followed by *Turn It Over* with bassist Jack Bruce; harder edged and more rock-orientated than its free flowing predecessor.

Lifetime broke up in 1971, amid much grumbling about conflicting egos, but the freewheeling spirit of the band lived on: in June 1972, Love Cry Want, a legendary jazz-rock group led by Washington DC guitarist Nicholas, with Larry Young on organ and drummers Joe Gallivan and Jimmy Molneiri, recorded an album–length statement live in Layfayette Park, across from the White House. *Love Cry Want* has Nicholas on a prototype guitar synth (which he would develop with Electric Music Laboratories) and is filled with the darkness and turmoil of the times, which were such that Richard Nixon himself had demanded that the plug be pulled on the concert. Equally impetuously driven was *Let's Be Generous* by Joachim Kühn on keyboards, Miroslav Tadic guitar, Tony Newton bass and Mark Nauseef percussion. It was a memorable reminder in the conservative 1990s what a dangerous beast jazz-rock could be when unconstrained by commercial consideration.

Even before Lifetime was wound up, McLaughlin had recorded *My Goal's*

Powerful, urgent music on Emergency! from Tony Williams Lifetime in 1969, featuring Tony Williams (drums), Larry Young (organ) and John McLaughlin (guitar). McLaughlin had made vast strides in just the few months since recording Extrapolation, as testified by his burning solos throughout this album.

Beyond under his own name in March 1971. For this album he head-hunted drummer Billy Cobham and violinist Jerry Goodman, with a view to inviting them to join a new band if he found they could work together. When they agreed McLaughlin approached two more musicians who were "excited at the prospect of playing music beyond category": keyboard player Jan Hammer, then Sarah Vaughan's accompanist, and bassist Rick Laird, with whom McLaughlin had played on the London scene before Laird put in road time with the Buddy Rich Big Band. The Mahavishnu Orchestra debuted at Greenwich Village's Gaslight Café in July 1971 and so mesmerised audiences that it was immediately kept on. The group exhibited an astonishing degree of ensemble cohesion at blisteringly fast tempi and was unconstrained by

unusual time signatures or abrupt changes of meter. McLaughlin's playing in particular was singled out for high praise: nothing like this had been heard in jazz before. He was soon acknowledged as the most influential guitarist in jazz since Wes Montgomery. His stunning virtuosity, linked to melodic and harmonic fluency, left fellow guitarists gasping.

Inner Mounting Flame was recorded in August 1971, featuring McLaughlin compositions that were often as complex as any bebop line, yet drawing on a wide range of influences, most notably the music of Eastern cultures, especially India. In the context of its time, *Inner Mounting Flame* turned out

Miles Davis amazed the jazz world in 1963 when he engaged 17-year-old drummer Tony Williams (above) to join his quintet. But Williams, already a master musician, was to be an integral element in the trumpeter's exploration of new forms which culminated in the great fusion albums at the end of the decade.

to be more influential than Miles Davis's best–selling album *Bitches Brew*. Gone were the periods of abstraction that were a part of McLaughlin's playing personality with Lifetime. In their place, collective ensemble interplay reinforced with an intensity that belied its spontaneity and a closely woven ensemble style braced by complex riff figures and dramatic counterpoint, given momentum by an earlier jazz device: two- and four-bar exchanges. The dramatic impact of the Mahavishnu Orchestra live – it was a very loud band – and its sheer visceral energy and new concept forced many leading musicians to reassess their approach to jazz. Both Larry Coryell and Chick Corea have acknowledged the impact of the Mahavishnu Orchestra on their thinking. Corea transformed his group Return To Forever into a guitar-orientated band in 1973, and in the same year Larry Coryell formed Eleventh House.

The problem of high intensity and dazzling virtuosity is that you can only make a first impression once. *Birds Of Fire*, released in 1973, honed the band's skills to a razor sharp edge, and the live *Between Nothingness And Eternity* stretched several compositions to the point at which they seemed to sag in the middle. After giving their final concert on December 29th 1973, the original Mahavishnu broke up. Their first three albums dramatically altered the landscape of the burgeoning jazz-rock movement, sparking off a host of imitators who exploited speed of execution and flashy riffs as an end in

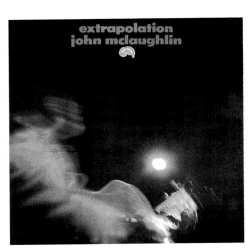

Eleventh House (1974 album, above) with guitarist Larry Coryell had strength but lacked the focus of other bands of the period. John McLaughlin finally pulled together all the strands evident in his previous work with Miles Davis and Tony Williams on The Mahavishnu Orchestra's Inner Mounting Flame LP of 1971 (centre). McLaughlin's 1969 album Extrapolation (right) was a turning point for the guitar in jazz, pointing away from bebop and towards complex time signatures and rock rhythms, using outside influences that ranged from free jazz to Indian music.

themselves. Guitarist Al DiMeola, for instance, confessed that he wanted to become "the fastest guitar player in the world". Such narrow artistic aspirations spelt the end for jazz-rock: in pursuing gloss at the expense of meaning the original promise of a jazz-rock union was undone by commercial excess as the music mutated into a consumer-friendly product known as "Fusion" that took up residence on commercial FM radio.

McLaughlin, meanwhile, went on to form a new version of Mahavishnu, but the somewhat pretentious aspirations of *Apocalypse*, recorded in 1974 with the London Symphony Orchestra conducted by Michael Tilson Thomas, seemed a reflection of the times, when "progressive" rock groups were filling stadiums with theatrical pomp, lights, costumes and elaborate sets. McLaughlin toured with a pared-down Mahavishnu ensemble but *Visions Of The Emerald Beyond* seemed to confirm that the band was coasting. McLaughlin appeared to have lost interest. While cutting *Inner Worlds*, the band's final album of the 1970s, in August 1975, he had already performed with Shakti, an acoustic group that fused jazz improvisation and Indian music.

Having all but defined jazz-rock in the late 1960s and early 1970s, McLaughlin's career subsequently went in a myriad of directions, with Shakti, the One Truth Band and an acoustic guitar trio with Al DiMeola and Paco de Lucia which produced *Friday Night In San Francisco* (1981) and *Passion, Grace And Fire* (1983). Then came another version of Mahavishnu, surprisingly lacklustre, in which he used a guitar connected to the Synclavier Digital Music System. As the decade progressed he returned to hard-bop on the soundtrack of the film *Round Midnight*, reawakened his symphonic aspirations with *Mediterranean Concerto*, acted as a producer for his wife, pianist Katia Labeque, and performed and recorded again with Miles Davis on *You're Under Arrest* and *Aura*. In the 1990s he formed a trio with percussionist Trilok Gurtu that produced *Qué Algeria* and performed a tribute to Bill Evans released on the album *Time Remembered*.

In contrast to McLaughlin's frenetic activity, Larry Coryell saw his career unfold in fits and starts as personal problems often stood in the way of capitalising on his promising beginnings with Gary Burton. "It's just that I

The Indian violinist L Shankar (above left) was an ideal partner for John McLaughlin in the group Shakti. The soaring melodic lines, complex rhythms and inventive dialogues between violin and guitar brought a fresh, exotic sound to Western audiences. In 1990 three members of Shakti – Shankar on violin, Zakir Hussain on tabla and Vikku Vinayakram on ghatam – displayed more Indian music traditions on their own album (above).

Paco de Lucia (above left) had breathed fresh life into the flamenco culture of his native Spain by opening its doors to outside influences. He found a soul mate in John McLaughlin (right). With the Guitar Trio – first with Larry Coryell and subsequently Al DiMeola – speed of fingers sometimes surpassed musical taste, but the project achieved enormous success and popularised the use of acoustic guitars in jazz.

had to rock out more, play loud, go through a phase where I almost lost my hearing. Everybody was out there for the perfect kind of acid trip, the perfect orgasm," he said. There was little discernible direction to Coryell's career at this time, but in 1969 he cut *Spaces* with a line-up that included McLaughlin, Chick Corea on electric piano, Miroslav Vitous on bass and Billy Cobham on drums. It is an album that includes many sublime moments by both Coryell and McLaughlin and although less well known, nevertheless numbers among the finest albums of jazz-rock.

However, Coryell was equally capable of some awful albums such as *Larry Coryell At The Village Gate*. In 1971 he formed a band with saxophonist Steve Marcus, but that eventually dissolved through alcoholic excess. However, in 1973 Coryell formed Eleventh House and the band's debut, *Introducing The Eleventh House*, promised much. A key figure in the line-up was trumpeter Randy Brecker, but when he left, Coryell was devastated and the direction of the band floundered. And while *Larry Coryell And Eleventh House At Montreux* from 1974 is somewhat self-indulgent, it does reveal Coryell's great talent. Subsequent albums lost the plot: *Level One*, for example, veered into disco territory as Coryell again failed to capitalise on promising beginnings.

Bouts of alcoholism and drug abuse in 1978 and 1981 interrupted three years of acoustic trio work, touring with Philip Catherine and Steve Khan, but in 1978 he recorded *Movies* with Mike Mantler, contributing a memorable solo on 'Four' on a jazz-rock album that came just too late for the recognition it deserved. In 1979 he recorded *Tributaries*, an acoustic album with Joe Beck and John Scofield that was a jazz/blues version of the flamenco orientated trio of McLaughlin, Al DiMeola and Paco de Lucia, with whom he later toured Europe, deputising for DiMeola.

Dates with Sonny Rollins, Charles Mingus and several weeks rehearsing with Miles Davis represented a genuine attempt to rehabilitate his career, which was followed by an adaptation of Rimsky-Korsakov's *Scheherazade* in

February 1982 followed by his transcriptions of three Stravinsky ballets, *Petrouchka/Firebird Suite* (1982) and *The Rite Of Spring* (1983). Although they contained few, if any, moments of jazz improvisation, they nevertheless represented a huge technical challenge for the guitarist. "It was the hardest thing I ever had to do in my life," he explained.

In the mid 1980s he returned to the playing style of Wes Montgomery, who had inspired him as a teenager, on *Comin' Home* (1984), *Equipoise* (1985) and, paired with Montgomery stylist Emily Remler, *Duos* (1985). Sadly the man who helped found jazz-rock never capitalised on it. Even a monster jazz-rock fusion blow-out, *Cause And Effect*, a 1998 trio album with Tom Coster and Steve Smith that shook the foundations of his earlier barnstormers with Eleventh House, seemed yet another incongruous addition to his sadly confused discography.

A couple of years earlier John McLaughlin had also returned to his musical roots – his days gigging on the London scene in early 1960s with the organ trios of Georgie Fame and Graham Bond. In 1993 he formed the power trio Free Spirits with organist Joey DeFrancesco and drummer Dennis Chambers, but McLaughlin did not adhere to any specific stylistic allegiance, regarding the band as a platform for hard, unequivocal blowing: it can be heard on *Tokyo Live* (1993) and *After The Rain* (1994) with Elvin Jones on drums.

In 1996 he recorded *The Promise*, a return to acerbic jazz-rock fusion. "Sometimes it's necessary to bring your past up to date, but this neo-bop thing is sometimes boring," he protested, reflecting on the retrospective musical climate of the times that had seen the pendulum of musical fashion swing in favour of acoustic jazz.

"It's as if records like *Jack Johnson* and *Bitches Brew* [by Miles Davis] don't exist... The new boppers all stop in '68 and then jump to '93! If anybody is the king of fusion it's Miles! Do we write that off? It's like, 'The paintings between 1970 and 1995 don't exist. It's that stupid!"

Emily Remler (above left) was only 32 when she died of heart failure in May 1990 while on tour in Australia. Citing Wes Montgomery and Pat Metheny as major influences, she received early encouragement from Herb Ellis and cut several fine albums. Remler's death cut short a flowering career and a highly individual jazz guitar voice. From the early 1980s Larry Coryell's fusion outings had become less frequent, and he began to perform more as a solo artist and in guitar duos. His partnership with Remler on Together (above) in 1985 was a highlight of this period.

KENNY MATHIESON

PAT METHENY

PAT METHENY MAY BE THE MOST VERSATILE GUITARIST YET, PLAYING EVERYTHING FROM FREE JAZZ AND WORLD MUSIC TO MINIMALISM AND NEW AGE. BUT AS LEADER OF THE PAT METHENY GROUP HE ALSO GIVES HIS FANS THE SMOOTH FUSION THEY CRAVE.

Many great musicians are difficult to pigeonhole, but Pat Metheny is particularly resistant to being pinned down. There are several sides to this immensely gifted guitarist's musical output, and some of them seem not only disparate but contradictory.

On the one hand, there is the most familiar Pat Metheny, the smooth jazz-folk-ethnic-rock fusion artist reflected in the bright, elegantly controlled harmonic and rhythmic textures of the Pat Metheny Group. Then there is Pat Metheny the dreamy impressionist, heard on his early ECM albums. There is Pat Metheny the conceptualist, heard on an extended composition like 'As Falls Witchita, So Falls Witchita Falls', or the later neo-narrative projects like *Secret Story* (1992) and *Imaginary Day* (1997).

And there is Pat Metheny the challenging jazz improviser, digging in with heavyweight company in trios with Charlie Haden and Billy Higgins or Dave Holland and Roy Haynes. Nor does it end there. There is also Pat Metheny the iconoclast, ripping through cutting-edge new jazz material with Ornette Coleman, or the dense sand-blasted free improvisations on *The Sign Of 4* (1997) with Derek Bailey, Gregg Bendian and Paul Wertico, or the feedback-laden noise-scape of his radical solo album *Zero Tolerance For Silence* (1994), which Geffen, his record company of the time, would only issue as a limited edition: only Metheny, however, could have induced them to issue it at all.

And there is more. Steve Reich's minimalist, multi tracked composition 'Electric Counterpoint' (1989), for guitar and tape, revealed yet another facet of his musical personality, and his work with the likes of Bruce Hornsby and Joni Mitchell yet another. He writes film soundtracks, too, and has played as a sideman or guest with a wide range of other jazz and Latin artists. It is possible – indeed likely – that a listener besotted by the Latin-inflected grooves of the electric group would run shrieking from his work with Coleman or Bailey, and vice versa, but for Metheny they are simply part of what he does, as he explained in an interview with this writer in 1997.

"I often hear people talk about me in terms of having two careers, but that's the easy way to look at it – the more challenging way is to try to deal with it as all one thing. That's the way it looks to me from the middle of it, and I certainly don't separate one thing from another. For me, it's all music. Of course, there are different vocabularies at work, there's no question about that, but the impulse and the spirit behind them is the same. I really believe that musicians should play the music they love, and try to communicate what they feel is important about life as it can be manifested through sound and music, and that has always been my goal.

"I never saw the project with Ornette, for example, as being all that

Pat Metheny on stage at the Shepherd's Bush Empire, London, in July 1998 (above left) and Metheny's keyboard collaborator Lyle Mays (above) at the same concert. Their enduring musical partnership dates back to the formation of The Pat Metheny Group in 1976.

different from what I usually do, just a little bit more out. When I first listened to Ornette's band as a kid, it seemed to me that they were just playing the music they felt strongest about, and playing it with incredible love and joy. It seemed very direct to me, and while most of the music I have played over the years is not stylistically close to it at all, that has always been the feeling I have tried to capture in my playing."

The various facets of Metheny's musical persona spill over into each other. The jazz improviser is often heard in the context of the electric group, while the textural exploration on a piece like 'As Falls Witchita...' is not far from the musical world of Steve Reich. When he has entered projects such as the collaborations with Ornette Coleman or Derek Bailey, however, he has thrown himself wholeheartedly into the musical challenges involved, rather than simply sounding like the familiar Pat Metheny pitched into an alien context.

Metheny was born on August 12th 1954, in the small town of Lee's Summit, Missouri, where he first discovered the music of Ornette Coleman in the local dime store, which sold off records in bargain lots: his elder brother, Mike Metheny, a jazz trumpeter, provided further exposure to the form. Pat took up guitar at 13, and began teaching – no, that's not a misprint – at the University of Miami at 17, and at Berklee College in Boston two years later.

In Miami he made the acquaintance of bassist Jaco Pastorius, who would

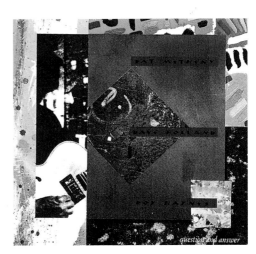
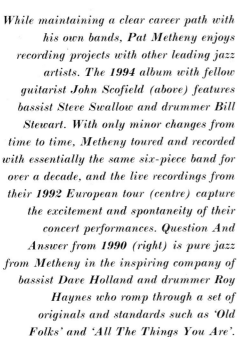

While maintaining a clear career path with his own bands, Pat Metheny enjoys recording projects with other leading jazz artists. The 1994 album with fellow guitarist John Scofield (above) features bassist Steve Swallow and drummer Bill Stewart. With only minor changes from time to time, Metheny toured and recorded with essentially the same six-piece band for over a decade, and the live recordings from their 1992 European tour (centre) capture the excitement and spontaneity of their concert performances. Question And Answer from 1990 (right) is pure jazz from Metheny in the inspiring company of bassist Dave Holland and drummer Roy Haynes who romp through a set of originals and standards such as 'Old Folks' and 'All The Things You Are'.

feature in the guitarist's recording debut, in a trio led by pianist Paul Bley, and again on Metheny's own debut album as a leader. At Berklee, he joined the band led by vibraphonist Gary Burton, and appeared on three of his albums for ECM. It seemed natural that Manfred Eicher's Munich-based label should pick up on the gifted youngster, and his first album as leader, *Bright Size Life*, a trio with Pastorius and Bob Moses, appeared in 1976.

It remains highly listenable today, although Moses told Jaco's biographer, Bill Milkowski, that it was a pale reflection of how they sounded live, something that has been said of other Metheny albums. The guitarist is a notably fluid, lyrical player (he has often acknowledged the melodic influence of Wes Montgomery and Jim Hall – as well as Ornette Coleman) with a finely honed sense of dynamic variation and control and immense technical powers. But the downside of that lyricism is a tendency to meander, which has seen some of his work tagged as New Age music, often with justification.

Watercolours (1977) fitted more closely into the stereotypical image of the so-called ECM sound, with its impressionistic wash of colour and instrumental texture, fed by Eberhard Weber's very European bass playing. It did well, and served as a platform for the guitarist to launch what has been one of the most enduring partnerships in contemporary music with the first appearance of the Pat Metheny Group, on a January 1978 an album of the same name. The band featured Metheny's characteristically bright, melodic guitar work alongside the keyboards of Lyle Mays, Mark Egan on bass, and Dan Gottlieb on drums. The Wisconsin-born Mays has a similar mid-West background to the guitarist, and has been a member of the group ever since, as well as featuring on the duo project *As Falls Witchita, So Falls Witchita Falls* (1981), an album which evokes their mid-Western childhood just as directly as *Beyond The Missouri Sky* (1997), Metheny's more recent folk and country-inflected duo project with fellow Missourian Charlie Haden.

Mays found a perfect setting in the Group (his own albums are rather anonymous), while Metheny found an equally ideal playing and composing partner, and one in sympathy with both his musical ideas and his growing fascination with electronic echo and delay effects. He made particularly lyrical but complex use of the so-called "chorus" device, in which a note is put through a variable time delay before being mixed back with the original sound. Metheney transformed it from a passing colour effect to a fully fledged improvising technique.

That ability to make fully realised musical use of technical advances has

Although he uses guitar synthesisers and a wide range of guitars (from six-string to 42-string) Pat Metheny (above left) still obtains his signature sound from his trusty Gibson ES-175D archtop, enhanced by delay units and other signal processing effects. Metheny's 1992 album Secret Story (above) was a large-scale project featuring a host of guests ranging from musicians from the Cambodian Royal Palace, the London Orchestra conducted by Jeremy Lubbock, harmonica master Toots Thielemans, and Brazilian percussionist Nana Vasconcelos.

marked Metheny out amid the mob of less imaginative technophiles, and is equally true of later developments, like his use of the Synclavier, which opened up full-blown synthesiser possibilities and came to play an increasing role in the group's characteristic sound, or the addition of the Roland vg-8 pickup he acquired in the late 1990s.

Many great guitarists have been content to concentrate on a single style of instrument, or even – like Wes Montgomery with his beloved Gibson L-5CES – a single model. Metheny has taken the opposite tack, playing not only the range of acoustic, archtop and solidbodied instruments (with six and 12 strings), but also such exotica as a 15-string harp guitar or the instruments he has devloped with the Toronto-based luthier Linda Manzer, including the remarkable 42-string Pikasso guitar and a fretless nylon-strung guitar, featured for the first time on *Imaginary Day.*

Manzer, he says "pretty much takes whatever I can dream up and accepts it as a personal challenge to make it happen". But his interest in exploring these instruments is based on an apparently insatiable curiosity and desire to expand his musical horizons, rather than frustration with the limitations of the conventional guitar.

"Frustration may not be the right word – there is of course always an element of frustration in trying to get what I hear in my head out in a clear way on any guitar, but I'm always interested in exploring the potentials of the guitar in ways that haven't been done too much before. One of the beauties of guitar is the incredible variety and amazing dynamic range that you have with it," he says.

He set about barn-storming around America with the group, travelling constantly and building up a big following which catapulted his music out of the confines of instrumental jazz and into the rock market in a way that few serious jazz musicians have ever managed. In the process, however, he maintained the pattern of contrasting record releases which have been characteristic of his approach, rather then taking the easier option of settling into a rigid but lucrative style. *American Garage* (1979) and *Offramp* (1981) respectively offered a rougher and more abstract alternative to the vibrant textures and Latin grooves of the Group, while the solo album *New Chautauqua* (1979) and the duo *As Falls Witchita, So Falls Witchita Falls* also rang the changes.

The biggest side step of the period came with *80/81* (1980), a straight jazz album that underlined the guitarist's jazz credentials in fast company –

Michael Brecker, Dewey Redman, Charlie Haden and Jack DeJohnette. Following the release of the live double album *Travels* (1982), featuring the Pat Metheny Group's then perennial guest percussionist, Nana Vasconcelos, which some critics feel is a better – and certainly more gutsy – representation of their work than the studio albums of that era, he echoed the *80/81* project in an exploratory trio set with Haden and Billy Higgins, *Rejoicing* (1983), which remains one of his best records.

His last album for ECM, *First Circle* (1984), was notable for bringing together the most stable and enduring group line-up, with Metheny and Mays joined by bassist Steve Rodby and drummer Paul Wertico. The Brazilian influence was strong in the group's music at this point, but other exotic textures from Asia and the Far East were creeping in. These would be taken further in the more ambitious projects of the 1990s, which saw him use a Cambodian orchestra and choir on *Secret Story* and Iranian folk music on *Imaginary Day*. Metheny placed a high premium on the sense of development-within-continuity which the group provided in his music.

"The Group is kind of like a family," he says. "It's very much an ensemble, and everyone in the band has an important role in the music. It has been stable, and that has let us develop together. The music we play in that band is based more on writing and concepts than on improvisation, and we also have a real strong percussion section, which is very important, maybe the most important element of all."

The guitarist left ECM for Geffen in 1984, but his next album was actually the soundtrack from the film *The Falcon And The Snowman*, issued by EMI in 1984. Metheny co-wrote the music with Lyle Mays, and it featured the group in characteristic form, as well as the guitarist playing with David Bowie on the theme song. It was not his first venture into soundtrack music – he had scored the television series *The Search For Solutions* in 1979 and the film *Little Sister* in 1983, and had been the guest soloist with the London Symphony Orchestra on *Under Fire* that same year – but it remains his best known work in the genre. He has composed several subsequent works for screen or stage, including *Twice In A Lifetime* (1985), *Lemon Sky* (1987), the ballet *Adieux* (1988), *Big Time* (1989), and *The Silent Alarm* (1993), and his music has been featured in several other films as well. His more recent large ensemble albums, like *Secret Story* and *Imaginary Day*, arguably also reflect something of the visual dimension of film and theatre music.

His debut for Geffen was his most controversial album to that point, and remains a classic of the era. In *Song X* (1985) he set aside the familiar sound of the Pat Metheny Group in a corruscatingly visceral meeting with Ornette Coleman which galvanised both men into remarkable responses, goaded on by the contributions of Charlie Haden on bass and drummers Jack DeJohnette and Denardo Coleman. The ethos and form of the music is Coleman's, but Metheny meets the challenge with a bite and ferocity seldom encountered in his own work, without throwing away his trademark melodic invention.

Many Metheny fans – including his mum – hated it, but it emphasised that the guitarist was his own man, even with a new label to accomodate. The Pat Metheny Group album which Geffen hankered for duly arrived in the shape of *Still Life (Talking)* in 1987, in which the distinctive harmonies and rhythms of Brazil provided the dominant note but which also included a powerful evocation of his mid-West roots. 'Last Train Home', echoing a strain of folk and country music which has provided an important element in his still-evolving musical tapestry. Its successor, *Letter From Home* (1989), was in a similar vein, but he ended the decade with another return to jazz roots in the album *Question And Answer* (1989), a trio set with Dave Holland and Roy Haynes, which had been recorded in fairly informal fashion in a single day in the studio. The results were more than enough to warrant release. And Metheny also toured with the trio, just as he had with Coleman (not that the peripatetic workaholic guitarist needs much persuading to go on the road).

The 1990s witnessed a similar pattern of varied releases. *Secret Story* featured an expanded band with the group at its core, as did *Imaginary Day*, and explored a plethora of ethnic and world music influences and idioms (with, in the case of the latter album, a pronounced rock feel in places as well), but without losing hold of the essential Americanness at the heart of these ventures. The group were featured in unadulterated form on the live album *Road To You - Live In Europe* (1993), and the subsequent studio sets *We Live Here* (1994) and the more reflective *Quartet* (1996). The latter was to be the last of Metheny's albums for Geffen. In 1997, he switched labels for the third time, moving to Warner Brothers, where he released *Imaginary Day*.

He had recorded an album on Blue Note with John Scofield, *I Can See Your House From Here* (1993), which did not quite live up to the expectations such a meeting inevitably created, and a lovely duo album with Charlie Haden, *Beyond The Missouri Sky*, for Verve, as well as the head-on collision with Derek Bailey enshrined on *The Sign Of 4*, which was issued on the Knitting Factory label.

He took the role previously held by Scofield alongside Bill Frisell on Marc Johnson's *Sound Of Summer Running* (1997), a project which added another radiantly beautiful chapter to his ongoing engagement with a lost, perhaps even semi-mythical, America. Space prevents any very detailed look at his work as a sideman or guest, which has been surprisingly prodigious for a major star, and included a reunion with Gary Burton in 1989, and another in 1998, as well as appearances with artists as diverse as Abbey Lincoln, Milton Nascimento, Akiko Yano and Joshua Redman.

Given his interest in the technological advances in music creation, it is not surprising that Metheny has also become involved in producing records, both for his own projects and with other artists, adding a further dimension to his already multi-dimensional career. The restless need to explore new things has driven a career which has brought him the kind of popular acclaim most jazz musicians can only dream of, and at the same time won him the admiration of his peers as a major creative force in the music.

His relationship to the central jazz tradition has seemed obvious at times and tenuous at others, but even in the Pat Metheny Group, he stresses that improvisation remains a crucial part of their chemistry, whatever idioms they may explore. His upbeat and idealistic music is not for those who need a whiff of angst in their listening, but it does have its roots in a jazz sensibility.

"It concerns me a little bit that jazz is becoming more like classical music in the late 1990s," the guitarist has said. "To me, jazz was always more than just a noun, it was more like a verb – it was this process of absorbing the realities of your time and manifesting them in sound for other people to hear, in a way that jazz guys are particularly good at through improvisation.

"For me, when I look at the jazz tradition, I see lots of examples of people using elements of the pop music of their time as a source of inspiration, and that is basically what we are doing."

FUSION: THE SECOND WAVE

THE FIRST FUSION GUITARISTS HAD CREATED AN EFFECTIVE MIX OF JAZZ AND ROCK IDIOMS. THE SECOND WAVE, ARRIVING IN THE LATE 1970S, BROUGHT A MORE ADVANCED HARMONIC UNDERSTANDING AND AN ENTHUSIASM, SOMETIMES SHORTLIVED, FOR ELECTRONIC EFFECTS.

John Abercrombie's versatility has led him from the jazz-rock of Gateway and acoustic guitar duets with Ralph Towner to a variety of projects on the ECM label that range from the impressionistic to out-and-out heavyweight fusion.

John McLaughlin and Larry Coryell were followed by others who mixed rock and jazz, but the second wave of fusion guitarists added other idiomatic flavours, new textures derived from evolving signal-processing technology and new harmonic dimensions.

With the exception of Allan Holdsworth (dealt with in Chapter 16), it was not until the 1980s that jazz-rock guitar caught up with the harmonic advances that modern jazz made in the 1960s. Many of the early guitarists in jazz-rock (for example Pete Cosey and Reggie Lucas in Miles Davis's early-1970s band) played Hendrix-influenced rock guitar in a nominally jazz-oriented setting. Even McLaughlin's lines in The Mahavishnu Orchestra typically owed more to rock than jazz. However, by the late 1970s many guitarists, working with the distorted sound of rock guitar and in rock or funk settings, were beginning to improvise chromatic phrases modelled on the way John Coltrane, McCoy Tyner, Herbie Hancock and others would approach modal (that is, single chord) material in the 1960s. Some were also extending the bebop and modern jazz idea of complicated chord changes, using the melodic minor and other scale types to generate a rarefied harmony, more abstract than that of bebop.

Mick Goodrick may be thought of as the father of what could be called the "Boston school of guitar-playing", a harmonically sophisticated style which came to inform much of the fusion guitar-playing of the 1980s and 1990s. Based in Boston, US, the home of the Berklee College of Music, Goodrick exerted a considerable influence, directly or indirectly, on several players who passed through the college and went on to become leading protagonists in 1980s fusion, among them John Abercrombie, John Scofield, Bill Frisell and Mike Stern. Although these players cite Jim Hall as a major inspiration for their lyrical side, they have much in common, harmonically, with Goodrick, a player little exposed on the world stage. His characteristic harmonic approach, and one which was clearly heard in the playing and writing of Scofield and Abercrombie around the same time, is well displayed on his 1978 album *In Pas(s)ing*. This is restrained, introspective "chamber jazz" rather than explicit fusion, but Goodrick applied a similar harmonic approach to his fusion work with Jack DeJohnette's Special Edition, on Gary Thomas's heavy-duty jazz-rock album *By Any Means Necessary* (where he is paired with Scofield), and on his own 1990 recording *Biorhythms*.

Ironically, some players in the second wave of fusion have recently severed their associations with the style. John Scofield has distanced himself from it, and John Abercrombie recently said categorically that he "hates" it. However, Abercrombie's aggressive, rock-oriented work with the pioneering fusion band

Dreams in the late 1960s, with Billy Cobham in the early 1970s, and on the track 'Lungs' on his own 1974 album *Timeless* (where he sounded a lot like John McLaughlin in Tony Williams's trio Lifetime) conspires with his position outside the jazz mainstream to draw him into the fusion category.

The label sits rather uneasily with the often introspective, esoteric work which has formed much of Abercrombie's output for the German label ECM, but on the other hand he is still capable of rocking (and does so with some force on 'How's Never' on the 1995 album *Homecoming*). He also only fairly recently abandoned the unlovely guitar synthesiser. His most tasteful use of that instrument can be heard on 'Secret Love' on Ron McClure's album *McJolt*, where he uses it to subtly shade his guitar lines.

Abercrombie was one of the second-wave players, especially in his 1970s ECM recordings, who imported ethnic flavours into his work. Acknowledging the influence of Coltrane, he would often play in what one might call an "ethnic modal" style, producing long, flowing, mode-based lines over a one-key vamp. The "ethnicity" of his lines lay in the fact that he would conjure an eastern flavour by using scales such as the harmonic minor or the Phrygian mode. Such a flavour is particularly evident on 'Opening', from the ECM

John Scofield (above left) will fill a performance with edge-of-the-seat excitement and an unpredictable, edgy guitar sound, employing loping grooves, harmonically-altered blues licks, angular runs, declamatory phrases and grinding chords. In contrast, Bill Frisell (above) in the rich tradition of jazz borrows from other forms of music, but in his case dares to draw from country music, a source of which conventional jazz wisdom disapproves. Frisell's iconoclasm extends to the use of signal-processing effects that are generally the province of the rock musician.

album *Gateway 2*. Abercrombie also made extensive use in the 1970s of the electric mandolin, and some of his most spirited playing can be heard on this instrument on Jack DeJohnette's 1979 album *New Directions In Europe*. In the 1990s, like many of his erstwhile fusion peers, Abercrombie returned to earlier styles, such as the jazz standard and the organ trio.

Along with Pat Metheny, John Scofield is one of the most original and influential fusion (or as he might now have it, "modern jazz guitar") players since John McLaughlin. His sound and vocabulary have been emulated by guitarists around the world.

Among Europeans who have shown a distinct Sco-tinge are the Swiss Harald Haerter, the young Dane Niclas Knudsen, the Austrian Wolfgang Muthspiel and, in earlier years, the Swede Ulf Wakenius. His influence is also discernible in the playing of a legion of younger Americans, among them Steve Cardenas, Kurt Rosenwinkel and Ben Monder.

Scofield is steeped in the post-1950s jazz mainstream (not only guitar players), and there lies the key to his style. Although he used high volume, distortion and rock and funk rhythms in the 1970s and 1980s on such classic fusion records as Billy Cobham's *Funky Thide Of Sings*, Chet Baker's *You Can't Go Home Again* and his own *Who's Who*, *Electric Outlet*, *Still Warm* and

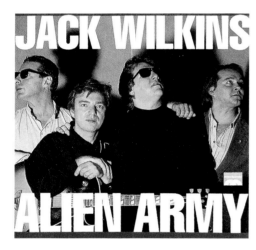

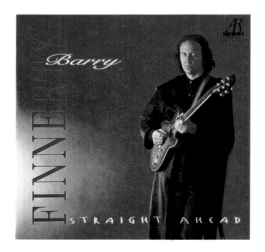

Long regarded for fluent, up-tempo lines and chord-melody elegance, New York guitarist Jack Wilkins shows another side of his musical personality on 1990's Alien Army (above), contrasting delicate balladry and boppish material with some blistering fusion. Barry Finnerty attracted plaudits for his late-1970s work with The Brecker Brothers, and on Straight Ahead (centre) from 1995 he stretches out on an attractively varied selection. A mentor for many aspirant guitarists through instruction and playing, Mick Goodrick contributes effectively to saxophonist Claudio Fasoli's adventurous city sound-portraits on this 1993 album (right).

Blue Matter, as well as playing a major role in Miles Davis's 1980s band, his harmonic sensibility was derived largely from early 1960s jazz.

After studying jazz at Berklee College in the mid 1970s, he had played as much in straightahead contexts (with Gerry Mulligan, David Liebman and others), and in his own rarefied chamber jazz trio and quartet as he had in jazz-rock. Although his playing on his first appearance on record (a Gerry Mulligan-Chet Baker reunion concert) was relatively conventional, there were already signs of the audacious harmonic approach and sound which came into full flower in the late 1970s. He further honed this language in the mid 1980s in his high octane fusion band, and the progression reached its peak in 1985 with the album *Still Warm*, in particular in the demonic 'Protocol' with its darting, chromatic bass line and angular, obsessive theme, based loosely on a diminished arpeggio.

Others players, such as Allan Holdsworth and Pat Martino, had developed strongly chromatic styles, but Scofield found a very personal way to fill the cracks between the ordinary notes. Yet no matter how far from home the harmony got, he almost always seemed to be playing the blues. Like Frisell,

Metheny and others, Scofield showed a fondness for country flavours, but a strong streak of Chicago blues has always given his playing a more metropolitan sound. If Metheny and Frisell developed a kind of "rural fusion", Scofield fostered the "urban" variety.

In later years Scofield rejected high-tech fusion in favour of a more jazz-like, often abstract style. His 1988 album *Flat Out* marked this departure, showing him once again in a conventional quartet setting with upright bass and playing such standards as 'All The Things You Are' and an adaptation of 'Softly As A Morning Sunrise'. However the set also included the countrified New Orleans funk of The Meters' 'Cissy Strut' and featured the Hammond organ. The country aspects and the organ were themes he developed further in later years. Country funk appeared later in 'Chariots' (the album *Meant To Be*) and other pieces with a New Orleans two-feel. A country feeling informed the Ornette-Coleman-styled pieces he wrote for his quartet with Joe Lovano, and in the 1990s he led several bands featuring Hammond organ in a sort of updated version of the 1960s organ trio.

Although he spent more time in the Hollywood film, TV and pop studios

By the mid 1980s Mike Stern (above left) had worked with the bands of Billy Cobham, Jaco Pastorius and Miles Davis, revealing an inventive, high-energy guitarist more than capable of working alongside saxophone heavyweights such as Michael Brecker and Bob Berg. Stern's Jigsaw album of 1989 (above) has saxophonist Bob Berg, keyboardist Jim Beard, electric bassist Jeff Andrews, plus Peter Erskine and Dennis Chambers alternating on drums. It's one of the most powerful fusion albums of the late 1980s, Stern mapping his course with assurance through tricky chord progressions, shifting rhythms and demanding tempos.

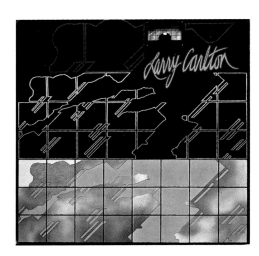

Larry Carlton (right) on stage at the Vienne Festival, France, in 1989. A studio musician in Los Angeles in the early 1970s, Carlton worked on albums by Joni Mitchell, Vicki Carr, Andy Williams and many other popular artists, but it was his lengthy association (and six albums) with The Crusaders and his work on Steely Dan's Aja album of 1977 that sealed his reputation. A student of the blues style of BB King and Eric Clapton, Carlton created a sophisticated string-bending style combined with a firm grasp of jazz harmony to carve out a distinctive style that was attractive rather than profound. He made a number of solo records, including the eponymous album pictured above that was made in 1978.

than on the road or playing original music, Larry Carlton was one of the most original and most imitated guitarists of the late 1970s and early 1980s. His style is an amalgam of the styles of the early 1960s blues revivalists, notably that of Eric Clapton, and of mainstream jazz guitarists, notably Joe Pass. From Clapton he took his beautifully fluid, singing, sustained sound, and from jazz players such as Pass his harmonic sophistication, especially his stunning command of extended arpeggios and bebop licks. In the complex chord sequences of Steely Dan, the heavily jazz-influenced rock band led by Donald Fagen and Walter Becker, Carlton found the perfect forum for his harmonic fluency, producing classic jazz-rock solos on such tracks as 'Kid Charlemagne'.

In the less demanding harmonic environment of The Crusaders, he could have contented himself with simple blues lines, but his jazz sensibilities allowed him to bring extra spice to the group's relatively simple soul-oriented style, notably on such tracks as 'Spiral' and 'Keep That Same Old Feeling'. His self-titled debut album (1978) was lighter in tone than his work with Steely Dan, but it contains acres of superb guitar playing. However, in his 1990s records he was engulfed in a wash of what he himself called "happy jazz" – sterile, funky easy-listening with only a residue of the vigour and attack of his early years.

While Carlton flourished in the studios on the West Coast, Steve Khan filled a similar role in New York. The son of the songwriter Sammy Cahn, he at first eschewed the chord sequences of the Broadway musicals that had been his father's living and opted for a career as a session rock guitarist. His first appearances on record, with the Breckers Brothers, and on his own albums, such as *Tightrope*, revealed a sophisticated blues/rock player with a powerful attack. In 1980, in some cool and stylish playing on 'Glamour Profession' and 'My Rival' on Steely Dan's *Gaucho*, Khan retained his characteristic biting rock sound but showed more harmonic depth than before.

With his 1980 recording *Evidence* (an exquisitely tranquil multi tracked tribute to Thelonious Monk, mostly on acoustic guitar) and in several records

Jeff Beck (left), the prototypical British rock guitarist, has proved an expressive player in jazz-rock; his playing is admired by John McLaughlin among many other of his fellow musicians.

with his trio or quartet Eyewitness (where he used a Gibson semi-acoustic rather than the modified Telecaster that had been his signature in the 1970s) his straightahead jazz leanings were fully confirmed. However, except in its instrumentation, Eyewitness was not a copy of earlier mainstream guitar trios. It mixed standards with more open-ended, sometimes vamp-based originals, but the intent – to play harmonically sophisticated, intimate music with the emphasis on improvisation – was derived from the jazz guitar tradition. Eyewitness produced some excellent music, although perhaps because of the space left for the guitar, Khan's playing lacked the focus which was his trademark in the 1970s.

Khan also did good work with synthesist Rob Mounsey, producing the album *Local Colour* in 1987, and in the mid 1980s he played in Joe Zawinul's short-lived Weather Update.

Despite spending time with The Brecker Brothers, Khan was denied the best showing any guitarist had with that band. That honour was bestowed on Barry Finnerty, who was lucky enough to be on hand for the brothers' sensational live album, the 1978 fusion classic, *Heavy Metal Be-Bop*. Finnerty's playing was a perfect match for the music, bringing just the right level of rock grit to Randy Brecker's ultra-complex bop-oriented themes and harmonies. However, Finnerty's playing did not at that time demonstrate the level of harmonic sophistication found in the brothers' playing.

Where the Breckers had developed all manner of bop-and-beyond phraseology, Finnerty was more typically a very good pentatonic rock player, and he played in much the same way on Miles Davis's 1980-1 comeback album *Man With The Horn*. However, two recent Finnerty issues, *Straight Ahead* and *Space Age Blues*, leave no doubt of his command of the chromatic vocabulary derived from bop.

Given their disparaging remarks, it seems that some observers couldn't tell the difference between Barry Finnerty and Miles's next guitarist, Mike Stern. Having studied at Berklee with Mick Goodrick, and played with Blood Sweat & Tears and Billy Cobham, Stern joined Davis's band in 1980 and walked into a wall of aurally-challenged critics who dismissed him as a Jimi Hendrix clone. Some of Stern's finest playing is to be heard on the 1981 album *We Want Miles*, yet several leading jazz writers were unable to step around his distorted rock tone and hear the sophisticated, bebop-derived lines which were at the heart of his playing.

Stern is a prime example of the second-generation fusion guitarist – a player with a keen awareness of the tradition (later he often played standards as sideman and in his own trios and quartets), integrating a post-bop vocabulary into a heavy rock and funk setting. He went on to produce a series of his own records featuring his personal mixture of rock and bop, of which the first, *Upside Downside*, remains the freshest and most striking example.

He was also often seen in the 1980s and early 1990s in a quartet with tenor saxophonist Bob Berg, tearing it up on such muscular R&B workouts as 'Friday Night At The Cadillac Club'. It may seem paradoxical that Stern cites the cerebral, mainstream Jim Hall as a major influence, but like other players from the "Boston school" Stern has a strong lyrical leaning, evidenced in various tender (if occasionally overworked) ballads on his solo albums.

Uniquely among the British 1960s rock players who influenced many of the Americans mentioned above, Jeff Beck himself moved towards jazz-rock in the 1970s. In 1972 he played a brief but soulful and intermittently jazzy solo on Stevie Wonder's 'Lookin' For Another Pure Love' on *Talking Book*, and in 1975 he appeared on two tracks on Stanley Clarke's *Journey To Love*, playing with special sensitivity on the title track.

His own putative jazz-rock records, *Blow By Blow* and *Wired*, confirmed that he was at his strongest on ballads, where lyrical, often chromatic ideas flowed beautifully. In Lennon & McCartney's 'She's A Woman' (*Blow By Blow*) and 'Goodbye Porkpie Hat' (*Wired*) he works in some delicate and indubitably jazzy ideas.

Keyboard player Max Middleton underlines the jazz intent on 'Scatterbrain' (*Blow By Blow*), taking his Fender Rhodes towards Herbie Hancock territory, and the group's jazzy aspirations are evident in the proliferation of funky rhythms and convoluted chord sequences, but when the tempo and volume are up, Beck tends to revert to the raw, unpolished approach of the blues-rocker. Beck's continuing affiliations with jazz were reaffirmed in 1995 when he applied his impassioned pentatonic style to John Lewis's 'Django' on John McLaughlin's album *The Promise*.

Fitting uneasily in any category, Bill Frisell is the archetypal post-modern guitarist. He incorporates the modernisms of the post-bop vocabulary and rock guitar, and he has made wide use of the latest music technology, including signal processing and guitar synthesisers, but at the same time he draws on the archaic resources of country music and mixes in avant-garde and art music ideas.

Frisell played extensively with the drummer Paul Motian, and like Motian he has a colouristic, painterly approach. Although he occasionally plays long, harmonically complex lines, he is more typically known for sustained, string-like sounds, often redolent of the pedal-steel guitar. Appropriately enough, the sound of country music has become more explicit in his writing and playing as his career has advanced, and in the late 1990s he recorded an album called *Nashville*. He did country-type shuffles and R&B with Joey Baron and Ginger Baker, and with Baker he also did some quite experimental, avant-rock playing. At the other extreme of the musical scale, he has fitted well with the tough, uncompromisng avant-garde playing of John Zorn's abrasive Naked City band.

New technology has been essential in the creation of Frisell's distinctive sound. His arsenal has probably been richer in signal processors than that of any of his peers. He has used delays and volume pedal to create a singing sustained sound and also at one point he used the guitar synthesiser. But, like many other players who experimented with that instrument, he had abandoned it by the late 1990s in favour of a simpler set-up.

Frisell has been described as an exponent of Americana, and the description seems fitting. One hears in his music shades of Aaron Copland's modern classical renditions of American folk music. Paradoxically, though, one perceives less of those other great American musics – jazz and blues. Frisell's contribution has been to exploit for jazz those musics previously neglected, indeed often vehemently rejected (one thinks of jazz drummer Buddy Rich's view of country music) by established jazz players. As a result of this eclecticism, many would call Frisell's playing anything but jazz, but few bars go by without it being apparent that jazz is his starting point.

Together with the players discussed in Chapter 16, those above have been the most prominent guitarists to emerge in the mature phase of fusion, but several others have played important roles too. Among them are Hiram Bullock, noted for his charismatic stage antics with David Sanborn, and Chuck Loeb, a smoothly fluent player formerly with Steps Ahead, the Bill Evans band and others.

Dean Brown, a notable force with Billy Cobham in the late 1970s, has made strong contributions to the re-formed Brecker Brothers band and Marcus Miller's band in the 1990s, and David Torn, like Frisell, has made a virtue of colouration. Of the later generation, the Austrian Wolfgang Muthspiel has merged jazz-rock with a highly individualised take on the avant-garde, and Jimi Tunnell, formerly with Steps Ahead, produced an impressive post-Weather Report album, *Trilateral Commission*.

In the 1990s, perhaps as a result of the burgeoning jazz education scene, there has been an explosion of technically well-equipped fusion players, among them David Gilmore (with M-Base and Wayne Shorter) and David Fiuczynski. In England, John Etheridge, Mike Walker and John Parricelli have all made strong contributions to the genre.

It is also encouraging to see women taking up the style, among them Leni Stern, wife of Mike Stern, and the young German Susan Weinert.

SHREDDING THE FRETS

THROUGHOUT JAZZ HISTORY, MUSICIANS HAVE TAKEN PRIDE IN BEING ABLE TO PLAY FAST. BUT SHRED-FUSION TOOK THAT TO NEW EXTREMES, BRINGING THE SOUNDS AND TECHNIQUES – AND SOMETIMES THE FASHIONS – OF HEAVY METAL GUITAR TO THE WORLD OF JAZZ.

The Swedish bad boy of shred guitar, Yngwie Malmsteen worked hard in his teens to build a formidable and innovative technique on the electric guitar by incorporating the music of Bach, Paganini and Vivaldi. He then proceeded to dissipate this facility in his twenties on a series of shallow, adolescent rock projects.

It could be argued that jazz guitar has always been about "shredding": playing as fast as possible. Ever since bebop placed a premium on virtuosity, good technique has typically been seen as a prerequisite of jazz guitar playing.

However, in the late 1980s a style of jazz-rock playing emerged which seemed to have something in common with the stratospheric flights of such heavy metal guitar players, or "shredders", as Eddie Van Halen, Joe Satriani, Steve Vai and Yngwie Malmsteen. Certainly in terms of sound (typically distorted), equipment (usually the solidbody "super-Strat" with very light action, an effects unit and powerful amplification), image (long hair and designer wear have not been unknown among modern jazz-rockers), speed of execution and the use of certain techniques (notably harmonics, and to a lesser extent the vibrato arm), the super-fluent jazz-rock players of the 1990s, such as Frank Gambale, Scott Henderson and the less well-known Parisian Nguyên Lê, seem to owe something to their hard-rocking cousins.

The Englishman Allan Holdsworth might also be included in that group, but he is a product of an earlier era, whose work has spanned three decades. Although he has something in common with the metal-shredders, his style was perfected long before shred-metal was conceived, and was in itself a major influence on later generations of shredders in both the jazz-rock and heavy metal worlds.

Despite the superficial similarities between the two styles, one important thing that sets the jazz-rock "shredders" apart from their rock counterparts is harmonic style. Without exception, Holdsworth, Gambale, Henderson, Lê, and other lesser known players have their basis in post-bop "changes-playing" or in the modal style developed by John Coltrane and others in the early 1960s. Leaving aside their sound and techniques, they are part of a tradition, distinct from rock, which stretches back through John McLaughlin to jazz pioneers on instruments other than guitar.

Where metal players tend to be primarily guitaristic, exploiting such uniquely mechanical aspects of the guitar as the vibrato arm (to create what is called a "divebombing" effect), two-handed tapping (as popularised by Eddie Van Halen) and "digital patterns" – visually symmetrical fingering patterns which are worked along the fretboard regardless of key – the jazz-rock shredders typically play in a linear style that reflects the underlying harmony. In this way they follow and extend a practice intrinsic to jazz since its conception.

Allan Holdsworth, active in England from the late 1960s onwards, is the most likely contender for the title of godfather of "shred-fusion". Until the advent of an energetic jazz education system in the US in the 1980s,

Holdsworth's magical combination of chromatic harmony and fluent legato technique set him in a class apart. It's interesting that had it not been for a perforated ear-drum, Holdsworth would not have taken up guitar. Clarinet was his first choice of instrument, but when ear-problems put an end to that, he worked, probably unconsciously, on developing on the guitar the legato sound of the clarinet.

In the 1980s he found in the SynthAxe, a guitar-shaped synthesiser controller, the perfect compromise between guitar and wind instrument. This allowed him simultaneously to play notes on the instrument's fingerboard and add expression by blowing into an attached tube.

However, resistance to it from his guitar-fixated followers seems to have

Scott Henderson (left) effortlessly transcends the boundaries between rock, blues and jazz, and merges their aesthetics in the highly energised music of Tribal Tech, the band which he co-leads with bassist Gary Willis. Yngwie Malmsteen's prodigious technique and classical influences are to the fore on the otherwise conventional rock album, Rising Force (above), from 1985.

caused Holdsworth to abandon it in the late 1990s in favour of the normal electric guitar.

Back in the late 1960s, when Holdsworth was shaping his sound, a large part of the equation in developing a fast, legato style was low action, light strings and sensitive amplification, and in this respect Holdsworth had much in common with the later shred-metal players. However, his vocabulary came from a quite different place. Although he has almost always played in rock contexts (one important exception was his late-1970s improvised work with the British drummer John Stevens), these have often been settings with jazz leanings, and Holdsworth's own inclination, from early days, was to put Coltrane's polytonal language on to the guitar. Evidence of his early success in this respect can be heard in his work with Soft Machine, in Tony Williams' Lifetime and with drummer Bill Bruford. Bruford's 1976 album *Feels Good To*

Steve Vai's Passion And Warfare album from 1990 (above) is a powerful and imaginative offering which distances Vai from his alter ego as guitarist with stadium-metal bands Whitesnake, David Lee Roth and Alcatrazz. Three years later his Sex And Religion LP (centre) was a further showcase for Vai's instrumental abilities and for his writing, with perhaps an occasional echo of his former boss, Frank Zappa. Joe Satriani's Surfing With The Alien (right) was an entertaining and impressive album from 1986 that fully represents the guitarist's well-honed guitar skills, and without the technical overkill of much of his later output.

Me is home to some of Holdsworth's most exquisite and creative work, notably that on 'Beelzebub', 'Back To The Beginning' and 'If You Can't Stand The Heat...'. Here, rather more than in his later work, Holdsworth makes characteristically subtle use of the vibrato arm for expression – some long way from the dramatic dive-bombing of the 1980s metallurgists.

Highlights such as these, along with ordinary everyday revelations, continued throughout Holdsworth's career. There was a drawback, though. In the 1980s, after moving to California, he began producing a long series of records under his own name in which it seemed he was trying to recreate in composition the complexity of his solo playing. However, the musicality of his best solos didn't seem to translate into his writing, and partly because of this, partly perhaps because he focused more on the SynthAxe than many fans cared for, and partly because he began allotting valuable space to vocalists, many of these records were not well-received. There were, nevertheless, some extremely good moments along the way, none less than in the perhaps significantly titled *Metal Fatigue* (had he had enough of tarring with that brush?). Though interrupted by a superfluous vocal, the title track has a magnificent, if ironic, heavy metal riff and a solo straight from jazz. But the best solo here, one of Holdsworth's finest creations, is the cliff-hanger on 'Devil Take The Hindmost', a masterpiece of pacing and technique.

On balance, however, it seems Holdsworth has fared more happily as a sideman, relieved of the pressure of writing and bandleading and free simply to improvise. He had several successful dates in this respect in the 1990s: the

refreshingly simple compositions and free improvisations of Chad Wackerman's *Forty Reasons* (1991) and *The View* (1993) give Holdsworth plenty of space to stretch out without worrying about the next chord change. *Truth In Shredding* (1990) is a stroke of imaginative genius from producer Mark Varney, which puts Holdsworth and Frank Gambale toe-to-toe in a set of 1970s jazz and jazz-rock covers, including tunes by the Brecker Brothers, Chick Corea and Wayne Shorter. And *None Too Soon* (1996) has Holdsworth in a set of standards – something his jazz-inclined admirers had long hoped for.

Holdsworth's pairing with Frank Gambale on *Truth In Shredding* was a minor historical moment. Here was the 44-year-old elder of jazz-rock guitar, in some ways a rather overlooked figure, brought into the spotlight alongside a leading player from the younger generation of shred-fusionists. The implied connection between the styles of the two men – that both are fast, fluent and modern, in other words, shredders – is real, but the differences are clear too. Holdsworth has frequently pointed out that he is not a bebop or changes player, and one thing that sets Gambale apart from Holdsworth is his comprehensive mastery of chord changes.

If Holdsworth is coming from Coltrane's modal 'A Love Supreme', Gambale is the modern guitar equivalent of his chord-packed 'Giant Steps'. In addition, whereas Holdsworth is noted for a smooth ligado-style left-hand technique in which the pick only plays a minor role, Gambale has made a science of picking, developing the "sweep-picking" technique to its highest level. (Sweep-picking entails striking successive strings in one direction only

An immensely capable musician, Joe Satriani is a rock guitarist who uses the full resources of the instrument and can out-gun almost any other of the fraternity. Like Yngwie Malmsteen, however, he often appears in need of a more substantial musical peg on to which to hang his hat.

Inspired by John Coltrane, Allan Holdsworth developed an innovative high-speed legato style on the guitar which he unleashed on the largely unreceptive London jazz scene in the early 1970s. On a good night, Holdsworth's playing could be quite breathtaking.

rather than picking alternately. By combining these strikes with a light action and hammer-ons and pull-offs, tremendous speed can be attained.) Thus although both men play at great speed, Gambale has the sharper, more staccato attack, a characteristic which links him with more conventional jazz guitar styles. It also creates the impression of greater rhythmic drive. Gambale had several good showings with Chick Corea's Elektric Band from 1986-93, notably on 'Little Things That Count' and 'Lifescape' from *Beneath The Mask*, on 'Time Track' from *GRP Super Live In Concert*, and on *Let's Set The Record Straight*, one of the excellent fusion albums by Tom Coster, the former Santana keyboard player. Except for *Thinking Out Loud*, his own records (such as *Thunder From Down Under* and *Note Worker*) tend to be weakened by the inclusion of vocals, and the best setting for shred Gambale-style remains *Truth In Shredding* and another superbly conceived Mark Varney production, *Centrifugal Funk*.

In the latter, Gambale is joined by two other shredders, Brett Garsed and Shawn Lane, in an orgy of over-the-top guitar-playing on such modern classics as Herbie Hancock's 'Actual Proof', Miles Davis's 'So What' and Marcus Miller's 'Splatch'. Quite by accident, this set is interesting in highlighting the contrast between shred-fusion and shred-metal. All three men play with extraordinary technique, but whereas Garsed's and Lane's rock-based playing becomes monotonous, Gambale is able to sustain interest through his superior harmonic resources.

There has, however, been a downside to Gambale's thoroughness, and that is the accusation that his playing is robotic, uncreative and lacking in feeling, an understandable charge in view of the generally breathless density of his lines. Perhaps aware of this criticism, he recorded *Thinking Out Loud* in 1995, an album of more relaxed, mid-tempo material modelled somewhat on the writing of Steely Dan. With the exception of one or two tracks, he plays a full-bodied Ibanez George Benson model guitar and gets an appropriately mellow sound. In 1998, perhaps following the same muse, or responding to the retrospective climate which has affected the playing of so many one-time modernists in recent years, he recorded an album with Steve Smith's Vital Information, *Where We Come From*, in which all the players, Gambale included, took a step back to the pop, funk and soul styles of the 1960s, with an attendant reduction in notemanship.

Although he may be classed as a shredder, Gambale plays with a cleaner tone than his predecessor in the Elektric Band, Scott Henderson. Like Larry Carlton, Gambale aims to achieve sustain through light distortion. Thus although he plays in rapid-fire shred style, he doesn't have the heavy rocking tone often used by Henderson. In this respect, and in his use of explicit heavy metal licks, Henderson technically comes closest of all the players in this section to shred-metal. A track like 'Torque' from the Tribal Tech album *Illicit*, with its raw, crunching distortion and power chord riffs, illustrates the point, but importantly it also shows that heavy rock is only one aspect of Henderson's range of sounds. Juxtaposed with the metal riffs are keyboard theme statements which could have been written by Joe Zawinul, and Henderson's solo, while beginning with heavily overdriven rock phrases reminiscent of his early inspiration, Jimmy Page, progresses to lightning-fast legato passages which have the intricacy and fluidity of Holdsworth lines.

Henderson's work in Tribal Tech, the band he has co-led with bassist Gary Willis since 1984, shows that while he comes closest to true metal, he is also one of the most eclectic of fusion guitar players. The group's 1995 album *Reality Check* illustrates his breadth of expression, ranging from the jazz standard (an updated reading of 'Stella By Starlight'), through heavy metal ('Stella By Infra-Red High Particle Neutron Beam'), smooth, clean-toned 1950s-style swing ('Susie's Dingsbums') and world-flavoured music reminiscent of Weather Report ('Speak'), to an exquisite blues performance on 'Nite Club'. Henderson's solo on the latter is a beautifully conceived example of his skill at building a storytelling solo. He begins with a few insinuating phrases in which touch and tone are nuanced to absolute perfection before building to a storming, virtuosic climax. It's a mark of his musicality that he introduces various jazz-derived harmonic colours into this setting without compromising

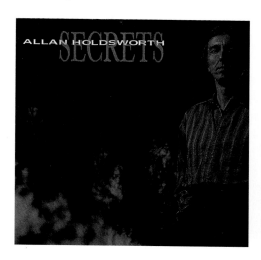

the authentic blues feeling. Shortly before recording this album, Henderson had begun leading his own blues band. It might have seemed impossible to find new angles on the time-worn verities of the blues, but Henderson's blues band has advanced this ostensibly static style. By working in some different notes and ingeniously stretching the blues form, his 1994 album *Dog Party* (named for his love of dogs) breathed vibrant new life into the old idiom.

In a jazz-rock setting, Henderson, like Gambale, is well-equipped to introduce chromatic bite, albeit in a more linear way. Where Gambale seems to focus on each passing chord as a separate entity, Henderson tends to play lines which flow right through the changes. Also, where Gambale's improvisations have a textbook purity, almost without style and only minimal inflection, Henderson in jazz-rock mode seems to integrate the styles of Jimmy Page, Allan Holdsworth and, in his particular manner of playing outside the underlying harmony, John Scofield. Of all the shred-fusion players, he is the most skilled at tonal manipulation, able to extract the most expressive range of sounds from his instrument, with or without effects.

Although lacking the public profile of Holdsworth, Gambale and Henderson, the Paris-based guitarist Nguyên Lê has developed a distinctly personal angle on shred-fusion. In a number of records as leader he has demonstrated an astonishing command of the standard jazz-metal vocabulary, complete with the harmonic mastery one would expect. However, to a vocabulary based in Hendrix, Holdsworth and perhaps Scofield, he has added a distinctive oriental flavour, reflective of his own Vietnamese background. This is specifically evident in his wide vibrato, percussive, koto-like attack and his individual use of pentatonic scales.

Allan Holdsworth's Secrets from 1989 (left) offers outstanding guitar and Synthaxe (guitar-synthesiser) work from Holdsworth, with excellent support from Jimmy Johnson (bass) and Vinnie Colaiuta (drums). Igginbottom was a shortlived group that Holdsworth formed in his home town of Bradford in Yorkshire, England. Igginbottom's Wrench from 1964 (centre) was his recording debut at age 21, his legato guitar style already formed and his compositions, in the words of Ronnie Scott's sleevenotes, "fantastic and strangely moving – full of unexpected twists and difficult intervals". Frank Gambale alternates between virtuosic attention-grabbing displays of rock guitar and musical statements of genuine beauty, inventiveness and depth on 1994's Passages (above). Fortunately, the latter are in the majority.

JOHN ZARADIN BRAZILIAN GUITAR

WHEN JAZZ CAME TO BRAZIL, IT MET AN ESTABLISHED TRADITION OF IMPROVISED MUSIC IN WHICH MANY STYLES AND CULTURAL TRADITIONS WERE MIXED. BUT CENTRAL TO ALL THE MUSIC OF BRAZIL IS THE NYLON-STRUNG CLASSICAL GUITAR, PLAYED WITH THE FINGERS.

The Brazilian guitar is the nylon-strung classical instrument. The music of Brazil owes much to the right-hand techniques of that instrument, and all the guitarists mentioned here are right-hand fingerstyle players, not pick players.

Brazil is a cultural melting-pot for three racial types: Indian, African and European. The native Indian has a substantial cultural presence in Spanish South America, but, because of Portugal's own colonial history, plays only a small role in the make-up of modern Brazil. Black Africans, meanwhile, were imported, until 1850, as slaves to do work originally imposed on the native Indian. In their evolution within their new territory, they have made a most significant contribution to the rhythmic character of the country's music.

The European colonists, who included Portuguese, Spanish, French, Italian, Austrian, Polish and even Scottish, brought with them their own customs, traditions and musical instruments. They maintained their interest in opera and theatre, continued to play their national dances – fandango, seguidilla, habanera, tango, waltz, polka and écossaise – and imported, amongst their instruments, the guitar.

The most numerous of the Europeans were the Portuguese and Spanish from the Iberian peninsula: both had inherited from Moorish occupation a great love of instruments that were plucked. The lute, guitar and vihuela, being such instruments, co-existed actively in their societies.

The vihuela, by repertoire and history, is really the father of the instrument that we now call the nylon-strung Spanish or classical guitar. The three basic kinds of vihuela were the vihuela de arco, played with a bow, the vihuela de peñola, played with a quill or pick, and the vihuela de mano, played with the fingers. Of these, the vihuela de mano was the most expressive and, having a greater number of strings than the guitar, accommodated more complex music.

In fact, the vihuela de mano became the most serious solo instrument of its day. It was played in the courts and in official venues, in contrast to the guitar, which had a much lower social profile and was used in the main for accompanying the voice and other instruments. The great age of polyphonic counterpoint in the 16th century was also the great age of the vihuela, and on this instrument was performed dedicated instrumental music – as opposed to arrangements or adaptations of vocal pieces. The common basic forms used for improvisation were the fantasy, which was a kind of free-form, and the theme and variations.

The period produced composer/performers who played publicly and were known for their ability to improvise. Narváez, Mudarra and Milán were three skilled players who wrote down their music and in consequence created

Charlie Byrd playing electric guitar early in his career (left). Byrd was to popularise the Spanish guitar through his bossa nova recordings with tenor saxophonist Stan Getz. On this early-1960s album (above), with not a single bossa in sight, Byrd plays jazz standards and a couple of originals on Spanish guitar. A swing jazz player at heart, he can dig in and play with the bluesy attack of a Big Bill Broonzy.

repertoire that is still in use today. Such musicians, performers as much as composers, could in one sense be considered the forerunners of many of today's jazz players.

During the 16th century the Portuguese began to occupy and colonise Brazil, bringing with them the vihuela. Brazil adopted the vihuela (whose name became violão), not the guitar, and it is this instrument, on which one could interpret written pieces and also improvise, that gave rise to a style of music recognised as being typically Brazilian. Today, the violão and the nylon-strung guitar are one and the same instrument.

In order to get a feel for the climate in which music existed at this time, we must remember that much of the colonisation was effected through European missionaries who, in endeavouring to establish Christianity, discouraged native expression and banned improvising. The imported African slaves were greatly affected by this. They had their own combined religious and musical rituals, which were unwritten and performed with improvisation.

This CD compilaton from the mid 1990s offers the Latin Impressions album, from 1962, and Once More – Charlie Byrd's Bossa Nova, from 1963. It's full of classic bossa nova compositions alongside several from Byrd's own pen.

They could accept the Roman Catholic impositions only by disguising their own customs and traditions in newly created routines and dances which were acceptable to the Church. In this covert fashion they kept them alive and laid the groundwork for what, in the samba and its variations, has become one of the world's most distinctive rhythmic idioms.

In 1739, the Church, through its Inquisition, cut the throat of Antonio José da Silva, and burned him as a heretic. He was born in Rio de Janeiro in 1705 and was one of the country's first celebrated composer/arrangers. He made a successful tour in Portugal and returned to Brazil with collections of fandangos, sarabandes, songs and so on. Having attended productions of Italian-style "Opera Buffa" in Europe, he re-created his own in Brazil. His productions satirised the Church, which became so upset that it felt obliged to kill him and destroy his scores and texts. The story of da Silva is not without a recent parallel when, in the 1960s and 1970s, many artists and musicians, including the guitarist/composer Chico Buarque, suffered interference from the country's establishment and were forced to leave Brazil because their work was not officially approved.

By the 18th century, however, music societies had been formed, and out of them grew small orchestras, groups and choirs performing a diversity of music in public festivals and events. Eventually, a music form unique to Brazil appeared: the chôros, "in which," to quote the composer Heitor Villa-Lobos, "are synthesised the different modalities of Brazilian, Indian and popular music reflecting in its fundamental elements the rhythm and characteristic elements of the people".

Chôro was first used as the name for a mixed instrumental ensemble, combining flutes, clarinets and trombones with guitars, the small cavaquinho and so on. But the description of the group gradually became the term for the music that it played: "the chôro of that time was intelligent improvisation. What is done today with jazz we did here in Rio years ago."

The music was originally based on dances from Europe – polkas, mazurkas and the like – which had repeating sections and therefore allowed variations to be made. The chôro musicians began to improvise on the forms: this would have had them imprisoned, at the least, not that many years before. The groups, being in direct contact with the African cultures now established in the populated areas, introduced colours and rhythms into their music that did not appear in the music of the Spanish colonies, and they used the portable violão/guitar both as a solo and as an accompanying instrument.

The repertoire, absorbing local influences, evolved styles of both song chôros and instrumental dance forms which were complicated and demanding of the players. It also provided a body of music for performers who could attract and entertain the public at large. Their world was the jumping off ground for modern Brazilian music and they played a great part in establishing an environment for improvising and the eventual absorption of jazz idioms from the US.

The bridge between the old samba and chôros forms and the new bossa nova was the success, in the 1950s, of the film *Orfeu Negro* ("Black Orpheus"). Set in Rio de Janeiro during carnival, it introduced to the world a music that was new yet recognisable, melodic, strongly rhythmic and harmonically interesting – perfect for improvisers and jazz players.

Looking at the lives and careers of some of the players involved with this awakening, we have mentioned Heitor Villa-Lobos, the best known of Brazil's classical composers, who was also a conductor and guitarist. He was born on March 5th 1887, and introduced to guitar, piano and clarinet as a child. At six, his father had built him his own guitar. But his father died when he was 12, and his mother banned further musical study, particularly of popular music, which she despised. Young Heitor ran off to join a chôros group, travelling throughout Brazil, playing guitar, improvising and beginning his huge catalogue of compositions.

Later he returned to formal musical study, in Rio de Janiero and then, from 1923, in Paris, where he wrote in the advanced idiom of the day. But on his return to Brazil, in 1930, he became involved in musical education and began producing a series of works dedicated to Brazil's new-found national pride and exploring the nation's fascinatingly mixed cultural identity. As a composer, he went on to become Brazil's great ambassador of music. He died in 1959.

The first Brazilian player to introduce the world to the guitar music of Villa-Lobos was Laurindo Almeida (1917-1995). His family, like that of Villa-Lobos, was musical but did not obstruct his guitar and music studies. In 1936 he sailed to Europe, performing on the Brazilian cruise liner Cuyaba. He heard the Quintet of the Hot Club of France in Paris and, upon his return to Brazil, joined the music staff of Radio Mayrink Veiga.

Leaving Brazil in 1947 for the US he settled in California, and gained his jazz credentials as a featured soloist with the Stan Kenton orchestra. In 1950 he left the Kenton band for a more diverse musical life, and during the years 1953 to 1954 he teamed up and recorded 'South Of The Border' with alto and flute player Bud Shank, one of the musicians playing bossa nova before it acquired its name.

Almeida was the first classical player to take the guitar to a wide audience, touring an arrangement of the adagio from Rodrigo's *Concierto de Aranjuez* in 1963 and 1964 with the MJQ. He worked continually as a composer, arranger and performer in the studios in California, and we hear his guitar voice in countless movie westerns. His recordings feature a variety of music from both jazz and classical repertoires, much of which exists in his own Braziliance Publishing Company catalogue. In the 1970s he found himself touring in jazz settings with the LA4 and in collaborations with Charlie Byrd.

After his 1962 hit 'Desafinado', with Stan Getz, Charlie Byrd was always associated with Brazilian music. But he is an American, born September 16th 1925, near Suffolk, Virginia. His professional career began in dance bands, having been taught plectrum guitar by his father. Although he quotes Charlie Christian as a main influence, he was very taken with the nylon-strung classical guitar and in 1950 moved to Washington DC and studied with Sophocles Papas before taking master classes in Siena, in 1954, with Segovia. Returning to the US, he joined the Woody Herman band, but felt increasingly drawn to the classical guitar and looked for a way of playing jazz on it.

He formed a guitar, bass and drums trio with Keter Betts and Bertel Knox and started up his own jazz club, The Showboat Lounge, in Washington DC. Here the trio played a jazz repertoire, but the shows also included classical guitar solos. In 1961, the US State Department sponsored a tour to South America for the trio and it was after that that Byrd's interest in Brazilian music really began.

The bossas that Charlie Byrd and Getz were playing, and Astrud Gilberto was singing, contained both the lyricism and the Afro rhythms of the old

Antonio Carlos Jobim (known as Tom Jobim in Brazil) was the most prolific of the bossa nova composers. His hits such as 'The Girl From Ipanema', 'How Insensitive', 'Wave' and 'One Note Samba' are now in the standard jazz repertory.

chôros and sambas, and these qualities are evidenced in the work of singer and guitarist João Gilberto. He made his name in Brazil when he took over from Luiz Bonfa in a group called the Quitiandinha Serenaders. He used his voice in an instrumental, jazz way and defined a guitar accompaniment style that persists to this day.

The music of 'Desafinado' announced its composer Antonio Carlos Jobim to the world and created in popular music a "new beat" – bossa nova. Jobim, born in 1927, was a trained composer and pianist who played the guitar and sang. He had contributed music to the film *Orfeu Negro* but, with 'Desafinado', he became Brazil's most popular composer – and world famous. His music is very much rooted in his country's history, and inspires every jazz

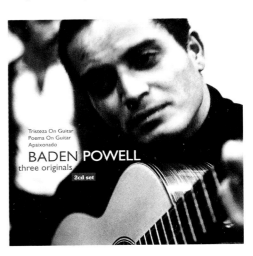

An excellent fingerstyle guitarist and composer, Luiz Bonfa co-wrote the film score for the movie Orfeu Negro (Black Orpheus) and many bossa nova classics including 'The Gentle Rain' and 'Menina Flor'. This album of Bonfa's (above) is from 1966. Classically-trained guitarist Laurindo Almeida moved from Brazil to Los Angeles to work as a studio musician, recording his own albums and performing with saxophone and flute master Bud Shank (1958 album, centre) in the LA Four. Three of Baden Powell's finest albums are on this early-1990s CD compilation (right): Tristeza On Guitar (recorded 1966), Poema On Guitar (1968) and Apaixonado (1975).

and Latin musician to play and improvise on it. In Brazil itself, however, the father of bossa nova is recognised to be Garôto (Anibal Augusto Sardinha) who died in 1955. In 1946 he recommended Luiz Bonfa for a contract with Radio Nacional in Rio, from which Bonfa emerged as the player to call upon both for sessions and for concerts, live and recorded. Luiz Bonfa was born on October 17th, 1922, and began to study the guitar at 11 years of age. His early teachers were his father and Isais Savio. He made a conscious decision to move from the classical world into the popular field of music and prompted a serious development to his professional career in 1957 when he went to live in the United States.

His arrival coincided with the explosion of bossa nova. He co-wrote, with Jobim, the music for the film *Orfeu Negro* (1958), and his songs from this film – 'Amanha Do Carnaval' and 'Samba Ofeu' – have become world-wide jazz standards. Working with the singer Mary Martin, he was exposed to jazz and made several successful recordings with Stan Getz. His life in California involved him with the TV and film industry, but in 1971 he returned to settle at his home in Brazil from where he develops his individual "romantic descriptive" style, synthesising melody and harmony with improvisation.

A player who is immediately recognised as Brazilian, but whose style owes much to jazz, is Bola Sete (1928-1987). He came from a musical family and studied at the National School of Music in Rio de Janeiro. In 1952 he took a sextet to Italy and worked there for almost four years in clubs and hotels, returning to tour throughout South America. Finally, in 1960, he decided to move to the US. After two years of hotel lounge work he was heard by Dizzy Gillespie and invited to play at the 1962 Monterey Jazz Festival. He was a

specialist performer in the bossa nova/jazz idiom with very strong Afro-Brazilian roots in his style. He has his own comments on bossa nova: "It's a samba with jazz feeling... Brazilian composers... have taken Brazilian music and put it with jazz music, which they love, and made something new with it that can be universal. Bossa nova is what the musicians have been playing for themselves in Rio: not in the country, but in the city. Like a jam session."

During the years 1966 to 1969 he toured within the US with his own Brazilian trio featuring music from *Orfeu Negro*, a recording of which is well heard on the album *Live At El Matador*. In 1971 he expanded his group to a quartet, and in 1972 started using the lutar, a guitar of his own design.

Of all the modern Brazilian jazz guitarists, none has a reputation to compare with Baden Powell, born on August 6th 1937. He stands on the shoulders of Paulinho Nogueira, who could be regarded as the founder of modern Brazilian finger-style, but Powell develops the idiom to make it his own. His father was a violinist and an admirer of Robert Baden Powell, the founder of scouting, and gave his son the same name. Baden Powell began to study the guitar at eight and was playing professionally at 15. In 1959 he co-wrote 'Samba Triste' with Billy Blanco and was thereafter employed as a session guitarist on samba and bossa nova recordings. In 1962 he teamed up with Vinicius de Moraes (1913-80), who went on to write lyrics for more than 50 of Powell's songs. He claims his influences were Reinhardt and Barney Kessel, but his natural music is obviously Afro-Brazilian with the samba as his declared favourite form.

Although he was well enough known in Brazil to keep working, his reputation did not extend abroad until the German writer and producer

Baden Powell in concert at the Lewisham Theatre in London, 1983. A brilliant and exhilarating performer, Powell combines classical technique and Brazilian rhythms with jazz savvy.

Joachim Berendt, visiting Brazil, persuaded Powell to record under his own name. His consequent success took him to Europe where his recordings and concerts have created a very loyal following. He now travels and performs between Europe and his native Brazil. His recordings and re-issues are numerous, but all demonstrate his unique style.

Of current players, Egberto Gismonti is probably the most unusual. He was born on December 5th 1947, and trained as a pianist and composer. His compositions, piano and guitar playing all feature in his concerts. His background is in the mainstream classical tradition, with (from the age of six) 15 years of piano training and composition lessons with Nadia Boulanger and Jean Barlaque in Paris. On his return to Brazil he decided to incorporate Brazilian folk roots and jazz into his work and, in 1967, began study of the guitar so that he could play chôros, counting Baden Powell as a decisive influence. In 1973 Gismonti took up the eight-string classical guitar for its extra range and, in 1976, having spent time with the Xingu Indians in the interior of Brazil, produced 'Danças Das Cabeças'.

Toninho Horta, on the other hand, born in Belo Horizonte on December 2nd 1948, was encouraged by his family to listen to jazz, and is professionally involved with contemporary jazz and rock rather than with traditional roots and samba. At the age of 13 he composed the song 'Flor Que Cheirava Saudade' and by 1970 was working with Milton Nascimento and later Flora Purim and Sergio Mendes. In 1980 he met Pat Metheny, moved to New York, and, with an interest in orchestration, studied at the Juillard School. He gained a reputation locally with his own trio (Mark Egan on bass and Danny Gottlieb on drums). In 1986 he went home to Minas Gerais, founded the "First Brazilian Seminar of Instrumental Music" and then, in 1992, returned to New York to work with his own quartet, including Kenny Barron on keyboards, Gary Peacock on bass and Billy Higgins on drums.

There are player/composers who make an important contribution to the Brazilian jazz guitar idiom by working only in Brazil or by travelling with shows in which they do not headline. Among them are Toquinho, who came to prominence with Vinicius de Moraes and plays very much in the Nogueira/Powell tradition, and Sebastião Tapajós, again in the same tradition, performing his own repertoire and working with a rhythm section.

Oscar Castro Neves was the guitar presence on the early records and tours of Sergio Mendes and is now involved with the guitar, MIDI applications and modern recording techniques. Jose Neto, who has his own group, Urban Oasis, is also seen in varied Latin rock settings with Tania Maria, Airto Moreira, Flora Purim and even Harry Belafonte. Rafael Rabello was centred in the chôros tradition but died unexpectedly in his twenties. Fortunately, his recordings with jazz saxophonist Paulo Moura stand as a fitting memorial to his playing.

There are so many excellent Brazilian jazz guitarists: but given the space restrictions of the chapter we can only mention a few. The players included have been chosen because, by recordings and touring, they have reached a wide public, and, as composer/performers and improvisers, they are today developing the Brazilian guitar in the tradition established by the vihuelistas of the 16th century. Musicians from widely differing backgrounds are attracted to the Brazilian jazz guitar and, with this instrument, they perform for and delight audiences, not just in Brazil, but throughout the whole world.

After studying composition in Europe, Egberto Gismonti (opposite, with Charlie Haden on bass) spent time in the Amazon rainforest studying the music of the Xingu Indians. His music reflects his diversity of interests – from Ravel to Brazilian music, from African music to jazz and blues. Jose Neto is pictured (above) at a Fourth World gig at Ronnie Scott's Club in London. After studying in his native Brazil, Neto moved to the US and has worked with Harry Belafonte, Tania Maria, Pacquito D'Rivera and Hugh Masakela. These influences – together with contemporary dance rhythms – help to shape the music of Fourth World, the band Neto co-formed with percussionist Airto Moreira and vocalist Flora Purim.

THE SESSION PLAYERS

THE RECORD PLANTS AND MOVIE LOTS OF NEW YORK AND LOS ANGELES HAD A VAST APPETITE FOR MUSICAL EXPERTISE. MANY JAZZ GUITARISTS TOOK THEIR INSTRUMENTAL TALENTS INTO RECORDING-STUDIO WORK – AND IN MANY CASES IT DID THEM NO HARM.

If Barney Kessel and Herb Ellis are the best known names amongst the guitarists who made their living, at least for a time, as studio players in Los Angeles, they were by no means the only ones.

In the 1950s and 1960s, studio work provided a reliable source of regular income for musicians on both coasts, and took a variety of forms. In New York, the radio and broadcasting networks maintained their own house orchestras, and hired musicians to enhance particular projects on a regular basis. Recording sessions provided another studio-based opportunity, at a time when singers were often featured with large studio ensembles. The real mecca of studio work, however, was in Los Angeles and the giant film studio complexes of Hollywood.

The colour bar was slow to break down on both coasts, and studio work went in the main to white musicians. They were liable to be called to play on anything from an advertising jingle to a full-blown jazz score by a Johnny Mandel or a Billy May – and all points in between. Playing jazz for a living is a fraught business, and the studio provided security, and occasionally a challenge: there were always the clubs, records, or tours in between your session commitments to keep your jazz "chops" in shape and your aesthetic principles sharp.

A number of guitarists have enjoyed careers centred on the studios, but have also been able to made their mark in jazz. One of the best known is Howard Roberts, although he has always been held in higher esteem by his fellow guitarists and guitar aficionados than by the jazz public at large, perhaps partly in consequence of the "invisible" part of his career spent playing commercial music in the anonymity of the studio.

Howard Roberts (1929-1992) took up guitar at the age of seven, and absorbed a wide-ranging technique and musical frame of reference. He began his professional career in his native Phoenix in the war years, and moved to Los Angeles in 1950. He had not been in town long when he was introduced to another prominent studio guitarist, Jack Marshall, at a local jazz club where both had gone to hear Barney Kessel play with Dave Brubeck. Marshall, a gifted guitarist and arranger, found him an opening, and started him on the road to a career in the studios which spanned two decades.

Roberts was able to adapt readily to the demands of the job, and contributed to literally thousands of recordings, film and television soundtracks. In the early 1970s, he switched his attentions to teaching, and co-founded the esteemed Guitar Institute of Technology in 1976, as well as producing and publishing a range of jazz guitar instruction books, writing a regular column for *Guitar Player* magazine, and endorsing the Howard

Roberts model guitar for Epiphone (later Gibson). Throughout all of these activities, however, he continued to play jazz.

Some of his later work fell into a slightly unconvincing fusion vein, but his more straight-ahead jazz work stands comparison with the best of the era. He is featured on disc with such luminaries as Chico Hamilton, Art Pepper and Thelonious Monk, but the finest examples of his work are to be found on the best of his own records, notably *Mr Roberts Plays Guitar* (Verve, 1957) and *The Real Howard Roberts* (Concord, 1977). He was a superior technician on the instrument in both single line and chordal playing, and an expressive exponent of jazz idioms, stretching from bebop to jazz-rock. His early absorption of the advanced harmonic and rhythmic ideas of composers like

 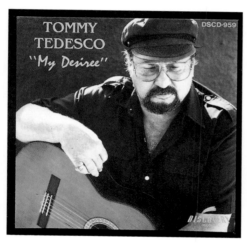 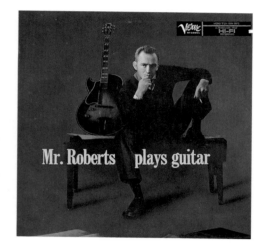

Bartok and Stravinsky fed into his own sophisticated musical sensibility in a jazz context: and he was not adverse to even more overt borrowings of classical sources, as in his use of a string quartet in *Mr Roberts Plays Guitar*.

The man who introduced Roberts to the studio trade, Jack Marshall (1921-1973), was a talented guitarist in his own right, and was equally highly thought of as an arranger and producer (his credits include Peggy Lee's major hit, 'Fever'). Marshall was brought up in Kansas, and played ukulele for three years before switching to guitar at the age of 13, inspired by the example of Django Reinhardt. His family uprooted to Los Angeles in the 1930s, and he took up electric guitar after finishing high school in 1938.

He sat in occasionally with the likes of Nat King Cole, Count Basie and Art Tatum in the thriving late night-club scene on Central Avenue, but began his studio career as part of a student broadcasting band in 1939. He was hired as a staff guitarist by MGM in 1940, and although he took an engineering qualification after the war, the studios were to be the focal point of his professional life. He built a formidable reputation for his work in that context (and for his lively sense of humour), with writing and arranging taking over as the principal focus of his interests.

At the same time as he was composing soundtracks and making sophisticated arrangements for singers like Peggy Lee and Vic Damone, he was also playing and recording with the luminaries of the West Coast jazz scene, including Shorty Rogers, Shelly Manne, Stan Kenton, and guitarists Barney Kessel, Al Hendrickson, Laurindo Almeida and Howard Roberts, all of whom featured in a collection of West Coast Guitar compositions he prepared as one of several instruction books (he was also a respected teacher). He never lost

Dennis Budimir duets with himself on the 1964 album Alone Together (left) and, on two tracks, with saxophonist Gary Foster. A strong, harmonically rich performance results, revealing influences from Bill Evans and John Coltrane. Tommy Tedesco flexed his formidable jazz guitar chops in 1989 for My Desiree (centre), alternately burning and caressing his way through a varied set: a modal tune, some jazz waltzes, 5/4 and 6/4 time, a fast samba, and a pretty ballad. One of the hot studio players to come up during the 1950s, Howard Roberts also made a solid reputation as a jazz guitarist with a series of albums for Verve, such as the 1957 outing Mr Roberts Plays Guitar (above). Always an incisive player, Roberts is heard here with a jazz quartet, occasionally augmented by string quintet arrangements from Marty Paich.

his appetite for performing, however, and in 1967 he talked the owners of Donte's nightclub into hosting a Monday night jazz-guitar gig which became a staple of the Los Angeles scene for several years.

Tommy Tedesco (1930–1997) was another guitarist who racked up a huge number of commercial studio recordings in Los Angeles. Like Roberts, he was a familiar enough name to guitar players, but is less familiar to the broader jazz public, and largely absent from the general jazz reference books. Born in Niagara Falls, New York State, he began to play the guitar at ten, but it was only in his mid-teens that he applied himself seriously to the task.

He came to Los Angeles as a member of a touring dance band in 1953, and decided to stay on, initially working in jazz clubs in the city with locally-based players like Chico Hamilton, Shorty Rogers, Art Pepper and Buddy DeFranco. In 1955, he began working in the studios, and effectively ceased to perform as a jazz artist for the next 25 years. He was hardly idle though, prompting one guitar expert, Maurice Summerfield, to conjecture that he might be the most recorded guitarist in the history of the music – even if much of it went uncredited. His contributions to film soundtracks, television shows and record albums certainly add up to a prodigious amount of picking.

There are other parallels with Roberts, too, including the fact that Tedesco taught at the Guitar Institute for many years, prepared respected instruction books and wrote a column in *Guitar Player*. Unlike Roberts, though, his self-imposed exile from active jazz work took him out of the scene for much of his career, and he has left a smaller recorded legacy of his own work in a jazz context. He did return in the late 1970s, gigging in the Los Angeles club scene and recording a number of albums on smaller labels, mainly Discovery Trend.

Not all of the Los Angeles based studio players plied their trade in the movie world, which began to have less and less call for live musicians in any case. A good studio guitarist had to be able to produce the goods in any situation, regardless of time pressures, and to fit whatever context his employer required. A more complex version of the latter quality is also required in the make-up of a good accompanist, and the recording studios provided work for many of them, often backed up by live engagements with the artists – mainly singers – whose albums they played on.

That was the case for the Pittsburgh-born guitarist Ron Anthony (b.1933), a classically trained musican on both bass and piano. An elegant stylist on guitar, he came to national notice as a member of George Shearing's Quintet in 1961-3 (and worked with the pianist again in the early 1970s), but settled in Los Angeles in 1965, where he worked with singer Vic Damone, a prelude to a nearly decade-long association with Frank Sinatra from 1985. An accomplished singer himself, he juggled these commitments with teaching, working for other band leaders and leading his own trio in the city's clubs.

Not all of the jazz guitarists involved in studio work were out-of-towners who chose to settle in Los Angeles. Dennis Budimir (b.1938) was born in the city, and was a member of trumpeter Harry James's band while still in his teens. He carved out impressive jazz credentials in the late 1950s, working in more adventurously modernist contexts with Chico Hamilton, Eric Dolphy, Bud Shank (Budimir replaced Billy Bean in the saxophonist's quartet for a time in 1961) and singer Peggy Lee.

Budimir was drafted into the army in 1961, and on his release, in 1963, began a studio career which saw him contribute to a host of recordings, beginning with singer Bobby Troup and taking in such names as Quincy

Tommy Tedesco's guitar has been heard by millions on the soundtrack of M.A.S.H. and countless other TV series and movies. His column in Guitar Player magazine revealed the strategies and skills of a top studio player... and the wages received.

Lee Ritenour (guitar) and Eric Marienthal (tenor sax) at the Royal Festival Hall, London, during the 1998 Oris London Jazz Festival (above left). Ritenour's pop-fusion guitar skills often distract attention from the jazz guitarist beneath. On Stolen Moments (above), a 1990 recording, Ritenour takes Wes Montgomery as his starting point, and leaves no doubt about his jazz credentials.

Jones, Don Ellis, Lalo Schifrin, Marty Paitch and Milt Jackson, as well as singer Julie London. A strong rhythm player who favoured a sparse, hard-edged development of bop style, his deft guitar work proved adaptable to many contexts, but his concentration on studio work left him under-exposed in his own right. The records he made for the Revelation label were, however, much admired by those who knew them.

Relative anonymity for those who chose the studio life was not the absolute rule. Others succeeded in combining a studio career with a major public reputation. Chief among them must surely be Lee Ritenour (b.1952), another Los Angeles native who revealed a precocious talent as a child, and was performing in a local big-band by the age of 12. By his own account a fanatical practicer as a teenager (he managed nine hours a day while in high school), he studied with a number of distinguished guitarists, including Joe Pass, Howard Roberts and Jack Marshall, and took over the latter's course at the University of Southern California – after Marshall's sudden untimely death in 1973. His first major break as a performer came when he was hired by Sergio Mendes's touring band in 1974, the same year he took part in a guitar summit presentation at the Monterey Jazz Festival, sharing a stage with Jim Hall, Mundell Lowe and Joe Pass.

All of this left him well equipped for a career as the consummate LA studio musician. His technical gifts and chameleon-like ability to blend into any setting have been put to use on literally thousands of recording sessions, and for an equally staggering range of artists, including Tony Bennett, Barbra Streisand, John Denver, Johnny Mathis, Aretha Franklin, Ray Charles and Stevie Wonder. His technique has not always been accompanied by the ability to project his own musical personality in any very individual or emotionally convincing fashion, however, and his recordings as leader have largely fallen into a rather bland pop-jazz fusion mould.

When he has moved in a more overtly jazz-oriented direction, however, he has done so impressively enough to leave the suspicion that there could have been much more to his playing had he chosen to go down that route. The influence of Wes Montgomery is never far away in such projects, notably in *Wes Bound* (1992) and the later *Alive In LA* (1997). His empathy with Brazilian music is heard to advantage on *Rio* (1979), and his meeting with Larry Carlton on *Larry & Lee* (1994) was an amiable if rather soft-focus addition to their rosters.

Too often, though, Ritenour has delivered a studio player's super-competent but rather anonymous performance when a more individual one was required. It has done him no harm at the cash register, however, and he remains a major name in the fusion world.

Another of Ritenour's early associations in Los Angeles was with guitarist John Pisano (b.1931). In 1976, Jack Marshall had set up his guitar night at Donte's, in Burbank, which became something of an institution in jazz guitar circles. Ritenour and Pisano performed as a duo at the club one night, and liked the experience enough to keep the duo going for over a year.

Pisano was born in New York City, and played piano before taking up guitar in his early teens. He opted for the musician's life after playing in an Air Force band in the early 1950s, and joined the Chico Hamilton Quintet

Robben Ford's effective blend of blues guitar and jazz has featured with Tom Scott's group LA Express, as well as The Yellowjackets, Miles Davis and David Sanborn. But it's Ford's blues-rock that cuts through on his own albums, notably Talk To Your Daughter.

(where he replaced Jim Hall) for his first important engagement in 1956. He settled in Los Angeles in the mid 1950s, formed a fine duo with guitarist Billy Bean, and worked with various luminaries of the LA jazz scene, including Jimmy Giuffre and Buddy DeFranco, and had an important association with Joe Pass. He can be heard playing sympathetic rhythm guitar on Pass's classic *For Django* album (1964), and filled that role again in the last five years of Pass's life.

Pisano's skills as a guitarist and wonderfully supportive accompanist inevitably found a welcome in Los Angeles, and if he was perhaps a little too self-effacing for his own good, the role seemed to suit him well enough. He worked for singer Peggy Lee throughout the 1960s, both in the studio and on the road, and was featured in an even more commercial context when trumpeter Herb Alpert recruited him for his Tijuana Brass in 1965, an association which also lasted until the end of the decade. He worked with Peggy Lee again in the 1970s, as well as guitarists Ritenour and Tony Rizzi.

More recently, he has worked with his wife, singer Jeanne Pisano, as The Flying Pisanos, and recorded two albums of collaborations with various friends for the Pablo label in the early 1990s, *Among Friends* and *Conversation Pieces*, which featured a number of guitarists, including Joe Pass, Lee

Ritenour, Phil Upchurch, and Ron Affif, the gifted nephew of Ron Anthony. They provide a good taster of his style, while tending to confirm the thought that his natural inclination was not to push himself into the limelight.

Phil Upchurch (b.1941) has established not one reputation as a studio musician, but two. The first came in his native Chicago, where his feel for the blues found him in demand on both guitar and electric bass (his first stringed instrument was the ukulele his father had given him when he was 11), especially after taking part in a hit record with singer Dee Clark. As well as contributing to countless blues and R&B sessions, he backed jazz musicians like Dizzy Gillespie and Stan Getz at this period.

After serving in the US Army in the mid-1960s, Upchurch returned to Chicago in 1968, where he worked with Cannonball Adderley and Grover Washington, among others. He was the house guitarist at Chess Records at this time, and played for blues legends like Muddy Waters, Howlin' Wolf and Otis Rush. In 1972, in a taste of things to come, he joined Quincy Jones in Los Angeles, but returned to Chicago after an earthquake soured him on the idea. In 1974, he recorded for the first time with George Benson, an old friend from the early 1960s, and contributed to several albums with the guitarist, including the spectacularly successful *Breezin'* in 1976.

The following year, Upchurch returned to Los Angeles, and this time he stayed, earning a second reputation as a studio musician in the West, and keeping his hand in as a soloist as well. He has gone on record as saying that he is not really a jazz player, a recognition that the foundation of his earthy guitar work lies firmly in the blues, which are never far from his fingers, whatever style he is featured in.

Like Upchurch, Robben Ford (b.1951) is another guitarist who is most often heard in a blues context, but possesses the necessary technical resources and improvisational flexibility to shine in a jazz setting as well. A California native from a musical family, he cut his teeth on rock-influenced electric blues in the 1970s, working with the likes of Charley Musselwhite and Jimmy Witherspoon as well as Joni Mitchell and Tom Scott's LA Express. In 1977 he became a founding member of the noted jazz-fusion group, the Yellowjackets, in an association which lasted until 1983.

Around this time, he also found himself much in demand for studio work (with Barbra Streisand and George Harrison among his satisfied customers), but succeeded in juggling the demands of the schedule to allow him both to form his own band, The Blue Line, and to hit the road with artists like Sadao Watanabe and, in 1986, Miles Davis. His strongest and most authentic work is arguably the driving blues-rock vein he explores with The Blue Line trio, although his singing is not as distinctive as his guitar playing.

All of these artists have combined studio careers with their own music to a greater or lesser degree. The qualities required of the studio musician are not the same as those of the great soloist or innovator, although they do overlap, and some musicians are more able than others to fulfill their potential in both of these fields.

If some of the guitarists highlighted in this chapter have never really gone beyond the technical polish and adaptability required in the studio to stamp their name on jazz in any very individual fashion, others – notably Howard Roberts – have made a major contribution to jazz guitar, and others, like Lee Ritenour, have found a mass audience. All have produced highly satisfying music along the way.

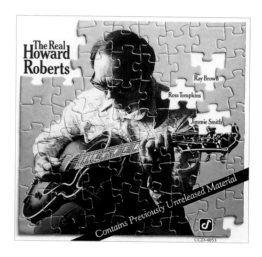

Recorded in the late 1970s and reissued later, The Real Howard Roberts is probably the guitarist's finest jazz album. Great phrasing, hard-swinging lines, funky blues licks and crystal clear chord-melody underpin a constant flow of great ideas, all executed with total assurance.

THE DECONSTRUCTIONISTS

JIMI HENDRIX HAD LITTLE DIRECT CONNECTION WITH JAZZ, BUT HIS REVOLUTIONARY IMPACT ON THE ELECTRIC GUITAR WAS FELT BY ALL WHO PLAYED THE INSTRUMENT. IT LEAD TO A NEW AND RADICAL SCHOOL OF JAZZ GUITARISTS, EAGER TO DITCH THE OLD CERTAINTIES.

Marc Ribot's guitar style is a hectic urban melange of Hendrix, noise guitar, teenage surf bands... and just about all the other points in between.

In its first heady flush, in the 1960s, rock music had no shortage of star players, but only Jimi Hendrix stood as a serious musical force.

With an emotional range far wider than that of any other contemporary guitarist, he demonstrated that the electric guitar was an electronic instrument rather than an amplified acoustic one, opening up a whole new world of musical possibilities that balanced energy and ingenuity, distortion, feedback, sustain and new fretboard techniques (most notably hammering-on) into vital and integral components of a new and integrated style. Just as Cecil Taylor redefined the piano or John Coltrane the tenor saxophone, Hendrix redefined the electric guitar. He was, as Gil Evans put it, a "sound innovator" who had a profound effect on jazz, although this has scarcely been acknowledged.

Just how significant an alternative Hendrix posed for the jazz world was actually acted out in living theatre at the old Scene Club in New York City on June 22nd 1968. "I saw [Larry] Coryell once. He was one of the few people who ever got up and tried to cut Hendrix," recalled drummer Robert Wyatt, then opening for Hendrix as a member of Soft Machine. "He was leaping backwards and forwards, his fingers flying, and Hendrix – when it came to his solo – just went 'ba-WO-O-O-OWWWW' and it just erased the last 10 minutes with one note. It was silly of Coryell to try. It was like walking into a blowtorch ... the fool!"

Under Hendrix's fingertips was a vast spectrum of guitar-playing sounds – blues, jazz, R&B, soul and rock – and the effect he had on open-eared jazz musicians was profound. "He was just running away with it," said Alan Douglas, Hendrix's friend, and, later, his record producer. "Everyone in jazz, blues and rock all felt lost. There were musicians in every genre who were very successful and took their music seriously and who found themselves icons of popular interest. In jazz it's Miles Davis.

"They felt they were evolving, making progress with their art, and all of a sudden here comes Hendrix and jumps seven miles ahead of them. There was envy, jealousy and admiration. They all began to question themselves, re-adjust to what they were hearing. Jimi sounded like a new age. I remember I was with Miles Davis at Fillmore East and we were both watching Hendrix perform, all he kept saying was, 'What the fuck is he doing? What the fuck is he doing?' over and over again, just mumbling to himself."

Even before Davis shocked the jazz world by embracing electricity, Hendrix's talent had been brought to his attention by his long-time collaborator, pianist and arranger Gil Evans, who had used Hendrix's 'The Wind Cries Mary' as the basis of the title track of Davis's 1968 album *Filles*

De Kilimanjaro. As Davis got to know Hendrix and began to form an understanding of his music, he gradually embraced electricity, to explore the sonic spaces opened up by the guitarist. Through Hendrix, Davis realised the potential of electronic improvisation at volume to change the face of jazz. Even after Hendrix's unexpected death on September 18th 1970, Davis continued to extend Hendrix's influence, albeit at one remove, with a series of albums that culminated in *Agharta* and *Panagaea* from January 1975. These live records, made the same day, suggested a new, electronic musical dialect through Pete Cosey's noise guitar and Reggie Lucas's incredible abstractions of Hendrix. They served merely to heighten speculation about what the guitarist's ultimate impact on jazz might have been had he been given enough time to have recorded, as he intended, with Roland Kirk and Gil Evans.

"It could have set a standard," said bassist and producer Bill Laswell. "I think it would have established a point of reference for the future." Yet even without a definitive statement from Hendrix in a jazz context, jazz musicians still saw enormous potential in his music. Paul Bley, for example, formed the electronic ensemble Scorpio, saying, "The implications for electronic instruments cry out for freedom just initiated by Jimi Hendrix."

Certainly Hendrix had done enough in his lifetime to suggest he was poised to make yet another step into the future. Already he had forced jazz musicians to consider volume as an aspect of authenticity and to weigh up how intensity in loud amplified sound could be enhanced by creative use of distortion. The avant-garde implications of 'Are You Experienced?', 'Castles In The Sand' and 'Driftin',' with their pre-recorded solos played backwards as an accompaniment to an orthodox solo, were echoed in the radical spirit that permeated much of the early jazz-rock of the late 1960s and early 1970s.

Drummer Tony Williams' Lifetime, for example, had first hand experience of Hendrix's playing since each member of the band – Williams, organist Larry Young and guitarist John McLaughlin – had jammed with Hendrix during the period of the trio's early rehearsals. McLaughlin's coruscating workout with Hendrix was preserved on the bootleg album *Hell's Session*, while Larry Young's work with Hendrix was released as *Nine To The Universe*. Williams jammed with Hendrix at his Electric Ladyland studios, but the results were apparently not recorded. Despite the simple set-up he used and the relatively primitive effects available to him, Hendrix was able to create quite astonishing guitar sounds, using simple techniques such as out-of-phase pickup settings, signal processing and devices such as the fuzz face, octavia, wah and delay, while his creative use of feedback extended the expressive range of the guitar even further.

Hendrix's scope was broad: he was well versed in R&B, learning the art at the music's front line, backing soul/R&B greats early in his career; he was equally well versed in the blues – his main influence was T-Bone Walker – while his "jazz" techniques included extensive use of pentatonic scales and modes at a time when they were considered more the province of jazz musicians. Clearly his playing represented a watershed of some kind and aspects of his style are a recognisable element in a wide range of guitarists throughout the 1970s, 1980s and 1990s, as well as being a source book of inspiration for more radical experimentation. Norwegian Terje Rypdal was in the European rock band Dream in the late 1960s when he first heard Hendrix, whom he says "blew my mind". Later, when the group included saxophonist Jan Garbarek and drummer Jon Christensen, Rypdal became more "sound"

Initially inspired by Hendrix, Norwegian guitarist Terje Rypdal uses the tonal resources of the electric guitar to create impressionistic sound pictures on this album from 1976.

orientated, playing some pieces using a violin bow on the strings, or playing the strings with pieces of metal. His rapid evolution into free jazz, and a brief period of study with George Russell in Oslo, led him into an abstract yet reflective form of expressionism. In 1971 he formed a trio with bassist Barre Phillips and Christensen, a format that provided the latitude he needed to develop his musical concepts.

One of the first artists to join Manfred Eicher's ECM roster, Rypdal appeared on Jan Garbarek's label debut, *Afric Pepperbird* in 1970. The following year he recorded *Sart* with a group that included Garbarek, Bobo Stenson, Arlid Andersen and Jon Christensen, and shortly afterwards made his own recorded debut as a leader with *Terje Rypdal*. While his early albums

Sonny Sharrock (guitar) and Peter Brötzmann (tenor sax) in Last Exit, an outfit offering extreme musical statements from two of the front-runners of the free jazz movements of the US and Germany.

reflected a post-*Bitches Brew* sensibility, and, on his third album *Whenever I Seem To Be Far Away*, long Mahavishnu-like passages over synthesiser textures, it was also clear that he was moving towards an impressionistic style of expressionism that reflected the stark imagery of nature near the Northern Lights. Yet this was done with the kind of sonic intensity Hendrix had pioneered on the fretboard, creating sometimes spiky, sometimes dissonant sound sculptures that used space for their effect.

At the end of the 1970s, Rypdal formed a quartet with Danish trumpeter Palle Mikkelborg, recording *Waves* in 1977, which consciously evoked European post-impressionism and the Hendrix-inspired music of Miles Davis. It reputedly became an influence on Davis's own *Aura*, which the trumpeter began recording in January 1985. Rypdal also recorded projects that found their context more comfortably within contemporary classical music such as *Eos*, a hypnotic, atmospheric 1984 collaboration with cellist David Darling. However, in 1984 he also formed the Chasers, a power trio with bassist Bjorn Kjellemyr and drummer Audun Kleive that evoked the honesty of the original jazz-rock union of the late 1960s and early 1970s but within a contemporary context. *Chaser* from 1985 presented tighter, often closed improvisational forms – as opposed to the open forms of his earlier moody impressionism –

and was followed up by *Blue*, one of his best selling albums, with forthright playing and even tighter, yet simpler, compositional constructs.

By the early 1990s, the Chasers were on ice, and in 1995 Rypdal responded to a commission from the Lillehammer Festival to write new music that would pay tribute to ECM's contribution towards defining a "Nordic Tone" within jazz. 'Sinfonietta' was performed at the festival, on February 16th 1996, which when recorded the following day became 'Out Of This World', the centrepiece of the album *Skywards*, a 16-minute composition, full of mood swings, that found room for Rypdal's highly individual guitar and long time collaborators such as Palle Mikkelborg, David Darling and Jon Christensen.

While Rypdal's playing immediately evoked a "Scandinavian" sound that

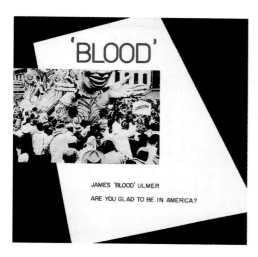

Eicher did so much to realise on recordings, then equally, Marc Ribot's playing personified the New York "Downtown" sound. Forming his band Rootless Cosmopolitans in 1990 with the likes of Don Byron on clarinet, Anthony Coleman on keyboards, Brad Jones on bass and Richie Schwarz on drums, the group touched base with Hendrix with their hair-raising takes of Hendrix numbers. However, Ribot also added the inspiration of Django Reinhardt to the mix, plus an eclecticism that embraced noise guitar at one end of the spectrum and a teenage love of surf bands at the other.

After moving from New Jersey to New York with a soul band, the Realtones, he joined organist Jack McDuff, but gravitated to the loose coalition of experimental Downtown musicians via New York's No Wave scene of the early to mid 1980s, through the Jazz Passengers and John Lurie's Lounge Lizards.

The Lizards were the archetypal Downtown band (Lurie was playing Downtown music before the term was even coined) and Ribot can be heard contributing striking solos on albums such as *Big Heart: Live In Tokyo* and *No Pain For Cakes*. On the former, recorded in 1986, his solos on 'Big Heart' and 'Fat House' marked him as a unique and distinctive soloist who delighted in asymmetrical phrases that weaved in and around the groundbeat.

Ribot can also be heard contributing his warped riffs and rude chords to the mid-1980s albums of such singers as Tom Waits, Elvis Costello and Marianne Faithful, and later Tricky and David Sylvian. However, on his own albums such as *Rootless Cosmopolitans* and *Requiem For What's His Name* he up-ended standard guitar practice with jagged-edge, odd-time takes that marked him out as an absorbing original. Later albums, such as 1998's *Marc*

Are You Glad To Be In America? (left) was a 1980 album full of powerful, urban statements from James Blood Ulmer supported by an appropriately heavyweight team that included drummer Ronald Shannon Jackson and saxmen David Murray and Oliver Lake. One of the founders of the experimental rock outfit Henry Cow in the mid 1970s, Fred Frith continues along his radical path, treading the boundary between experimental rock and free jazz, as epitomised on his 1980 recording Gravity (centre). Uwe Kropinski is one of the leading figures of the vibrant free-jazz scene which flowered in the enforced isolation of the former German Democratic Republic where Kropinski developed a highly personal, virtuosic style, demonstrated on this 1985 album (above).

Ribot Y Los Cubanos Postizos, that tapped the spirit of the music of Cuban maestro Arsenio Rodriguez, appeared alarmingly polite by comparison. But it was with his group Shrek (the Yiddish word for horror) that he moved closest to the edge. Playing music that took its inspiration from the music of Albert Ayler, he once had the alarming experience of being pelted with plastic beer glasses when Shrek opened for the Red Hot Chilli Peppers.

The 'New Thing' implications of the 1960s provided the starting-point for Sonny Sharrock, who in 1965 moved to New York to find himself the sole electric guitarist in America playing free jazz. Making his recording debut on Pharoah Sanders' *Tahid*, he made an uncredited appearance on Miles Davis's seminal *Jack Johnson* while at various times between 1967 and 1974 providing moments of occasional musical disruption in Herbie Mann's otherwise lightweight combo. After receiving constant knocking for being "too far out", he quit music in the 1970s to work with the emotionally disturbed, until producer/bassist Bill Laswell introduced him to New York's Downtown scene in the 1980s, enabling him to enjoy something of a career renaissance until his death in 1994.

He initially appeared with Laswell's experimental avant-jazz-rock ensemble Material on *Memory Serves* in 1982 and subsequent Laswell-produced Sharrock albums included *Guitar, Seize the Moment, Highlife* and a bracing work-out with Nicky Skopelitis on *Faith Moves*. However, it was as a member of the memorable post-modern quartet Last Exit that he provided some of his most enduring moments.

On albums such as 1986's *The Noise Of Trouble* his "shards of splintered glass" provided the perfect backdrop for Peter Brötzmann's saxophone outrages, Laswell's country-inspired basslines and Ronald Shannon Jackson's cavalry charges that gave shape to a modernist vision of collage to destroy the traditional "organic" unity of art. By refusing to provide meaning in its conventional sense, Last Exit revelled in their destruction of art's traditional autonomy. It was quite a band.

While Sharrock's *Sturm und Drang* was echoed in the more outré outbursts of Bill Frisell (most notably with John Zorn) and Jean-Paul Bourelly, James Blood Ulmer respun Sharrock's deconstructionist urges into a more tightly focused style that emerged through his association with saxophonist Ornette Coleman in the mid 1970s. On Ulmer's 1974 album *Tales Of Captain Black*, one of the few times Coleman plays on record as a sideman, the guitarist sounds for all the world like the return of a cutting-edge Jimi Hendrix, with a style full of tonal distortions and savage riffing.

By the end of the 1970s, Ulmer's playing was not totally unrelated to the punk guitarists. Indeed, his own working group had no trouble finding work in New York's punk joints, and certainly Ulmer's music had much in common with punk's dissolution of rock's certainties. *Are You Glad to Be in America?* with Ronald Shanon Jackson on drums, bassist Amin Ali and a front line of saxophonists Oliver Lake and David Murray prompted one reviewer to quip, "They're like the Bar-Kays gone berserk."

With fusion bottoming out in the early 1980s, Columbia began showing interest in the avant-garde, and signed Ulmer in 1981. During his stay with the label he made three albums, emerging as a spacey conceptualist and post-Hendrix funkster on *Black Rock* and *Odyssey*. In 1995 he joined bassist/producer Bill Laswell's group Third Rail, recording *South Delta Space Age*, and his jarring energy had begun to sound out of place amid the neo-

With the energy of a hard-hitting blues player and an espousal of Ornette Coleman's arcane Harmolodics, James Blood Ulmer developed a raw, dissonant style into a distinctive voice in the 1970s.

conservative conformity that had descended on American jazz, with most of his work in his own right coming from Europe and Japan.

When Ulmer left Prime Time, Ornette Coleman's experimental electric ensemble, his replacement was Bernie Nix, who took up the saxophonist's theory of harmolodics on *Dancing In Your Head*. Essentially any system of cadences was abandoned in favour of polymodality and polyrhythms; several simultaneous tonal centres allowed Coleman's melodic brief to roam free on the impulse of the moment, the rhythm section converging around him like a drum choir with each instrument acting rhythmically in a way that forsook conventional harmonic thinking. With Nix joined by Charles Ellerbee, albums such as *Body Meta* and *Of Human Feelings* essayed Coleman's often genial approach to freedom rooted in the blues that allowed him to communicate beyond the usual following, suggesting he had become the *vox populi* of free jazz. Later in the decade, Prime Time opened for the Grateful Dead, such was the regard lead guitarist Jerry Garcia had for Coleman's playing – indeed, Garcia guests on Coleman's 1987 album *Virgin Beauty*.

If Coleman's approach to free jazz was an often genial, pumping, body music, then the British guitarist Derek Bailey's work with his continually evolving ensemble Company was an altogether different affair. Creating a

A tireless champion of free improvisation, English guitarist Derek Bailey (above left) became dissatisfied with the content and structures of conventional jazz in the 1960s, which he regarded as too restrictive. Using dissonance, note-clusters and harmonics, Bailey built an atonal vocabulary for the guitar and introduced fresh approaches to collective improvisation. On these live recordings (above) from a 1986 British concert tour with Dutch percussionist Han Bennink, Bailey offers totally spontaneous improvisation captured on record.

dense, often atonal vocabulary for the guitar, making use of dissonance, note clusters and whistling harmonics. Bailey also created new forms to frame the improvisatory process, through collective approaches that explored propositions advanced in 1937 by composer John Cage: "I believe that the use of noise to make music will continue to increase until we reach a music produced through the aid of electronical instruments which will make available for musical purposes any and all sounds that can be heard... Whereas in the past the point of disagreement has been between dissonance and consonance, it will be, in the immediate future, between noise and so-called musical sounds."

Bailey's Company created an aesthetic of interaction that did away with the background/foreground or soloist/accompanist approach to improvisation and, indeed, most accepted common practises of jazz were either transformed or discarded. Bailey stretched his guitar to the limit and, in so doing, the nature of sound itself – which had the effect of removing conventional "meaning" from what he played. Bailey's style was as unorthodox as it was internally coherent, something that becomes clear when comparing his self-produced *Solo Guitar Volume 1*, made in 1971, with *Solo Guitar Volume 2* made 20 years later. Bailey's music found several levels, in high volume duets with drummers Han Bennink and Milford Graves, or by introducing classically trained non-improvising musicians to Company, such as Ursula Oppens, Antony Pay and Philip Eastop.

In the 1980s Bailey became championed by Downtown avant-gardists John Zorn and Eugene Chadbourne, the latter a guitarist who took much inspiration from Bailey's style and appeared with Bailey during 1990's Company Week at the Palace Theatre in London. Chadbourne's own group Shockabilly revealed his love of improvisation, country & western and good old-fashioned rock'n'roll. On Hal Willner's tribute to Thelonious Monk, *That's The Way I Feel Now* from 1984, Shockabilly contributed a memorable version of Monk's 'Criss Cross' which sounded for all the world as if the tune had been written specially for them. Their own startling originals, leavened by large doses of humour, were perfectly captured on *Shockabilly Live...Just Beautiful*.

Chadbourne and Zorn's group 2000 Statues featured their unorthodox version of the avant-garde and their album *The English Channel* included the British guitarist/bassist Fred Frith. He was a founder member of the avant-rock band Henry Cow, which was formed in 1968, lasted ten years, and recorded six albums for the Virgin label that revealed an eclectic brand of highly orchestrated, structured rock. When the band wound up, Frith promptly began exploring unstructured improvisation, howling and scraping with an array of prepared guitars. On the *Guitar Solos* series from 1976 and 1978, he can be heard collaborating with Chadbourne, Bailey, Henry Kaiser, Hans Reichel and others. In the early 1980s he appeared on *Memory Serves* by Bill Laswell's group Material and on two albums with Brian Eno.

Later in the decade he gravitated towards New York's Downtown scene, and appeared on bass as a member of John Zorn's memorable post-modernistic group Naked City. By then the Downtown scene was a hotbed of deconstructionists, with Marc Ducret among the vanguard of younger guitarists to whom the status quo was an anathema; his 1997 solo *Un Certain Malaise* and his 1998 collaboration with drummer Bobby Previte *In The Grass* revealing his imperious disregard of convention. Equally, from the West Coast Bay Area, Will Bernard adopted a gritty world view by letting reggae and salsa mingle with rock in a hard boiled vision built on strong rhythmic underpinnings.

Ultimately, however, it was Bailey's voice that became perhaps the most distinctive in the forum of European improvised music, which had evolved quite different characteristics to the model of American jazz and improvised music. The cultural isolation in East Germany, for example, meant that after the popularity of Dixieland and New Orleans jazz in the 1950s, subsequent styles of jazz had little impact. Indeed, American jazz as a whole was frowned on by the authorities. With the reunification of Germany, this repression found voice in a jazz scene that leapt from New Orleans to freedom in one stride, producing such distinctive voices as Uwe Kropinski.

Generally, European improvised music tended to be more radical and adventurous than the increasingly conservative United States jazz scene. That was increasingly involved in appropriating jazz to form part of the nation's cultural heritage, with many musicians effectively acting as custodians dedicated to reviving great moments from jazz's recorded history or participating in a music with clearly proscribed parameters (hard bop). As colleges and universities produced more and more students conscious of a limit to their art, musicians appeared less eager to participate in staking out new ground. Indeed, some, such as Wynton Marsalis, go so far as to express impatience and intolerance with the contemporary, refusing to acknowledge its place in the narrative of jazz history. As American jazz paused in the 1980s and 1990s to move towards "an alternative conservatory style for the training of young musicians" and "an artistic heritage to be held up as an exemplar of American or African-American culture", it seemed apparent that academicism was breeding revivalism while innovation was held in check.

Yet away from the glitzy revivalism at Lincoln Center aimed at wealthy Manhattan socialites, away from the limited ambitions of major recording companies concerned not with art but with potential sales, and away from the pages of an increasingly conservative jazz press that acted as a kind of service industry to the major recording companies, it was the deconstructionists, refusing to march in step with a safe accessible mainstream, who continued to explore the future. Bailey, the arch deconstructionist of all, continued to move in mysterious ways, performing and recording *Saisoro* with the Tokyo rock duo Ruins, and improvising with jungle DJs. In early 1996 producer/bassist Bill Laswell and co-producer John Zorn engineered a meeting in the studio between Bailey and drum legend Tony Williams. *The Last Wave*, cited by *Wire* magazine as "One of the year's most sensational moments", was an onrush of astonishing sound that was a logical continuum of the progressive and multi-textural jazz-rock fusion proposed by the original Lifetime. "I had talked to Tony about creating another environment where we could produce that kind of energy again in a setting where he could play more aggressively and more expressively in an area that's not formatted in the usual jazz way," explained Laswell. Bailey created a climate in which Williams' drumming sounded dangerous again, rather than merely virtuosic as it had within the hard bop environment.

In a collision of willpower and free-associating idealism, both guitarist and drummer were forced to match each others' movements in fields of competing energy as Williams attempted to impose rhythmic strategies into Bailey's dark, often frightening world, where it's possible to lose yourself in a maze of sonic reverberations.

CHARLES ALEXANDER **THE ACOUSTIC GUITAR IN JAZZ**

*SINCE CHARLIE CHRISTIAN, THE GUITAR IN JAZZ HAS
GENERALLY BEEN ATTACHED TO AN AMPLIFIER. BUT NOW THE
ACOUSTIC PLAYERS ARE HITTING BACK, PERFORMING MUSICAL
MIRACLES WITH NOTHING MORE THAN A FEW STRINGS
STRETCHED ACROSS A WOODEN BOX.*

Since the first recordings of Charlie Christian with the Benny Goodman band, in 1939, the predominant sound of the guitar in jazz has been that of the amplified instrument. Oscar Moore, Barney Kessel, Johnny Smith, Tal Farlow, Jimmy Raney, Herb Ellis, Kenny Burrell, Wes Montgomery, Joe Pass and many more great players all popularised the sound of the electric guitar in jazz.

The emergence of the electric guitar as a jazz voice in the 1940s coincided with the end of the swing era and the decline of the big bands. Those bands had provided steady work for rhythm guitarists, pumping out chords on their Gibson L-5s and Strombergs, full-bodied archtop guitars designed to be audible alongside powerful brass and saxophone sections. But these guitars were not suited to small group work, where the guitar was a frontline instrument. Many superbly crafted instruments were consigned to the attic.

The warm, sweet, jazz chord voicings plucked on the Spanish guitar by players such as Charlie Byrd, Joao Gilberto and Laurindo Almeida were central to the bossa nova music of the late 1950s and early 1960s. But in spite of the enormous popularity of the bossa nova, the Spanish guitar remained peripheral in jazz. Kenny Burrell brought it to the fore in his 1965 album *Guitar Forms*, fronting a big band in atmospheric arrangements by Gil Evans. But this was a temporary deviation from his usual archtop electric guitar.

The predominance of the electric guitar in jazz during the 1960s was reinforced by the popularity of the organ-guitar-drums groups, such as those led by Jimmy Smith and Brother Jack McDuff, with the guitar comping in the background and injecting bluesy fills and solos. Nor could jazz ignore the opening up of popular music during that decade – the awakening interest in blues music, the rise of rock, the preference for even eighth-note rhythms over the swing phrasing of jazz, and the new sounds being generated by the electric guitar. The blending of these and other influences with the improvisational tradition and the harmonic vocabulary of jazz led to the emergence of a new form: "jazz-rock", or "fusion". The solidbody electric guitar was to play a vital role in this music, with John McLaughlin leading the way through his recordings with Tony Williams's Lifetime and his own Mahavishnu Orchestra.

But McLaughlin's creativity was not limited to high-energy electric music. On *My Goal's Beyond* (1971), he demonstrated the expressive possibilities of the acoustic guitar in jazz with a series of powerful solo performances including the Charles Mingus classic 'Goodbye Pork Pie Hat', which he recorded over his own guitar accompaniment. On the Mahavishnu Orchestra's *Inner Mounting Flame*, alongside the explosive excitement emanating from his double-neck six-string and 12-string solidbody guitar, there was the reflective, subdued passion of his acoustic guitar on 'Lotus On An Irish Stream'. For

Shakti's blend of Indian music and Western forms McLaughlin commissioned Abraham Wechter to build an acoustic guitar with extra drone strings set transversely across the body – one of many instruments he aquired from Wechter.

In the late 1970s McLaughlin joined the extraordinary flamenco guitarist Paco De Lucia and Larry Coryell to form the all-acoustic Guitar Trio. Coryell was soon replaced by Al DiMeola, and the strong-willed virtuosi, with their pot-pourri of influences, were an enormous success, firmly establishing the acoustic guitar as more than an accompaniment for singer-songwriters.

A Guitar Trio concert could be an intense experience, in part because of the awesome strength and emotional charge of the music but also on account of the competitive spirit of the three participants. Although the music could at times descend into gladitorial displays of technical prowess, it could also achieve peaks of passion and beauty, as evidenced on two albums, the 1981 live recording *Friday Night In San Francisco* and *Passion Grace & Fire* from 1983. Re-forming the trio in the late 1990s may have been a financial success, but the artistic unity of 15 years earlier had all but dissolved.

For several years from the mid 1980s, McLaughlin performed extensively on acoustic guitar with the remarkable Indian percussionist Trilok Gurtu.

The talents of Al DiMeola (above left) surfaced in the early 1970s when he was guitarist with Chick Corea's group Return To Forever. Di Meola went on to score international success with albums such as Land Of The Midnight Sun and Elegant Gypsy, while still in his mid-twenties. For many years Paco De Lucia (above) has toured and recorded with his own Sextet. Although rooted in flamenco, De Lucia takes the wider view and incorporates elements of Argentinian tango as well as Brazilian and Cuban influences.

Gurtu combines the Indian rhythmic tradition with that of jazz and, with the addition of a bass player such as Jeff Berlin or Dominique Di Piazza, provided the guitarist with a stimulating framework. The partnership is captured on the 1991 album *Que Alegria*. On quite a different scale, the 1990 CD *The Mediterranean Guitar Concerto*, produced by George Martin, featured John as soloist with the London Symphony Orchestra. His admiration for the music of pianist Bill Evans was expressed on *Time Remembered*, released in 1993, on which he performed a programme of Evans's compositions on solo acoustic guitar, with the accompaniment of the Aighetta Quartet of classical guitarists.

With his powerful intellectual and physical energy, and a preparedness to tackle a range of demanding projects (such as Shakti and its successors) which

*Al DiMeola headlines with bandoneon player Dino Saluzzi on **Heart Of The Immigrants** (above), a 1993 acoustic tribute to Astor Piazzola. Recorded live in the studio with no overdubs, it is a superb, passionate performance. Ralph Towner's classical and 12-string guitars feature on **Music Of Another Present Era** (centre), an album from the early days of the group Oregon in 1973 that includes several fine compositions by Towner. Michael Hedges widened the language of American acoustic guitar music with a range of techniques, many displayed on his **Aerial Boundaries** album (right) from 1984. Some were of his own invention, others developed by guitarists in contemporary classical music and free-jazz.*

few other guitarists, if any, could even contemplate, John McLaughlin stands in a category all of his own.

Like John McLaughlin, Al DiMeola is a virtuoso on both electric and acoustic guitars. In spite of his obvious brilliance, however, it can be a frustrating experience to search for the person behind the music when listening to his electric guitar work. A series of albums for Columbia in the early 1980s demonstrated his skills as a guitarist and his willingness to examine the possibilities of the guitar synthesiser. But, with slick technical display too often substituting for depth, his overriding concern seemed to be to impress rather than to offer a musical experience. A switch to the Manhattan label offered a new direction. His 1985 album *Ciello E Terra*, inspired by British classical guitarist Julian Bream, was a happy marriage of his acoustic guitar skills and some of his best writing to date.

In 1986 DiMeola met the Argentinian tango composer Astor Piazzolla and began a friendship that lasted until the composer's death. Tango music started in the dance halls and bars of Buenos Aires but evolved into a form that could become complex and yet passionate – never far from its dance-rhythm roots but at the same time musically rewarding. Tango can be traced back to Naples, Italy, and the musical traditions imported by Italian immigrants to Argentina. Like DiMeola, Piazzolla had roots in Naples, and this encouraged the guitarist to explore the culture of tango and the music of his own Italian heritage. Staying on acoustic guitar, he recruited bandoneon player Dino Saluzzi (a bandoneon is similar to an accordion) and recorded *World Sinfonia*, featuring several Piazzolla compositions.

After two years of touring, this ensemble returned to the studio and emerged with *Heart Of The Immigrants*. Not long before he died, Piazzolla had sent the guitarist the score of his *Tango Suite* and DiMeola included this challenging piece as a tribute to his mentor and friend. Arguably DiMeola's finest album, it draws on his own emotional experience to create music in which, finally, both his heart and his head are equally represented.

Ralph Towner (b.1940, Chehalis, Washington) has trodden a unique path in contemporary jazz. Little known until a guest appearance on the 1971 Weather Report album *I Sing The Body Electric* sparked interest in his unusual and sophisticated use of the 12-string guitar, his music draws on sources, influences and compositional traditions that lie outside jazz. Towner performs mainly on six-string classical guitar, and also on the 12-string guitar

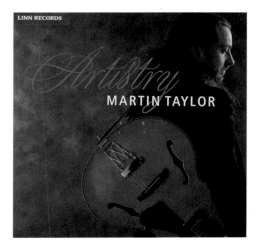

and piano. He played piano and trumpet as a child, and it was only at the age of 22, in his final year at the University of Oregon (from which he received a BA in composition in 1963), that he took up the guitar. In 1964 he went to Vienna to study for a year with classical guitarist Karl Scheidt, returning in the late 1960s after a period of post-graduate study at Oregon. At this time Towner also discovered Brazilian music, notably the guitar of Baden Powell.

In 1971, after three years in New York playing mainly piano with Miles Davis, Keith Jarrett and other leading jazz artists, and as a member of the Paul Winter Consort, he formed the group Oregon with bassist Glen Moore, woodwind player Paul McCandless and percussionist and sitarist Colin Walcott (with percussionist Trilok Gurtu joining in 1985 after Walcott's death in a road accident). Using purely acoustic instruments, Oregon has set its own unique agenda for more than 20 years, drawing upon influences from Brazil, India and 20th century classical music to create a music of depth and beauty that is as adventurous as the best of jazz but which seeks less familiar structures, harmony and sounds.

Towner's writing, always to the fore in Oregon's music, has also contributed to the success of many collaborative projects on the German label ECM, with which he has enjoyed a long association. One of the most striking albums of the early 1970s was *Solstice*, which brought Towner together with saxophonist Jan Garbarek, bassist Eberhard Weber and drummer Jon Christensen: uncluttered statements delivered with quiet emotional intensity. In the mid 1970s he toured and recorded as an acoustic duo with fellow guitarist John Abercrombie. He has also recorded with vibraphonist Gary Burton, trumpeter Kenny Wheeler and with drummer Peter Erskine. Before

From the R&B of 'Louie Louie' and 'Grooves of Joy', where Tuck Andress emulates a slick funk rhythm section with just one guitar, to the chordal richness of 'Body And Soul', Reckless Precision (left) from 1990 is solo-guitar mastery all the way. Early in his career, English-born guitarist Laurence Juber played jazz with the National Youth Jazz Orchestra and rock with Paul McCartney's Wings. A formidable acoustic guitarist, his driving, melodic style is displayed on this 1997 recording (centre). Artistry by Martin Taylor (above) is a tour-de-force of solo jazz guitar from 1992. Its breathtaking up-tempo work, tenderly explored ballads, quick-witted improvisations and imaginative arrangements confirmed Taylor's status as a major guitarist.

his partnership with Ralph Towner, John Abercrombie (b.1944, Portchester, New York) had already gained solid jazz experience with Johnny "Hammond" Smith, Gil Evans, Gato Barbieri, Dave Liebman, Chico Hamilton and Billy Cobham. *Timeless*, his debut album for ECM in 1974, featured keyboardist Jan Hammer and drummer Jack De Johnette, and showed Abercrombie as both a resourceful composer and a guitarist capable of lyrical statements, flowing lines and tough, blues-inclined phrases. Abercrombie is a sophisticated harmonic thinker who creates subtle chord voicings and progressions far removed from the bebop idiom, but still retains the energy and swing of earlier jazz forms.

Equally adept on electric and acoustic guitars, John moves easily from forceful fusion to more abstract structures, and was selected by Gunther Schüller for the guitar chair in the posthumous orchestral performance of Charles Mingus's 'Epitaph'. Gateway, and his other touring bands, have consistently attracted leading musicians, such as bassists Dave Holland and Marc Johnson and drummers Jack De Johnette and Peter Erskine.

Earl Klugh (b.1954, Detroit, Michigan) came to the guitar through the music of Chet Atkins, and the sweet tone of his nylon-strung guitar over a rhythmic, synthesiser-tinged background became one of the signature sounds of the late 1970s and 1980s. Although he recorded with Yusef Lateef at age 15, it was his contact with George Benson that effectively launched his career. Klugh appeared on Benson's 1971 album *White Rabbit* and joined his band in 1973, still aged only 19. The following year found him with Chick Corea's Return To Forever on both electric and acoustic guitars but by the mid 1970s he was enjoying success in his own name. By 1995 he had chalked up more than 30 albums as a leader.

Klugh is a skilful composer and arranger. His writing can be interesting – always melodic, harmonically aware and cleverly constructed – but too often his music is emotionally bland. A typical composition begins with a simple melodic hook over a light funky background, which moves smoothly to a mild conclusion, like a bus journey through a pleasing landscape. Given the right company, however, Klugh can scale the heights, as evidenced on the 1987 album *Collaboration* with George Benson. Here he discards "smooth jazz" to play with a depth and intensity that is rare in his own projects.

The sudden success of the guitar duo Acoustic Alchemy came as a surprise both to Greg Carmichael and Nick Webb and to their record label MCA, when their 1987 debut release, *Red Dust And Spanish Lace*, began to shift in its thousands, helped by endless radio play. The two English guitarists had met at the London College of Music and began to perform and write together, blending the sound of Nick's steel-strung guitar with that of Greg's nylon-strung. Their influences and interests, including the contemporary folk styles of John Martyn, Bert Jansch and John Renbourn, the repertoire of classical guitar and flamenco, and the music of Miles Davis, John Coltrane and Jimi Hendrix, are all reflected in their music.

With a rhythm section laying down light Latin and funk grooves, Alchemy had created a sound with wide appeal. For ten years they enjoyed a pattern of six months touring and six months writing and recording, and a string of strong-selling albums. Only the death of Nick Webb in 1998, after a lengthy illness, brought the partnership to a close. With Webb's encouragement, Carmichael plans to continue Acoustic Alchemy with other guitar partners.

It is hard to pinpoint exactly when the career of guitarist Martin Taylor began. Perhaps it was when the six-year-old joined in on rhythm guitar when his father, Buck Taylor, had a gathering of fellow musicians at home. It's possible, however, that the enterprising proprietor of a High Street music shop in his home town of Harlow, England, launched Martin's career at the age of 11, when he paid him simply to sit in the shop window on Saturday afternoons and play his guitar. Not only did the talented youngster attract customers, he also inspired a feature in the local newspaper.

There's no doubt that his career had been running in the right direction for several years by the time bassist and producer Peter Ind invited him to record his debut, *Taylor Made*, in April 1979. Still only 22, Martin had already worked with drummer Lennie Hastings's band, travelled to New York as a musician on the Cunard liners (playing with the Count Basie Orchestra on one memorable occasion), and had made his mark on the London jazz scene. His duo with veteran guitarist Ike Isaacs had enjoyed a two-year residency at The Pizza On The Park and Isaacs, recognising the innate talent of this youngster, had passed on to Martin his accumulated musical wisdom and experience.

But 1979 was to be a watershed for Taylor for another reason. Violinist Stephane Grappelli asked him to join his quartet, in place of Diz Disley who had suffered a hand injury. This was the start of an association that was to introduce Martin Taylor to audiences world-wide.

If *Taylor Made* announced the arrival of a new voice in the world of jazz guitar, mature beyond his years, with a confident grasp of the harmonic and rhythmic language, then the album *A Tribute To Art Tatum* (1984) revealed another side to him. Here, Taylor played solo and, like the great pianist, supplied melody, chords and bass line simultaneously for a series of jazz standards. But this was no mere technical display, for the arrangements were inventive – beautiful introductions, unfolding eloquently-stated melodies, with subtle re-harmonisations, unexpected key-changes and breathtaking double-time passages.

With *Sarabanda*, recorded in Nashville in 1987, Taylor was teamed with a first-class rhythm section, allowing him to lay attractive melodic lines over Latin-tinged rhythms. This album hit the top of the US radio airplay charts. Meanwhile Taylor's career was accelerating. He toured in a duo with Emily Remler in 1982, recorded with Chet Atkins in 1987, substituted for Herb Ellis alongside Barney Kessel and Charlie Byrd in The Great Guitars in 1989, and performed with Joe Pass in a duo a year later.

The release of the album *Don't Fret* in 1990 marked the beginning of a fertile nine-year association with Linn Records. *Artistry*, produced by Steve Howe and released in 1992, showcased his solo guitar style to dazzling effect. One of only a handful of guitarists to perform entirely solo, his one-man jazz concerts now became a significant part of his annual schedule. Taylor's stunning, almost orchestral, interpretations of jazz standards, his relaxed delivery and beautiful guitar sound appealed to jazz aficionados but also found a resonance with a much wider audience.

Two years later Martin formed a quintet, Spirit Of Django, comprising himself on solo guitar, a saxophonist, a rhythm guitarist and a bassist, plus Jack Emblow, a much-admired veteran of the British music scene, on accordion. Inspired by the music of Reinhardt and Grappelli, this unusual line-up dipped into the Hot Club repertoire and clothed the music with lively, fresh arrangements and no-holds-barred solos. By now he was a consistent award winner, widely acclaimed as one the leading jazz guitarists on the world scene. In April 1999 he signed a six-album recording contract with Sony, the first British artist to be signed by the label for 30 years.

Tuck Andress (b.1952, Tulsa, Oklahoma) is best known as one half of the duo Tuck & Patti (his vocalist wife Patti Cathcart being the other half). The release of their album 1988 *Tears Of Joy* on the Windham Hill label revealed that here was a musical partnership of distinction, propelled by a guitarist of extraordinary ability. Not only did their repertoire span the classic jazz standards as well as groove-based pop hits, the guitarist could re-harmonise those standards with sensibility while supplying an interesting bass line and, in his solo breaks, adding a melody line. On the funky side of things, he could add percussive effects by striking the strings with his thumb, lay down a James Jamerson-style bassline, and create on one guitar the overall effect of a Motown rhythm section.

At 17, after playing rock'n'roll guitar for three years, Tuck Andress discovered Wes Montgomery, George Benson and Miles Davis and switched to jazz. After gaining live gigging experience with a number of R&B bands, he enrolled at Stanford University, majoring in classical guitar. Working in commercial bands, he began to experiment with combining the parts of the rhythm section instruments (and, on occasion, the horns) and replicating them altogether on his guitar.

Tuck first met Patti in 1978 at an audition for a show: they started to perform as a duo in restaurants and coffee shops to earn some money to form a band. It soon became clear that with Tuck's unique guitar style there was no need for a band. Tuck's 1990 solo album *Reckless Precision* confirmed that and the duo's follow-up album *Dream* led to international touring. Equally matched in performance skills, Tuck & Patti – just the two of them – can hold the attention of a 2,000-strong concert audience for over three hours and still have them shouting for encores.

The Italian guitarist Antonio Forcione was born in 1960 and began leading his own band at 14, having taken up guitar three years earlier. He immersed himself in the folk music of southern Italy and performed on mandolin at festivals throughout the country, before moving to Rome to study jazz guitar. In 1983 he moved to London to develop his career. There he began to work with Spanish flamenco guitarist Eduardo Niebla in an acoustic guitar duo, quickly graduating from the streets of Covent Garden to the club circuit. Word quickly spread about their virtuosic, passionate performances combining influences ranging from flamenco and Brazilian rhythms to contemporary jazz.

After their fourth album, in 1992, the duo split up, allowing Antonio to concentrate on his own solo and group projects, including his Acoustic Band, which features pianist Huw Warren. In 1993, Antonio formed a new duo, Acoustic Mania, with Neil Stacey, another guitarist of equivalent technical ability, established writing skills, and with a comparable spread of musical interests. Stacey was already well regarded for his role as guitarist in the Kimbara Brothers, a group that takes the Reinhardt tradition as its starting point, although his own influences extend to Hendrix in one direction and Joe Pass and Pat Metheny in another. Few, if any, duos can match Acoustic Mania for precision and virtuosity, the quality of their compositions, and the sheer vitality and expressiveness of their music.

The acoustic guitar players profiled so far in this chapter have their musical feet more or less firmly within the area we know as jazz, but there is a whole wealth of music making on acoustic guitar which draws on traditions,

The blend of Greg Carmichael's nylon-string guitar and Nick Webb's steel-string guitar – along with their talent for writing accessible, light fusion tunes – spawned a string of successful albums for their group Acoustic Alchemy, including Back On The Case, an outing from 1991.

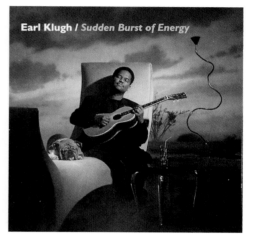

The sweet sound of the nylon-string guitar of Earl Klugh (above left) over light, funky grooves has earned the guitarist commercial success at the easy-listening end of the jazz spectrum. But for a taste of what Klugh can really do, turn to an external project such as his 1987 album, Collaboration, with George Benson. On his own Sudden Burst Of Energy (above) from 1996, Klugh's talent as a highly-skilled composer, arranger and performer in the pop-fusion idiom is clear, and his pretty nylon-string guitar strolls effortlessly through the entire album.

backgrounds and cultures further afield. The influences here may be Celtic music or the blues, the music of the Balkans or American bluegrass, the oud music of the Arab world or the ragtime of Scott Joplin.

Fine guitarists in this area include Bert Jansch and John Renbourn, who emerged in the 1960s and inspired a generation of aspirant guitarists with their work in Pentangle. Peppino D'Agostino, from Italy, and Pierre Bensusan, the Algerian-born wizard of the DADGAD tuning, bring compositional flair to their music. While Belgian-born Jacques Stotzem and the American, Duck Baker, gained their early inspiration from American blues and acoustic guitar traditions, there is more than a trace of jazz in their work. Laurence Juber performed with Britain's National Youth Jazz Orchestra before a stint with Paul McCartney's Wings, a Los Angeles studio career and subsequent re-emergence as a brilliant acoustic stylist.

Finally, the premature death of Michael Hedges in a road accident in 1998 robbed the world of one of its most original and innovative guitarists, a man who single-handedly extended the soundscape and technical boundaries of the acoustic guitar and prepared it for another century of creative development.

THE NEW MAINSTREAM

GUITARISTS UNMOVED BY THE RISE OF FUSION DEDICATED THEMSELVES TO BREATHING LIFE INTO THE TIME-HONOURED STRUCTURES AND REPERTOIRE OF JAZZ. THESE SO-CALLED MAINSTREAM PLAYERS ALSO FAVOURED THE TRADITIONAL ARCH-TOP SEMI-ACOUSTIC GUITAR.

The rise of rock music in the 1960s placed the solidbody electric guitar firmly in the vanguard, and threatened to eclipse the more established jazz approaches entirely. Many jazz guitarists turned to the new jazz-rock fusion genre as a response, but a sizeable post-fusion generation of players have shunned that option in favour of an engagement with the structures and repertoire of jazz, stretching from traditional jazz and swing through to bebop and hard bop, and usually with the favoured instrument of jazz players, the hollow-bodied arch-top guitar.

The generic classification applied to many of these players has been the increasingly vague "mainstream". As a definition of a style, it has its origins in the post-swing era, when the big-bands increasingly gave way to smaller groups playing in a style with its roots in a mixture of traditional jazz and swing, often with a leavening of the harmonic sophistication of bop. The label gained revived currency with the growth of a new generation of so-called mainstream musicians in the mid 1970s, led by saxophonist Scott Hamilton in New York. It became apparent as the 1980s came and went that there was a significant group of musicians dedicated to preserving the established frameworks of jazz, and both to playing and extending the repository of tunes associated with those frameworks. Guitarists have been at the forefront of that development. Some of them have been second-generation inheritors of a tradition handed down by illustrious guitarist fathers. That is true, for example, of Doug Raney, son of Jimmy Raney, and John Pizzarelli, son of Bucky Pizzarelli. As well as inheriting the mantle, both have also sometimes collaborated with their fathers.

Doug Raney (b.1956) cut his teeth on rock guitar before turning to jazz, and studied informally with Barry Galbraith for a time in New York. He developed into a well-rounded jazz stylist but is by no means a straight copy of his father in stylistic terms. He draws on swing, as well as a flavour of the single-note bop style favoured by Jimmy, and employs imaginative chord voicings to forceful effect on the best of his many albums for SteepleChase, including *Introducing Doug Raney* (1977), *The Doug Raney Quintet* (1988) and *Raney '96* (1996). John Pizzarrelli (b.1960) has a more direct connection to the swing influence, and if he is best known as a singer in the Nat King Cole mode, he is also a fine guitarist. Like his father, he favours the seven-string guitar inextricably associated with the late George Van Eps, which allows extra bass presence and the possibility of playing an accentuated piano-style bass line against the melody.

Both are excellent swing players, and in duo (or with brother Martin on bass) they reveal the kind of empathic intimacy honed in many evenings spent

John Pizzarelli at the Pizza On The Park, London, in 1998 (above left). Sharing his father Bucky's love for the American swing guitar tradition and a penchant for the seven-string guitar, John has also enjoyed success with his relaxed and gently ironic vocal style. He performs with his own Trio and has recorded some fine guitar duets with his father. Frank Vignola is an all-rounder, rooted in mainstream jazz guitar but with more contemporary leanings. On his 1994 record Let It Happen (above) Django tunes stand alongside such chestnuts as 'Tico Tico', 'String of Pearls' and 'Spanish Eyes' as well as jazz classics by Horace Silver and Sam Jones. Mandolinist David Grisman makes effective contributions to several tracks.

playing in the family home. Long before he took up the instrument, John has memories of hearing the likes of Zoot Sims, Joe Venuti and Joe Pass jamming in the front room, and although he started out playing in a rock band, genes and that subtle indoctrination eventually won out. He has recorded instrumental duet albums with his father, working within a common swing idiom, juxtaposing hard-driving chords in octaves with delicate, cleanly-picked single line extemporisations, as well as vocal albums under his own name, and has relished the opportunity to work with a big band as well.

Howard Alden (b.1958) also favours the seven-string guitar, and is perhaps the most symbolic example of a younger musician who grew up in the rock era but chose instead to play a revitalising role in mainstream jazz. He grew up in Los Angeles, where he taught himself to play, and was heavily influenced by the likes of Charlie Christian, Barney Kessel and, of course, Van Eps, but relocated to New York in 1982, and began a long association with one of the principal standard bearers of the "new mainstream", Concord Records.

Alden has mined the rich vein of the standard repertoire in beautifully lucid fashion, alongside the work of great jazz composers like Duke Ellington, Thelonious Monk and Bill Evans, all of whom rate very highly in his personal pantheon, and an album of compositions by the banjo virtuoso Harry Reser. He has worked regularly with various members of the Concord stable, including trombonist Dan Barrett and clarinetist and saxophonist Ken Peplowski, and also teamed up with Van Eps for the label. Their relaxed

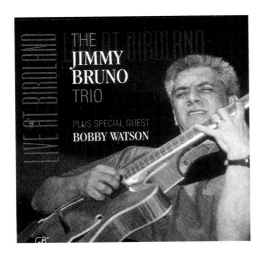

Howard Alden, at the Brecon Jazz Festival in Wales during 1991 (above right) with the Ruby Braff Trio. Wielding his seven-string Benedetto guitar, Jimmy Bruno lays down muscular, uncompromising bebop-inspired lines on this live recording (above) from 1997, with Bobby Watson guesting on alto sax. A highlight is their duet on 'These Foolish Things'.

interplay is heard on several albums, beginning with *13 Strings* (1991), arguably the strongest of their collaborations. Van Eps's masterly command of chordal playing has been an important influence in the development of Alden's style, but his single-line playing is an even more impressive feature.

He plays ballads with a ravishing grace, and exhibits a characteristic subtlety and control in his use of dynamic variation. At fast tempos, his flowing, superbly liquid lines on the higher strings and immaculately placed chordal punctuations underline his innate lyricism, but he is equally capable of pushing into unexpected harmonic territory, especially on material by Monk. Alden's records have been consistently strong, and almost any will give a good representation of his playing. His tribute to Bill Evans, *Your Story* (1994), is a delight, as is *Take Your Pick* (1996), while the sets with Van Eps hold particular interest from a guitar perspective, as do two other releases, *Concord Jazz Guitar Collective* and *Full Circle*, to which I will shortly return.

Concord's focus on mainstream swing has also brought several other guitarists on board, including Cal Collins (b.1933) and the younger Gray Sargent (b.1953). Collins is a gifted, melodic player with an attractively light and fluent approach, and roots firmly planted in the swing era. He joined the Benny Goodman Orchestra in 1976, and made his Concord debut with *Cincinnati To LA* in 1978. It began a three-year tenure in which he cut a half-dozen solid albums, one of which, *Interplay* (1980), also featured Herb Ellis.

He returned to Cincinnati in the early 1980s, although he did make another album for Concord in 1990. Gray Sargent had studied at Berklee College and worked with a range of musicians (including Illinois Jacquet) by the time he teamed up with another Concord mainstay, pianist Dave McKenna, in 1979. Sargent's approach is not notably original, but he is a clean and sure-fingered stylist with a relaxed but swinging feel which is heard on his own rather understated *Shades Of Grey* (1993), but possibly to better advantage on albums with Dave McKenna, Ruby Braff and Scott Hamilton.

Jimmy Bruno (b.1953) and Frank Vignola (b.1965) are two more important East Coast guitarists to have featured in several contexts on the Concord roster. One of those was the Concord Jazz Guitar Collective, a scintillating project with Howard Alden captured on a studio album under that title in 1995. Alden and Bruno both played seven-string guitars for the session, but Bruno switched to acoustic on four cuts, while Vignola, best known as an acoustic specialist, is heard on electric on four others.

As well as being a thoroughly enjoyable session in which the trio (plus bass and drum on eight tunes) work their way through a set of material which includes classic tunes from Django Reinhardt, Jimmy Giuffre, Charlie Parker, Bud Powell and Tadd Dameron, using a similarly broadly-based frame of stylistic reference, it also provides an intriguing opportunity to sample all three guitarists in a single shot. Alden's fuller sonority and flowing lines are easily distinguished from Bruno's tougher sound and more robust articulation, while Vignola takes a gentler tack on both instruments. Bruno's father was also a guitarist (he worked with Nat King Cole, among others), and his interest in the instrument was encouraged at home. His first significant professional engagement was with the Buddy Rich Big Band, where he doubtless picked up some of that toughness (if only in the interests of self-preservation). He has earned a deserved reputation as a teacher as well as a performer in the ensuing decades.

He is serenely comfortable at even the most exhilarating of tempos, firing off blistering and imaginative single-note lines coloured by the odd chordal interjection or Montgomery-style octaves. His own albums include *Burnin'* (1994), a powerful trio set, and a collaboration with fellow Philadelphian Joey DeFrancesco on the fiery *Like That* (1996), in which his penchant for speed is exercised to the full, although his own evocative 'Night Dreamer' also emphasises his craft at slow tempos. *Live At Birdland* was recorded in 1996 with alto saxophonist Bobby Watson as a special guest. Bruno also recorded another album with Howard Alden, *Full Circle*, which was issued as a double CD in combination with the first ever Concord release, featuring Herb Ellis and Joe Pass, to mark the label's 25th anniversary in 1998.

The rather younger Frank Vignola is also the son of a guitarist, and fell under the sway of Django Reinhardt's music as a youngster. The urbane, technically polished swing style he developed has been built on the Hot Club foundation, but with all manner of modernist inflections and directions, as well as a distinctly flamenco-like classical touch. His albums include collaborations with tuba player Sam Pilafian as the duo *Travelin' Light*, work in a more modern vein with his Unit Four quartet, and his trio-plus-guests sessions *Appel Direct* (1993) and *Let It Happen* (1994). It goes without saying that the hot-house New York jazz scene has thrown up – or taken in – a number of important players working in the swing-to-bop (and sometimes beyond) mainstream style.

One of these is the Canadian-born Peter Leitch (b.1944). He was inspired to turn to jazz by hearing artists like John Coltrane, Thelonious Monk and Wes Montgomery play live in Montreal. He was assisted initially by a local Canadian guitarist named Ivan Symons, and the rather better known Belgian guitarist René Thomas, who was a resident of Montreal in the 1960s.

Leitch has been involved in various projects in New York since moving to the city in 1983, and was the musical director of Guitarists Play Mingus, the five-guitar offshoot of the Mingus Big Band project, until a falling-out over their musical direction. He plays a biting, harmonically sophisticated brand of bop-rooted single-line jazz guitar, and has recorded a number of albums for the Concord, Reservoir and Criss Cross labels, in settings ranging from a duo with pianist John Hicks on *Duality* (1995) through to the septet featured on *Colours And Dimensions* (1996), where he explores the guitar's role in the ensemble as well as its capacities as a solo instrument. He plays both electric and acoustic on this album, and it provides a fine introduction to both his expressive playing and imaginative music. Leitch is also famous in guitar

Canadian-born Peter Leitch (above) delivers a tough, well-informed brand of hard-bop guitar playing.

circles for the instrument he plays. His Zoller guitar, a big hollow-bodied instrument made by the Hofner company, was designed by and named for the late Atilla Zoller, and is one of only two such models in existence (the other was owned by the great Jimmy Raney, and passed on to his son, Doug).

Vic Juris (b.1953) found his way into jazz after hearing a record by Johnny Smith at his guitar teacher's house. The New Jersey native has had a varied career, working with fusion musicians like Eric Kloss, Barry Miles and Richie Cole, organ greats like Don Patterson, Wild Bill Davison and Jimmy Smith, the progressive saxophonist Dave Liebman and the singer Mel Torme. He has also collaborated with guitarists Larry Coryell (including a Five Guitars Play Mingus project in 1997) and Bireli Lagrene. A handful of recordings in his own name reflect his sophisticated bop-rooted side.

Like Juris, Dave Stryker (b.1957) can also point to an apprenticeship with a jazz organ great. The Nebraska native moved to New York in 1980, and was eventually hired by organist Jack McDuff for a two-year stint in 1984. When they were not on the road, they played a regular four-night residence at Dude's Lounge in Harlem, where the guitarist came to the notice of his next employer, saxophonist Stanley Turrentine. The guitarist joined Turrentine's band in 1986, staying almost a decade while also building his own career.

Stryker's tough, driving, blues-rooted tone, and aggressive but fluent bop-influenced soloing, was tailor-made for both these settings (he played with Jimmy Smith and Lonnie Liston as well), and has been reflected in his own discs as a leader for the SteepleChase label. They range from organ trio to big band, and he has also co-produced a tribute to Grant Green on the Evidence label, as well as championing the music of the obscure Omaha-born guitarist Billy Rogers. Like many of these players, Stryker also teaches guitar.

Ron Jackson (b.1964) is another fine guitarist who also belongs in this informal grouping. He was born in the Philippines, where his father was serving in the US Army, and was weaned from his initial leanings toward rock and R&B by discovering Pat Metheny and George Benson in his teens. He moved to a more central jazz idiom firstly at Berklee College and then in two years spent in Paris working regularly with pianist Bobby Few, before settling in New York in 1987. He possesses a clean, decisive touch even at very fast tempos, and a fertile sense of harmonic development which is firmly rooted in bop chord structures, and is also a sensitive interpreter of slower material.

He made his recording debut as a leader in 1991 with an album for Muse, but the best example of his work on disc is *Song For Luis*, an album of duets with the great bass player, Rufus Reid. Jackson took part in the Mingus tribute project led by Larry Coryell, as did another highly regarded member of the new mainstream, Russell Malone (b.1963). The Georgia native cut his teeth on church music, and was yet another player converted to the jazz road by hearing George Benson. He established a local reputation, then joined organist Jimmy Smith's trio, followed by a stint with Harry Connick Jr, which led to his cutting a couple of solid discs for Columbia, with *Black Butterfly* (1993) slightly the stronger of the two.

His profile was raised again by his participation in Robert Altman's film *Kansas City* in 1996, but he is currently best known for his work with singer Diana Krall in her trio, which also features another Connick sideman, bassist Ben Wolfe. On disc, and even more so live, the trio reflects the benefits of playing together on a steady basis. They make familiar standards of a distant era seem simultaneously authentically classic and cooly contemporary, while

Joshua Breakstone keeps good company: on this 1986 album he has Kenny Barron on piano, Dennis Irwin on bass, Keith Copeland on drums and Pepper Adams on baritone sax. With a firm grasp of the bebop language, Breakstone nevertheless avoids its cliches, instead unfolding a storyline in his solos, all the while building interest with economical, elegant lines and sustaining longer notes with a clear, rounded guitar sound.

Guitarist Russell Malone is pictured (left) with vocalist/pianist Diana Krall. Malone has an in-depth appreciation and understanding of all styles and periods of jazz guitar, from Lang, Kress and McDonough to Moore, Montgomery and Benson. His excellent accompaniment and soloing skills have attracted a succession of high-profile bandleaders, including Jimmy Smith and Harry Connick Jr. Since the mid 1990s his recording and international touring with Krall have in particular won him a large international following.

the trio provides an ideal context for the guitarist's polished playing, spanning from the gentlest filigree of tapped-out harmonics to hard-driving swing and imaginative soloing.

Joshua Breakstone (b.1955) has racked up around a dozen album releases since making his recording debut back in 1979. Another teenage convert to jazz, he studied at Berklee and with guitarist Sal Salvador, and has developed into a fine keeper of the flame of bop guitar. Many of his albums feature eminent guests from that tradition, including Pepper Adams, Jimmy Knepper, Kenny Barron and Tommy Flanagan, and have featured themed tributes to Grant Green and Thelonious Monk, although he has also varied things by cutting albums devoted to fluid bop-based interpretations of the music of The Beatles and, on *Walk Don't Run* (1991), the surf band The Ventures.

Peter Bernstein (b.1967) is another significant contributor to the New York scene, both as a sideman with artists like Larry Goldings, Jim Hall and Joshua Redman, and in his own projects. He came to jazz through rock and blues, with the influence of Wes Montgomery proving a decisive factor in his conversion: he was later able to record with Montgomery's regular Indianapolis organ man, Melvin Rhyne. He contributed to the Grant Green tribute co-produced by Dave Stryker, and his fluent stylings have kept him very busy, but has yet to make a really striking record under his own name.

Ron Eschete (b.1948) made his name on the West Coast rather than the East. A Louisiana native, he came to jazz through an early interest in blues, and began his westward drift when hired to accompany singer Buddy Greco in Las Vegas in 1969. The following year he settled in Los Angeles and has worked extensively in the studios there (as well as teaching at the Guitar Institute of Technology), but has also found time to amass an impressive roster of jazz collaborations with artists like Ray Brown, Gene Harris, Dizzy Gillespie and Hampton Hawes, as well as several eminent guitarists.

Eschete is another player who favours the seven-string instrument (he played with George Van Eps in California), and is a deft improviser with a particular feel for blues, a quality put to good use in the Gene Harris Quartet. His own albums feature the guitarist in several settings, including the solo album *A Closer Look* (1994).

The continuing productivity of these players, and the emergence of even newer names like Barry Zweig and Kenny Poole, bear testimony to the enduring legacy of the styles which make up this new mainstream. These players have not simply preserved the structures and repertoire of the swing and bop era, however, but have recast them in fresh guises. In the process, they are extending the vocabulary, without abandoning the original language.

THE LEGACY OF DJANGO

DJANGO REINHARDT LEFT BEHIND NOT ONLY A STACK OF RECORDINGS BUT A SEEMINGLY INEXHAUSTIBLE APPETITE FOR MUSIC IN HIS GYPSY JAZZ STYLE. COUNTLESS ADMIRERS AND IMITATORS HAVE SOUGHT TO FOLLOW HIM – BUT IT DOES HELP TO BE A GYPSY.

When Django Reinhardt died in 1953 he left the world more than 850 recordings of his virtuosic playing. These ranged from his 1928 debut on banjo to the "electric" bebop-influenced sessions of the 1950s. But it was the Quintet of the Hot Club of France recordings with Stephane Grappelli that have proved the most enduring and influential.

Using the previously unheard line-up of violin, solo guitar, two rhythm guitars and bass, this group recorded its hybrid of American jazz and Gypsy fire in the 1930s to immediate critical acclaim. The music has a timeless quality that, like a good wine, even improves with age. The driving four-to-the-bar rhythm of the rhythm guitars, supporting a fluid violin solo and guitar improvisation, created a sound that is even today recreated for film soundtracks, TV advertisements and modern CD releases.

For centuries the European Gypsies have been persecuted because of their way of life, and as recently as 50 years ago thousands perished alongside the Jews under the Nazis' "final solution". It is then somewhat paradoxical that at that time Reinhardt, a Manouche Gypsy, was heralded across the world as the greatest living guitarist. Not surprisingly, Django became and remains a Gypsy icon, whom many Gypsy musicians aspire to emulate but none expect to better.

It is argued that to master Django's guitar style and technique you have to be born and raised a Gypsy. Such is their cultural reverence for the master that they gravitate to the acoustic guitar or violin in the way British and American kids kick a ball to emulate their sporting heroes. Even today, it is common to find four generations of players, each with a battered Maccaferri-style guitar, bashing out Reinhardt compositions like 'Minor Swing' or 'Douce Ambience' on a Gypsy caravan site.

It is the opportunity to practice and develop the technique to make the acoustic instrument an audible solo voice that is perhaps the most important aspect of the Gypsy musicians' training. There must be a genetic advantage, too, but hour after hour of constant practice can only assist a budding guitarist in the quest to master the style.

Gitane Gypsy Boulou Ferré (b.1951) and his brother Elios (b.1956) no doubt started their musical education this way. Their father was Pierre "Matelot" Ferret (1918-1989) and their uncle Baro Ferret (1908-1976), both regular rhythm guitarists in the Quintet of the Hot Club of France. Boulou, however, deviated from Gypsy tradition in 1963 and entered the Conservatoire National de Paris to begin many years of classical training.

Hailed as a child prodigy and "the next Django" he survived this potentially damaging early adulation and is today one of the most accomplished players in the true Django style. Boulou still works in a duo with his brother Elios playing Favino Maccaferri style guitars or Gibson semi-acoustics and archtops, usually an ES-330 and ES-175.

When a duo has been active for more than 30 years it comes as no surprise that the interplay and counterpoint is nothing short of telepathic. Couple this with a jaw-dropping technique and you have arguably the finest guitar duo on today's jazz scene. As with most of the current Gypsy masters their work is woefully under-recorded but their output for the Danish label SteepleChase should give the listener an idea of their virtuosity.

The early life of Boulou was mirrored 15 years later when another astonishing child prodigy burst on to the scene. Born in 1966, Bireli Lagrene

Babik Reinhardt in performance at Juan les Pins, France, in 1998 (left). Son of the legendary Django – a hard act to follow – Babik prudently developed an electric-guitar style that was sufficiently personal and far-removed from that of his father to allow him his own identity and to avoid unwanted comparisons. This 1985 album (above) by Boulou and Elios Ferré has the two Gitane Gypsies heading in directions guided by their classical training and an interest in bebop and post-bop styles, despite both being able to play brilliantly in the Django idiom. Their father, Pierre "Matelot" Ferret, and his brother Baro both played rhythm guitar with Django, and while Boulou and Elios continue the musical tradition of their family, they do not allow it to restrict them stylistically.

began his life as a Sinti Gypsy in the Alsace region of France. No doubt tutored in the traditional way by his guitarist father, by the age of 12 Lagrene was a true virtuoso of the acoustic Django-style guitar. As a teenager he toured continuously perfecting the Hot Club style, but the influence of Wes Montgomery, Jimi Hendrix and Jaco Pastorius steered his playing into less traditional areas as his recordings of the late 1980s and 1990s show.

The concept of the "heir-apparent" to Django playing distorted rock guitar solos on his Yamaha solidbodied instrument must have disillusioned many die-hards, but Lagrene has lost none of his original ability. In the same way his fluent English is spoken with an American accent, his native tongue will always be French, and his spiritual music will forever be Django-influenced jazz guitar.

If there is an argument for the theory that talent is purely inherited then Babik Reinhardt (b.1944) should be the greatest living Gypsy jazz player. Despite being the second son of Django, Babik has demonstrated little interest in recreating his father. Drawing on American players as a main influence, he rarely plays the acoustic guitar, favouring a Gibson ES-175 to produce modern

lines inspired by Jimmy Raney and Wes Montgomery. Forever pushing at the boundaries, Babik has recorded film soundtracks and collaborated with the cutting edge of fusion players, including Larry Coryell and Didier Lockwood.

Fapy Lafertin was born in 1950 on a Manouche campsite in Courtraie, Belgium. Like every other Gypsy great, he began his studies as an infant and blossomed into one of the second generation of players most responsible for keeping Gypsy jazz music in the public eye.

With his group WASO he toured constantly during the 1970s, establishing himself as a festival favourite throughout Europe. A master of many instruments, including the notoriously difficult 12-string Portuguese *guitarra*, he continues to play and record in the Django style, most recently with the British band Le Jazz.

The Manouche (or Sinti) gypsies have settled in many European countries, including Holland, home of the Rosenberg dynasty. Stochelo Rosenberg (b.1968) leads a trio of cousins, with Nous'che Rosenberg on rhythm guitar and Nonnie Rosenberg on bass, that has become one of the most internationally respected purveyors of the true Django style. From their early days on Dutch children's television and Gypsy festivals this trio has risen to the dizzy heights of playing the Carnegie Hall in New York as part of Stephane Grappelli's 85th birthday celebrations.

The CD of this concert demonstrates the impact this purely acoustic trio had on the unsuspecting Americans, the audience whooping and cheering with delight after every tune. While the trio is still very much together, Stochelo is exploring other forms of music, later releases exhibiting strong classical influences in both his guitar playing and the use of a full orchestra for accompaniment.

The latest Rosenberg virtuoso is Jimmy (b.1980) who made his TV debut at nine, rattling through Django standards in the TV documentary *The Django Legacy*. A product of the campsite training ground that has produced so many virtuosos, Jimmy Rosenberg is something extra special.

While it is common for talented players to learn Django's solos note-for-note as part of their learning process, Jimmy, even as a 12-year-old, surpassed this and was creating his own masterpieces, demonstrating a genius and maturity beyond his formative years. Married at 16, the chain-smoking, beer-drinking teenager seems to live every part of his life ahead of time, yet still remains unfazed by the constant adulation heaped on him.

Guitarist Jon Larsen of the Hot Club of Norway has long been a tireless supporter of Gypsy jazz, and as owner of Hot Club records was able to record Jimmy from his earliest days. In addition to his work with his trio Sinti, Jimmy is still a regular visitor to the Hot Club Studios and has produced two recent releases collaborating not only with Jon's group but with Angelo Debarre and Romane.

Frenchman Angelo Debarre (b.1962) is a Hot Club Records artist and one of the true Gypsy stylists to remain unswervingly loyal to his roots. A master of the Gypsy waltz, his recorded output and regular festival appearances keep the traditional flame burning. In contrast, Romane is a true innovator, pushing forward the boundaries of what is defined as Gypsy jazz.

Born Patrick Leguidecoq, he rediscovered himself as the enigmatic "Romane", adopting the airs and graces of his Gypsy idol, growing a look-alike moustache and living in a house a few metres away from Django's old home in Samois-sur-Seine. Romane is not a Gypsy but one of the few

Born in 1966 into a Gypsy family in Alsace, Birelli Lagrene (opposite) made the successful transition from child prodigy in the Django Reinhardt mould to mature, virtuosic player with a style rooted in today's music.

outsiders that the Gypsy community has accepted as one of their own. He is arguably the most accomplished non-Gypsy playing in this style, this achievement being testament to the practice he must have undertaken away from the usual Gypsy playing schools. His formal training comes through in his magnificent compositions, the Debussy-inspired 'Dans Le Regard Du Laura' being a modern classic. His CDs are masterpieces of both composition and performance, by both himself, his virtuoso violinist Florin Niculescu and his rhythm guitarist "Doudou" Cuillerier. These three musicians are currently involved in a new band with Babik Reinhardt. Calling themselves the New Quintette du Hot Club de France, they are recreating the original tunes but with modern arrangements and discarding the traditional acoustic Maccaferris in favour of modern arch-top electric guitars.

In recent years two events have influenced the non-Gypsy community to

Many Gypsy guitarists play in the style of Reinhardt, but few bring to it such artistic depth and sheer musicality as Fapy Lafertin (right). He also performs fado music on the 12-string Portuguese guitarra. This 1991 album (above) is an excellent representation of Fapy's artistry, encompassing his evocative Django-inspired playing and his fado stylings on the guitarra, as well as Argentinian tangos, Brazilian music and, on the title track 'Fleur de Lavende' his own writing skills.

produce their own brand of Hot Club music. The first happened in the early 1970s when skiffle guitarist Diz Disley (b.1931), a lifelong Reinhardt devotee, convinced Stephane Grappelli to leave the hotel music circuit and rediscover the sound that had originally inspired them.

Grappelli had been working successfully with pianists, playing his own style of polite jazz in commercial environments but, intrigued by Disley's offer, set off on a short tour, leading Diz and Denny Wright on acoustic guitars and Johnny Hawksworth on bass.

Drawing from his 1930s repertoire, the experiment was a complete success and led to a high profile 25-year period for the violinist during which time he assisted the careers of guitarists John Etheridge, Martin Taylor and Mark Fosset. Grappelli never looked back, and even in his last year of life was touring the world with veteran American guitarist Bucky Pizzarelli and bassist John Burr, getting the reverence his contribution to the genre deserved.

The second important event was a television show, shown in 1991 on Channel 4 in the UK and subsequently released world-wide on video. Entitled *The Django Legacy*, it featured events around the 1990 jazz festival held annually in Samois-sur-Seine, the last home of Django. Every year Gypsy families, musicians and enthusiasts converge on this sleepy riverside village to watch great jazz, but more importantly to meet and play with fellow enthusiasts in the many campsites and cafés.

John Jeremy's documentary portrayed events perfectly and, in showcasing the previously unheard-of Stochelo Rosenberg Trio to the world, created a new guitar hero overnight. Many young players, tired of the Van Halens, Vais and Satrianis, found in Rosenberg and Lagrene a fresh form of virtuosity and, most importantly, a guitar style to emulate. Django CDs disappeared from the cut-price record bins and a whole generation of players learned the solos from 'Dark Eyes' and 'Minor Swing' with the enthusiasm previously reserved for 'Eruption' or 'Surfing With The Alien'.

Wayne Jeffries, a young guitarist based in Nottingham, England, personifies this phenomenon. With his cropped hair and Motorhead tattoos, he looks the antithesis of a 1930s jazz fan but when jamming with the Gypsies produces music that belies his appearance.

Another young British player who has dedicated his playing career to Gypsy jazz is Robin Nolan (b.1968). Robin abandoned his studies with Adrian Ingram at Leeds College of Music to form a Hot Club Quartet in Amsterdam. Now based permanently in Holland, Nolan mixed acoustic guitar-driven Gypsy jazz, bebop harmony and a pop sensibility to great success, particularly on the streets of Amsterdam, where his band busked for the tourists. Today Robin has six CDs to his credit and appears at major European festivals.

The festival scene is not only necessary for Gypsy music to flourish but for luthiers to exhibit their new reproductions of the classic Maccaferri-designed guitar. Most European countries have a dedicated event, usually run by enthusiasts in an attempt to get the music to as large an audience as possible. The French festival at Samois is probably the most popular, no doubt because of its Django connection, but successful events also occur in Augsburg, Germany, and Oslo, Norway.

The German festival is run by the publishers of the excellent *Hot Club News*, a magazine dedicated to the German Gypsy jazz scene. Promoter Bernhard Gierstl presents his annual Django Reinhardt Memorial Concerts each April to showcase the incredible talent of German gypsy players. Lulu

Noted as a strong player in the Reinhardt style, Diz Disley (in 1961, above) helped to re-ignite Stephane Grappelli's career in the early 1970s, touring with the violinist for almost ten years. Disley's fine swing guitar style also suggests an awareness of Teddy Bunn and Oscar Moore.

Reinhardt. Ziroli Winterstein and Wedeli Köhler are examples of the world-class performers featured over the last few years. Jon Larsen of Hot Club Records runs a similar series of concerts each January in his hometown of Oslo. This festival gives his group The Hot Club of Norway a chance to perform with the leading Gypsy players from France, Belgium and Germany, and gives Norwegian jazz fans a rare chance to hear the world's best on their own doorstep.

Perhaps the most encouraging developments in the Gypsy jazz world are occurring in North America. The US has for a long time had its Django Reinhardt fans, but has until recently showed little interest in recreating or developing the style of music. Some 15 years ago, four musicians working in Disneyland, Los Angeles, decided to form a new group to alternate with their bluegrass sets. Being proud owners of Selmer guitars, they recreated Hot Club favourites for the unsuspecting tourists.

Today the three guitarists still share the same enthusiasm for their idol. John Jorgenson is currently in Elton John's band, and a world class guitarist in almost every style, yet still enjoys gigging and recording Gypsy jazz. Raul Reynoso and Doug Maddocks are active also, Reynoso recently releasing *Royal Streets*, a Django-inspired collection of swing tunes, to critical acclaim.

Jorgenson's current high profile has no doubt helped encourage guitar fans to seek out Django's music, and today we find a "Hot Club of..." in most major American cities. Paul Mehling leads the most established of these, The Hot Club of San Francisco, recreating the classic line-up, his Dupont Maccaferri replica playing Django's lines with an American accent.

Seattle has spawned many influential guitarists, including Hot Club revivalists Pearl Django, a successful quintet playing festivals and doing lucrative corporate work in the Pacific North-West area of America. Featuring guitarists Dudley Hill, Neil Andersson and Shelley Park, their prolific output of American-influenced radio-friendly Gypsy swing is proving a big hit with the Middle of the Road record buyers as well as Gypsy jazz fans.

New Yorker Frank Vignola (b.1965) is another young player who is pushing at the boundaries of the style. Playing his trusty Favino acoustic, his love of Django shines through with every well-hit pick stroke, yet he is equally at home with his Benedetto electric producing seamless bebop lines. His recent appearance at Carnegie Hall with Jimmy Rosenberg, and the subsequent release of the video and CD, will no doubt produce greater interest in Django's music such is the virtuosity of both players.

The current availability of tuition videos, Django re-issue CDs and related books continues to fuel the growth of this unique music. Any guitar style that contains great technique, strong melodic content and, dare I suggest, a competitive element in the soloing is bound to succeed with young male guitarists out to impress. I am aware of only a couple of women playing in this style. Perhaps this is where the genre is heading in the future? One can certainly hope so.

The recent revival in the popularity of the Django style has had interesting effects on the market for new and vintage guitars. Fewer than 1,000 original Selmer Maccaferris were made between the 1930s and the early 1950s and many have subsequently been lost or damaged. As any schoolboy will tell you, if demand for a product goes up, and the supply is fixed, the price goes through the ceiling. The price of an original Selmer is now beyond the average musician, with asking prices of $15,000 commonplace. This has resulted in a proliferation of small independent luthiers entering the market, producing good quality replicas to meet this growing demand.

In 1932 the Henri Selmer company of Paris entered into a partnership with Italian guitarist/designer Mario Maccaferri to produce a range of guitars. Maccaferri designed a nylon-strung classical, a harp guitar, a slide guitar for "Hawaiian" use and a steel-strung "jazz" model, this being the large D-hole 12-fret model.

Following a dispute, after only 300 or so guitars were made, Maccaferri parted company with Selmer. Wishing to continue with guitar production, Selmer modified the Maccaferri design, increasing the scale length (producing a neck with 14 frets clear of the body), dispensing with the internal sound

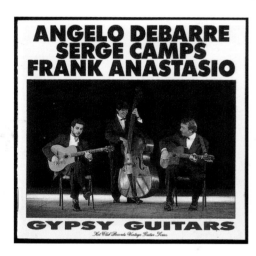

chamber and reducing the soundhole to a small oval shape or "petite bouche". This revised design, first produced around 1936, became the chosen guitar of Django, thus establishing the currently desired pattern.

The first replicas, strictly speaking, were those produced by the luthiers who lost their jobs when Selmer closed down. Familiar names like Favino, Di Maurio and Anastasio began producing similar designs Favino became a prolific maker, a tradition passed on to his son, who currently makes excellent Selmer-style guitars.

Of the current French makers, Maurice Dupont is probably the best regarded. From his workshop in Cognac he produces replicas that, when aged by the passage of time, are practically indistinguishable from the originals.

In the UK established luthiers John le Voi and Doug Kyle have been joined by David Hodson and John Smith in producing replicas of professional quality for less than a tenth of the price of an original. Similarly in America, luthiers have specialised in Selmer replicas, Shelley Park and Michael Dunn being the longest established. A new company called Dell-Arte now manufactures a range in Mexico that is surprisingly good in tone yet sells for less than $1,500.

It may strike some as suprising the home of the copy guitar, Japan, has yet to fully rise to the challenge of producing a good Selmer replica. A few false starts in the 1970s, commissioned by a European importer, produced a decent guitar but the current line manufactured by Saga can at best be considered as entry-level only.

It appears that a good acoustic tone does not come cheaply. Most current professional players use a hand built replica by one of the above makers.

Angelo Debarre plays solo guitar on 1989's Gypsy Guitars (left), a dazzling programme of Hot Club favourites, Gypsy melodies, a Fapy Lafertin waltz, traditional Hungarian and Romanian music and a stunning Csardas. A young English guitarist now resident in Amsterdam, Robin Nolan (1996 album, centre) is hailed by many as one of the brightest young stars in the Django firmament. Hot Club stylists from Toulouse, France, the group Latcho Drom play on La Verdine (above) with energy and verve, but it is the work of their solo guitarist Christophe Lartilleux which gives them their competitive edge.

THE BRITISH SCENE

JAZZ GUITAR HAS A SIXTY-YEAR HISTORY IN BRITAIN, AND BRITISH PLAYERS HAVE MASTERED ANY NUMBER OF DIFFERENT STYLES, FROM TRAD AND BIG-BAND SWING TO BEBOP AND FUSION. NOW YOUNG PLAYERS ARE BUILDING LINKS WITH TODAY'S DANCE MUSIC.

Britain has produced its fair share of important players in the six decades since the guitar became established as a solo instrument in jazz, and in a wide diversity of styles and influences.

There will be much debate over who is the father of British jazz guitar, but one strong – if largely forgotten – candidate may be the Trinidadian guitarist Lauderic Caton. Caton died in London in 1999, at the age of 88, having lived as a virtual recluse since giving up music in 1959. The writer and photographer Val Wilmer, who was one of Caton's few contacts in the final decades of his life, noted that he "played a key role in establishing the electric guitar in Britain", while his recordings with the West Indian All-Stars and broadcasts with clarinettist Harry Parry brought many listeners their first real taste of the instrument.

Caton, who had learned several instruments in his native Trinidad, arrived in London in 1940, and quickly installed himself on the local scene, playing jazz, Caribbean and Latin music. His trio with pianist Dick Katz and bassist Coleridge Goode at the Caribbean Club in Soho achieved considerable cachet, while his Charlie Christian-influenced technique and fluid horn-like lines attracted a lot of attention among other guitarists (Django Reinhardt was among those who dropped by to check him out and sit in.) Ray Ellington eventually took over the trio, but Caton became disenchanted with touring and quit the band. He continued to work throughout the 1950s, often with saxophonist Louis Stephenson, but had given up by the end of the decade.

Among those who benefitted from his example at the Carribean Club, however, were the two main pioneers of bebop guitar in Britain, Dave Goldberg (1922-1969) and Pete Chilver (b.1924), the former sadly unrepresented on disc. Goldberg grew up on Merseyside and began playing there, but began his professional career after his family moved to Glasgow while he was in his late teens. He picked up gigs with dance bands, and joined Ronnie Munro's Scottish Variety Orchestra. While serving in the RAF, he spent some time in America, and later joined the Ted Heath Band.

He remained with Heath until 1949, when he emigrated to America, and spent the early 1950s working back and forward across the Atlantic, earning a living in dance bands, studio and film work, and touring with dancer Katherine Durham, all evidence of his technical command and versatility. He settled in London in 1954, working with Geraldo's celebrated dance band, and later Jack Parnell's ATV Orchestra. At the same time he was honing his jazz chops in small groups with progressive musicians including saxophonist Ronnie Scott, trumpeter Dizzy Reece and drummer Phil Seaman.

Goldberg's American adventures earned him a reputation beyond the

British scene before his untimely death from a drug overdose in 1969. But Pete Chilver's early retirement from professional music has confined his renown to a smaller circle. Born in Windsor, he took up guitar under the influence of Django Reinhardt, and by his late teens was playing regularly in a band with pianist Ralph Sharon. He trained as a draughtsman before becoming a professional musician in 1946 with the Ray Ellington Quartet, and played extensively in London where he shared a flat with Dave Goldberg.

Having racked up an impressive list of associations (including Ted Heath, Stephane Grappelli, Benny Goodman and George Shearing), Chilver moved to Edinburgh in 1950, where he set aside professional music and took over the management of the family's hotel and restaurant. He maintained an active

Lauderic Caton (left), the British-based pioneer of the electric guitar, performing with the Ray Ellington Quartet in the late 1940s. By the time the distinctive guitar solos of Denny Wright (above) had earned him a slice of skiffle stardom with Lonnie Donegan in the 1950s, he had already paid his dues in the bands of Carl Barriteau and Kenny Graham, and had founded the Hot Club Of London. From 1973 to 1978 Wright worked with Stephane Grappelli alongside Diz Disley, before forming the quartet Velvet with trumpeter Digby Fairweather, fellow-guitarist Ike Isaacs and bassist Len Skeat.

link with jazz by promoting the music at his famous West End Cafe, a legendary venue in Scottish jazz, but he never resumed his playing career.

While Goldberg and Chilver mixed swing with the emerging bop style in their playing, others chose to take a more conservative approach. Denny Wright (1924-1992) was a contemporary of both men, but his work as a guitarist, pianist, singer and arranger was heard in more traditional contexts. He alternated touring with studio work, including leading his own group in the late 1940s and 1950s. His principal associations (in a very long list) included working with singer and skiffler Lonnie Donegan, trumpeter Digby Fairweather, the bluegrass band led by Johnny Duncan, Hot Club-style bands with Diz Disley and Stephane Grappelli, and a duet with violinist Johnny Van Derrick. But he also worked with more modernist figures on occasion, including saxophonist Bruce Turner in the 1950s, and briefly with Kenny Graham's Afro-Cubists in 1967. A solid stylist with the ability to adapt convincingly to many settings, he remained much in demand.

Jim Douglas (b.1942) is rather younger, but also took a traditional line. Born near Edinburgh, he turned professional in the early 1960s with the

With his acute harmonic insight and fine musicianship, Ike Isaacs was soon in demand as a guitarist on the London music scene after his arrival from Burma in 1946. From the early 1960s he contributed a technical column for guitarists in Crescendo magazine, and taught and encouraged any young guitarist who showed a serious desire to develop. One such was Martin Taylor, with whom Isaacs performed as a duo for several years at London's Pizza On The Park.

Hidden Town Dixielanders, and played with clarinettist Pete Kerr and the Clyde Valley Stompers before joining the Alex Welsh Band. He became a core member of that group, one of the best of the British traditional jazz outfits, contributing cogent, rhythmically powerful guitar and banjo until 1981, shortly before the leader's death. He has featured with a number of other British bands, including the Alex Welsh Reunion Band and the Great British Jazz Band, but has also worked with visiting American musicians, including cornetists Ed Polcer and Warren Vache.

Both Goldberg and Wright did a great deal of session work, and several other talented British jazz guitarists followed a similar course. That list would include Judd Procter (b.1933), a fine Doncaster-born guitarist and singer whose career in the studio did not prevent him putting in jazz time with Ray Ellington, Benny Goodman and Don Lusher. But the best known players in this category are Ike Isaacs and Ray Russell. Ike Isaacs (1919-1996) was born in Rangoon, Burma, and died in Sydney, Australia, where he had taken up a professorship at the Sydney Guitar School. But he spent much of his working life in Britain, where he established a considerable reputation as a skilled jazz and studio musician.

Isaacs came from a musical family, and survived a horrendous overland journey from Rangoon to Calcutta after the Japanese invasion of Burma, where his professional career began. He arrived in London in 1946, and became a familiar figure on the jazz scene. Ike worked extensively with the Ted Heath Band and the BBC Showband over a long period, and was part of a quartet for the weekly BBC *Guitar Club* broadcasts.

His impeccable technique and finely honed musicianship guaranteed him a regular supply of studio work, in a wide variety of musical settings. He suffered from nerves in front of an audience, but he was involved in a number of important projects, the best known of which was his tenure with the great French violinist Stephane Grappelli, who had resurrected the Hot Club format at the instigation of another English guitarist, Diz Disley, in 1972. Isaacs was recruited for a subsequent edition of that band, and played with the violinist on numerous occasions in the 1970s, when he also toured as a member of Velvet with trumpeter Digby Fairweather and fellow-guitarist Denny Wright

For many years Ike Isaacs wrote an influential column on aspects of guitar technique for *Crescendo International* magazine. He taught extensively and played the role of unofficial mentor to a number of aspiring guitarists.

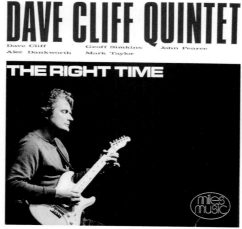

These included Martin Taylor, who recalled that Isaacs's house in London "was a real meeting place for guitarists. We were all fascinated by his immense knowledge of chords and harmony, and also his famous Burmese curries! Ike was never all that keen about performing in public, but he loved to suggest things to guitarists that they might play in their own way, and took pleasure in hearing his ideas emerge in that context".

Ray Russell (b.1947) also enjoyed a successful career as a freelance studio musician, arranger and musical director, and established a lucrative sideline as a composer of music for television and films. Born in London, he took up guitar at 12, and was a member of Georgie Fame and The Blue Flames in the mid 1960s. He worked with Graham Bond in the late 1960s, and went on to play with such jazz luminaries as Harold Beckett, Mike Gibbs and Gil Evans, as well as working in pop and rock contexts.

Outside of the studio, though, much of his attention has been directed to leading his own groups, which have served as a showcase for his composing and arranging as well as his guitar work. Russell cut a number of significant records, including *Turn Circle* in 1968, which have been hard to find in recent years. But in a welcome development in 1999, Columbia reissued two of his long unavailable albums, *Rites And Rituals* and *Dragon Hill*. He continues to record in a jazz context, both solo and with the rhythm team of Anthony Jackson and Simon Phillips.

Stylistic definitions are usually less than precise indicators in jazz, and the group of players who came of age in the heyday of hard bop in the late 1950s and early 1960s, and might be loosely gathered under that heading, is a diverse one.

Terry Smith (b.1943) was born in London, and began playing local gigs as a teenager, but his first regular engagement came in a six-month spell with

At the same time as John McLaughlin was developing the musical ideas laid down in Extrapolation, fellow London-based guitarist Ray Russell (1968 album, left) was also exploring new forms and shifting time-signatures, and discarding the hollow-body guitar in favour of the solidbody variety. A major jazz guitar voice on the contemporary British scene is Dave Cliff (1987 album, centre). Cliff's musical preferences are clearly indicated by the composers represented here: Jimmy Raney, Wes Montgomery, Jimmy Heath, Sonny Rollins and Horace Silver. Meanwhile, returning to Django territory to pay tribute to his former bandleader Stephane Grappelli, John Etheridge (1998 album, above) shines on the quartet tracks and the duets with violinist Christian Garrick, but his solo interpretation of 'The Nearness of You' is a miniature masterpiece.

Jim Mullen's unorthodox Wes-like thumb-picking technique drives a highly personal style that blends the raw with the sophisticated to great effect. Interweaving an innate feeling for the blues into harmonically-aware contemporary jazz lines, Mullen typically rounds off his phrases with a broad vibrato. His performances never fail to ignite, and he remains one of the most expressive players on today's UK scene, equally effective in fusion or straight jazz settings.

trombonist Roy Brooks's dance band in Doncaster. On his return to London, he worked for a time with pianist Roy Budd, drummer Trevor Tomkins (Budd's cousin), and bassist Tony Archer in a small group setting, and took part in the Ronnie Scott Big Band in 1967. Like many other players at the time, he was also drawn into the burgeoning pop and rock scene, and toured internationally with the Walker Brothers, and later with Scott Walker.

His principal jazz associations, however, were with two other stalwarts of the UK scene, organist Mike Carr in the late 1960s, and saxophonist Dick Morrissey in the early 1970s. If, the imaginative jazz-rock band he co-led with the saxophonist from 1969, lasted until the mid 1970s, and was in some respects a forerunner of the successful Morrissey-Mullen. An accident to his hand forced Smith to stop playing for a time, but he was eventually able to return to the instrument. His collaborators have been many and varied, including blues singer Jo Ann Kelly and numerous touring American musicians, as well as top UK bop-based players like Don Weller, Peter King and Tony Lee.

Phil Lee (b.1943) was another wartime baby who discovered jazz as a teenager in the late 1950s, and he began playing guitar at 13. His early associations included commercial work as well as the John Williams Big Band, but he also worked with more adventurous spirits like Graham Collier (as a bassist) and Mike Gibbs in the late 1960s, and was featured in a number of more experimental jazz and jazz-rock settings in the 1970s, including Henry Lowther's Quartenity, the John Stevens Quintet, the jazz-rock band Gilgamesh, the Michael Garrick Sextet, and Axel, a band he co-led with saxophonist Tony Coe.

He has proved a sympathetic accompanist of singers as different in their approaches as Norma Winstone and Marian Montgomery, and has provided support to a range of American visitors, as well as racking up a long list of home-based associations spanning several generations of players, from Jimmy Hastings through to Julian Stringle, and including the London Jazz Orchestra. He has been much in demand as both a session player and a teacher, notably at the Guildhall School of Music, and has recorded as leader for the Spotlite and Cadillac labels, which issued his subtle duo album with bassist Jeff Clyne, *Twice Upon A Time* (1987).

Dave Cliff (b.1944) was born a year later than Smith and Lee, and at the other end of England, in Hexham, Northumberland. He took up the instrument at 14, and cut his teeth professionally in an R&B band in Newcastle. He enrolled on the jazz course at Leeds College in 1967, where his tutor, bassist Peter Ind, introduced him to the music of Lennie Tristano. The pianist's cool, rather cerebral approach has remained an important facet of the guitarist's mature style, and it was logical enough that when Ind was putting together a band to accompany Tristano's best known disciples, saxophonists Lee Konitz and Warne Marsh, on a UK tour in 1975, the guitarist should be included.

Ind was a friend and mentor when Cliff moved to London in 1971, and helped him find a foothold in the capital's jazz scene. He was not slow to take advantage, and quickly established his standing as an inventive and adaptable soloist. He has worked equally comfortably in driving hard bop (with Tommy Chase or Mike Carr), more mainstream settings (Bob Wilbur and Humphrey Lyttelton), and traditional jazz (Alex Welsh). He is a regular first-call for visiting Americans like Warren Vache and Kenny Davern, and has evolved a

John Etheridge achieved recognition in the early 1970s for his imaginative electric guitar contributions to progressive rock bands Curved Air and Soft Machine. In 1977 he revealed another, largely hidden side of his musical personality when he brought a Django-style acoustic-guitar virtuosity to Stephane Grappelli's touring group. Since then Etheridge has run his own fusion quartet, toured with bassist Danny Thompson, duetted with Pat Metheny and with ex-Police guitarist Andy Summers, and performed extensively on classical violinist Nigel Kennedy's jazz projects. In 1998 Etheridge formed a new acoustic quartet that featured violinist Christian Garrick.

refined association with alto saxophonist Geoff Simkins. He also teaches, and has recorded a number of albums over the years, including an intriguing exploration of *The Music Of Tadd Dameron* (1996) with Simkins, and a meeting with guitarist Howard Alden on *When Lights Are Low* (1997).

Other guitarists who should be included in this informal grouping are Adrian Ingram (b.1950), who is known not only as a fine performer in both jazz and classical styles, but also for his work as guitar tutor at Leeds College of Music and his writings, including a book on Wes Montgomery; Amancio D'Silva, who played with more overt experimentalists like Joe Harriott and Stan Tracey; Welsh guitarist Trefor Owen (b.1944), who has made something of a speciality of touring with visiting guitarists like Mundell Lowe, Doug Raney and Louis Stewart; and Esmond Selwyn (b.1948), who has led his own groups and worked with Don Rendell and Robin Jones.

The superstars of the jazz-rock field, John McLaughlin and Allan Holdsworth, are both dealt with elsewhere in this book, but other guitarists also made their mark. John Etheridge (b.1948) grew up in London, and taught himself the instrument as a teenager. He began playing with

progressive rock groups in the early 1970s, often with violinist Darryl Way, and joined Soft Machine in 1975, an association which lasted throughout the decade. At the same time, however, he was working regularly as part of Stephane Grappelli's touring band. That adaptability has been a recurring feature in a career that has ranged from mainstream swing to free jazz.

He led his own band Second Vision for a time in the early 1980s, and continued to work in a jazz-rock context with Gary Boyle. He has led his own bands on occasion since then, while other important associations include work with two virtuoso bassists, Brian Torff and Danny Thompson, tours with guitarists Bireli Lagrene, Jim Mullen and Andy Summers, and work in the group led by classical violinist Nigel Kennedy. He has been an inventive contributor in all these settings (and many others) on both acoustic and electric guitar, while his own infrequent albums have allowed him to air his own compositions, notably on *Ash* (1994).

Jim Mullen (b.1945) was born in Glasgow, and began playing in local bands as a bassist before switching to guitar and forming his own trio. He moved to London in 1969, and established a strong reputation in jazz-rock with Pete Brown, Brian Auger, Herbie Mann, the Average White Band and Kokomo, as well as co-leading Morrissey-Mullen with saxophonist Dick Morrissey, a notably successful outfit for a decade from the band's formation in 1975. In the 1990s he worked with a variety of artists, including singer Claire Martin and pianist Gene Harris, but concentrated more on leading his own excellent jazz group. He has evolved into a highly musical and notably imaginative stylist. His lyrical guitar work is full of unexpected harmonic twists and turns, and he employs a distinctive Wes Montgomery-inspired thumb style which helps to give him an instantly identifiable sound, heard to advantage on albums like *Rule Of Thumb* (1995) and *We Go Back* (1996).

The UK scene continues to throw up new names in jazz guitar. The most promising of the musicians to emerge in the 1990s is Mike Walker. He took up guitar relatively late, at the age of 17, but was quick to make up lost time, and attracted a lot of positive attention working with the Manchester-based Creative Jazz Orchestra, trumpeter Kenny Wheeler, pianist John Taylor and saxophonist Julian Arguelles.

He is a highly talented player, but is the first to admit that he is not exactly driven in career terms. However, he was persuaded to put together a sextet and write his own music for a tour of Scotland in 1998, which revealed facets of his work that had not been obvious from his previous associations, harking back to his early interest in the jazz-inflected rock of Joni Mitchell and Steely Dan and the bright, soaring textural interplay of Weather Report. It proved highly effective, and may be springboard to further developments.

Other contemporary names to watch include Phil Robson, best known for his work with Julian Arguelles, and Kevin MacKenzie, a Scottish guitarist whose music includes fusion projects with both folk and funk components as well as more straight-ahead jazz. Tony Remy has played with musicians like pianists Julian Joseph and Jason Rebello and saxophonist Jean Toussaint on the London scene, but is best known for his contemporary fusion work with the band Desperately Seeking Fusion and his own groups, Lateral Thinking and the Tony Remy Band. Ronny Jordan has been even more closely associated with a smooth fusion of jazz and contemporary dance music which can be heard on his albums *The Antidote* and *The Quiet Revolution* albeit at the cost of a certain blandness.

Esmond Selwyn (opposite) was born in London but studied guitar in New York with Chuck Wayne, Sal Salvador and Allen Hanlon. On returning to England he performed with saxophonist Don Rendell and the Robin Jones Quartet as well as his own groups. A high-energy improviser with a refined chordal style, Selwyn has also contributed technical guitar columns to several British magazines. Ronny Jordan (pictured at the Town & Country Club, London, in 1992, above) achieved commercial success by pairing elements of Wes Montgomery's style and guitar sound with contemporary dance rhythms and rap.

CHRIS BURDEN **THE EUROPEAN SCENE**

EVERY COUNTRY IN EUROPE NOW HAS A CLUSTER OF JAZZ GUITARISTS. LARGELY CUT OFF FROM THE LUCRATIVE AMERICAN MARKET, THESE PLAYERS HAVE DRAWN ON THE CONTINENT'S OWN MUSICAL RESOURCES: GYPSY, GALLIC, SCANDINAVIAN AND CELTIC.

Whenever jazz guitar aficionados congregate and the talk turns to the great players, more often than not the names mentioned in reverential tones are of the great American legends. For these are the players who have, over the past 60 years or so, become familiar names to the jazz guitar enthusiast.

Since those pioneering days, names such as Eddie Lang, Dick McDonough, Carl Kress, Charlie Christian and later on Kenny Burrell, Jim Hall, Joe Pass and others have woven wondrous and sinuous paths through the American songbook. Along the way, they've transformed many great tunes into jazz standards that have become the mainstay of any self-respecting jazz outfit.

So deep has been the influence of these seminal players that we tend to forget that, since the 1930s, a parallel world of jazz guitar has existed on the other side of the Atlantic. This world has produced players of stature to rank alongside their American colleagues. For a number of reasons, however, many of their names – and indeed their very existence – are virtually unknown to the jazz guitar fraternity elsewhere in the world.

As the American pioneers of jazz guitar came to be known in Europe, first by word of mouth and then, as they became more and more available, on record, they inspired countless guitarists to take up this new and exciting music. Some kept strictly to the faith, others stamped their own individuality onto the music. However, while many of the American guitarists eventually conquered the world, almost all of their European cousins spent their musical lives in relative obscurity.

There were many reasons for this: lack of promotion over the years has meant that there has been, and still is, an ignorance of the European players in the rest of the world. This has been especially true in the US, historically the biggest market for jazz. Indeed, even today, the history of European jazz guitar, its development and personalities, is virtually unknown outside Europe itself. There are now, and have been, many world-class European jazz guitarists who have worked tirelessly from one corner of the continent to the other and beyond. To get the holy grail of wider promotion usually meant signing to a major label prepared to issue jazz guitar recordings, and until fairly recently, those weren't easy to find in Europe.

The US labels quite naturally tended to foster home-grown talent. As a consequence, very few European jazz guitarists, particularly in those early days, were offered recording contracts with the major American labels. The lucky few who did receive the exposure, including players such as the richly gifted René Thomas who recorded for the Jazzland label in America, found their profile sufficiently raised to lift them clear of the pack.

On the other side of the coin were the players who had none of these advantages. As in the US and elsewhere, many of these recorded for a myriad of tiny labels which sprang up and died almost without drawing breath. Historically, it wasn't until the arrival of such independent labels as SteepleChase, Demon, Hot Club and Enja that opportunity opened for the European jazz guitarist.

While many of the countries of Europe have produced one or more gifted jazz guitarists, that hasn't necessarily had anything to do with the size of the country. There have been many surprises. One musical influence that seems to have taken no account of national borders is the style of music known as "Gypsy". The nomadic lifestyle of the Gypsies meant that they have lived in nearly all of the countries of Europe. Their love of music, and of the guitar in particular, has meant that, from the time of Django Reinhardt onwards, their passion and eclecticism has reached out to touch almost all of the guitarists who followed, either knowingly or otherwise.

Perversely, one of the smallest countries in Europe has produced arguably the greatest of all European players. That country is Belgium and the player is Django Reinhardt, who is covered elsewhere in this book. To many people, this country is the birthplace of another truly world-class player, the wonderful Rene Thomas (1927-75). Thomas received early encouragement from Django but soon turned toward bebop, inspired by Charlie Christian recordings and then the stylings of Jimmy Raney and Jimmy Gourley, whom he met while working in Paris between 1949 and 1951. Like Christian, he played on a Gibson ES-150, creating a broad, clear tone. Capable of weaving intricate, boppish lines, Thomas always played with passion. His recorded performances of 'You've Changed' or 'Body And Soul' are jazz guitar balladry of the highest order.

One modern jazz guitarist in Belgium who has become an important and potent voice in jazz guitar around the world is Philip Catherine. Born in England to an English mother and Belgian father, Catherine (b.1942) started out under the influence of John McLaughlin and Larry Coryell but has since encompassed jazz-rock, bebop and other styles. He is, without doubt, one of Europe's most gifted modern players.

The Netherlands, meanwhile, has its own rich history of jazz guitar. This is an area steeped in the Gypsy tradition, to the extent that the jazz guitar community there has elevated Reinhardt into a god-like figure. This intensity of adulation for one player is certainly unknown anywhere else in Europe. Beyond that, though, the jazz guitar has continued to throw up great players. The name of Willem "Wim" Overgaauw (pronounced "Over-choe") is the one that has exerted the greatest influence. Overgaauw (1929-1995) was first-call guitarist in the 1950s and 1960s for all the visiting US jazzmen. He toured Europe with Wes Montgomery and later was instrumental in setting up his country's guitar education programme when he became tutor in jazz guitar at the famed Hilversum Conservatory. Overgaauw recorded several well-received albums for Columbia but somehow never got the recognition outside of Europe he undoubtedly deserved.

The Conservatory programme was a rich breeding ground for the young aspiring players in Holland and today, guitarists such as Jesse van Ruller and Maarten van Der Grinten owe a great debt to Overgaauw, who became their tutor and mentor.

Van Ruller (b.1972) is certainly one of the new names to watch. In 1995 he won the guitar section of the prestigious Thelonius Monk competition in

With the success of Pork Pie, the group which he formed with American saxophonist Charlie Mariano and Dutch keyboardist Jasper Van't Hof in 1973, Philip Catherine (above) became one of the best-regarded guitarists on the European scene. His extensive recording credits include albums with Chet Baker, Charles Mingus, Larry Coryell, Niels-Henning Orsted Pedersen, Birelli Lagrene, Stephane Grappelli and fellow-countryman and harmonica star, Toots Thielemans.

Washington DC and has since recorded a wonderful debut CD which highlights his bebop leanings. His friend Van der Grinten (they now play together as a duo) came to prominence when he recorded with four other guitarists (Louis Stewart, Doug Raney, Heiner Franz and Frédéric Sylvestre) as the European Jazz Guitar Orchestra. Another hard-swinging bebop player, Van der Grinten (b.1963) has also recorded a number of quirky CDs with one of his ensembles, The Van Der Grinten/Herman Quartet, which mixes guitar with C-melody saxophone, tuba and valve trombone.

The countries of Scandinavia have been rich breeding-grounds for jazz guitar, producing a string of world-class players. The family tree has at its head the godfather of Swedish jazz guitar, Rune Gustafsson, and goes on

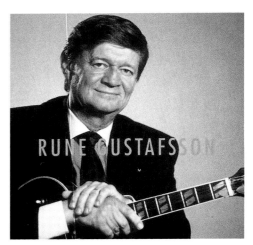

Belgian guitarist Rene Thomas had lived in Canada and then New York for five years when he returned to Europe in 1963 to perform with drummer Kenny Clarke at the Blue Note Club. Meeting Mister Thomas (above) was recorded with French musicians at that time. Jesse Van Ruller sustains interest throughout this 1997 CD (centre) as he twists and turns through a set of standards and originals with total assurance and a clear sense of purpose (and with excellent support from pianist Julian Joseph). Rune Gustafsson is the father figure of bebop guitar in Sweden, and this 1993 CD (right) showcases his work in quartet and duo formats.

down through Ulf Wakenius, Peter Almqvist and Staffan William-Olsson from Sweden, Doug Raney, the son of Jimmy Raney, who lives in Copenhagen, Jukka Tolonen from Finland and Pierre Dorge from Denmark.

Gustafsson (b.1933) is another icon on the European jazz guitar scene. He won awards in the US back in the early 1960s for his album *Move* and since that time has worked with some of the great names of European jazz including Arne Domnerus and Niels-Henning Orsted-Pedersen.

The Pedersen link goes on through Ulf Wakenius, one of the most exciting players to have emerged on the jazz guitar scene in Europe for many years. With his musical partner Peter Almqvist, Wakenius (b.1958) came to prominence in Guitars Unlimited in the late 1970s. This acoustic duo wowed audiences wherever they played and helped to establish both players as names to watch. Since then Wakenius has enjoyed a prominent association with Pedersen, before becoming guitarist for Oscar Peterson: a well-deserved accolade for a gifted player. Over the years, Wakenius has released albums that have ranged from jazz-rock to bebop to pure acoustic solo guitar. Such is his phenomenal facility on the instrument that Wakenius is at home in whichever style he chooses.

Peter Almqvist (b.1957), Wakenius' musical partner for many years in Guitars Unlimited, has become somewhat overshadowed by the former's success, but is a world-class bebop player in his own right with several excellent solo albums to his name.

One player sure to make his mark in the future is Staffan William-Olsson, who these days makes his home in Norway but hails originally from Sweden. As a member of his organ-based group, The Real Thing, and as a soloist,

William-Olsson takes his bebop leanings and adds that hard bite so typical of today's modern players. But he has such an innate drive and swing, plus the mainstream hallmark of a fat, warm sound, that he simply begs to be heard. Many of these Swedish players grew up in the same neighbourhoods in Gothenburg and Stockholm, went to the same schools, became great friends and digested the same musical influences. Without doubt, Sweden has a rich and continuing tradition of jazz guitar.

One of the great names of Scandinavian jazz guitar is Robert Normann (b.1916), who died only recently in 1998 at the age of 81. Normann has long been revered in Norway and is without doubt one of the country's most famous jazz luminaries. A shy, reclusive man, Normann was a gifted player who shunned the limelight, content to stay and work in his own country. This was a player who so impressed Django Reinhardt when he visited Norway in 1939 that, when he was asked back, he is reputed to have remarked, "What business do I have there? You have Robert Normann."

Normann's style is certainly unique: he plays three or four melodic lines at the same time, using elements of Russian Gypsy music, jazz and Norwegian folk music. After his long years out of the limelight, the jazz guitar world has recently started to realise in recent years what an original talent Robert Normann was. His recordings, now out on CD, bear testament to one of Europe's top players.

Doug Raney, son of jazz guitarist Jimmy Raney, was born in New York in 1956 but has made his home in Copenhagen, Denmark. Like many of the younger generation of jazz guitarists, he was weaned on a diet of Hendrix, Beck and Clapton before the influence of his father's music began to assert itself. In the late 1970s, he started to work with this father on club dates before coming to Europe both to perform and live. It soon became apparent that he had inherited much of his father's facility on the instrument and has long been acknowledged as a major talent in his own right.

Jukka Tolonen (b.1952) has almost singularly represented the Finnish jazz guitar scene since coming to prominence with well-known rock band Tasavallan Presidentti in 1969. Something of a recluse, Tolonen is a player of wide musical tastes who treads the line between rock and jazz very successfully although there are many who have felt that glimpses of the real man are seen in his gentle acoustic work with Danish guitarist Christian Sievert, with whom he first recorded in the late 1970s.

One of the finest bebop jazz guitarists in Europe, Louis Stewart emerged self-taught from the unlikely background of Irish showbands with a superb technical command of the guitar and a refined jazz sensibility. An authoritative improviser with a style that hints of the influence of Montgomery and Burrell, Stewart performs as a member of the European Jazz Guitar Orchestra, assembled by Heiner Franz.

Ireland is steeped in the lyricism and romanticism of Celtic music, and it seemed inevitable that it would throw up a world-class jazz guitarist. It did so in spades when Louis Stewart burst onto the European scene in the 1960s. Born in Waterford, Ireland, in 1944, Stewart's initial exposure to the guitar came through the recordings of Les Paul and Barney Kessel. After establishing a solid reputation around the Dublin area, which highlighted his potential, he cemented this in 1968 when he was voted Outstanding European Soloist at the Montreux Jazz Festival.

Shortly after that, he began a fruitful association with the legendary saxophonist Tubby Hayes, a move which brought him international exposure. Stewart is a richly-gifted, lyrical player seemingly at ease with all jazz guitar styles. He remains Ireland's one player of world renown, although in recent years several others, including the fine Dave O'Rourke, are beginning to be heard outside of the country.

France is another country steeped in the Gypsy tradition. Its players have brought to the guitar that touch of Gallic flair coupled with a good deal of idiosyncrasy. It's a country which loves jazz guitar, but in recent years it has swung away from bebop to embrace much more of the post-bop, hard bop and fusion trends that have also enveloped many of the jazz-loving countries of Europe. This is nowhere more apparent than in the astonishing rise of the Vietnamese fusion guitarist, Nguyên Lê, who has made his home in Paris and who has achieved considerable success both in France and world-wide. Lê is a player of brilliant facility on the instrument, and embraces a multitude of styles and effects which he hones into a whirlwind blend of fusion, bebop and everything in between. Listening to Nguyên Lê in full flight is not for the faint hearted.

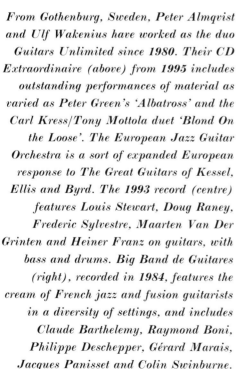

From Gothenburg, Sweden, Peter Almqvist and Ulf Wakenius have worked as the duo Guitars Unlimited since 1980. Their CD Extraordinaire (above) from 1995 includes outstanding performances of material as varied as Peter Green's 'Albatross' and the Carl Kress/Tony Mottola duet 'Blond On the Loose'. The European Jazz Guitar Orchestra is a sort of expanded European response to The Great Guitars of Kessel, Ellis and Byrd. The 1993 record (centre) features Louis Stewart, Doug Raney, Frederic Sylvestre, Maarten Van Der Grinten and Heiner Franz on guitars, with bass and drums. Big Band de Guitares (right), recorded in 1984, features the cream of French jazz and fusion guitarists in a diversity of settings, and includes Claude Barthelemy, Raymond Boni, Philippe Deschepper, Gérard Marais, Jacques Panisset and Colin Swinburne.

One of the most important figures to have emerged in France in recent times has been Christian Escoudé. Yet another player of Gypsy origin, Escoudé (b.1947) was, like most of the European players, influenced by Django Reinhardt but, like Django's son Babik, has generally veered away from the Gypsy style to embrace elements of bebop, although there is in his playing a very obvious Gypsy element. Nowhere is this melange of styles more apparent than in his recordings with bassist Charlie Haden, where Escoudé mixes textured layers of acoustic Gypsy lines with bebop overtones. Conversely, Escoudé has made several well-received pure Gypsy-style albums in the past which have shown his complete mastery of the instrument.

A pivotal player in French jazz guitar, Pierre Cullaz (b.1935) started playing in Paris in the late 1940s, performing with many of the seminal French jazz musicians of the period including Eddy Louiss, Martial Solal, Claude Bolling and Michel Hausser as well as prominent artists such as Sarah Vaughan and Art Simmons. An excellent teacher and a prolific writer and arranger, Cullaz was instrumental in forming the fine French jazz guitar group, Guitars Unlimited (not to be confused with the later Guitars Unlimited duo of Ulf Wakenius and Peter Almqvist) with Francis Lemageur, Raymond Gimenez, Victor Apicella and Tony Rallo, which recorded several excellent albums for the Barclay label in France.

Certainly the French have had a penchant for guitar big-bands. Apart from Guitars Unlimited, there have been several excellent outfits, such as the guitar quintet featuring Sacha Distel, Jimmy Gourley, Jean-Pierre Sasson, Henri Crolla and Jean Bonal, a veritable *Who's Who* of French jazz guitarists of the time. In the 1970s, Pierre Laurent got together a six-piece outfit that paid tribute to Django Reinhardt. But the largest of these bands was undoubtedly Gérard Marais' Big Band de Guitares which featured a stellar line-up of Marais, Claude Barthélémy, Jacques Panisset, Phillipe Gumpowicz, Colin Swinburne from the UK, Philippe Deschepper, Benoit Thiebergien and a young player who was to go on to become one of the mainstays of Heiner Franz's European Jazz Guitar Orchestra, Frederic Sylvestre.

Another rich vein of European jazz guitar has surfaced in Germany. Here jazz guitar has to a great extent taken on a hard post-bop edge, as exemplified by players such as Volker Kriegel, Michael Sagmeister and Norbert Scholly. In contrast, players such as Heiner Franz, Russ Spiegel, Paul Shigihara and Helmut Nieberle play in a more mainstream manner, mixing

 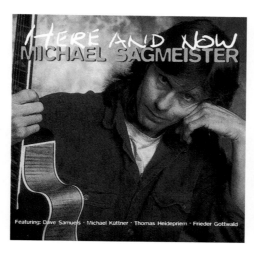 

bebop with acoustic and finger-style guitar. Volker Kriegel (b.1943) started playing at the age of 15 and within five years was leader of an outfit voted best band at a major amateur festival in Germany. It was whilst at University that Kriegel first began to meet players such as Albert Manglesdorff.

Shortly afterwards, his big break came when he was chosen for the guitar seat in vibraphonist Dave Pike's quartets. Although he acknowledges the influence of bebop players such as Jim Hall and Kenny Burrell, Kriegel has moved much more in recent years into the ground populated by players such as John Scofield and John McLaughlin.

Michael Sagmeister (b.1959) traded his expensive bike for a schoolmate's cheap guitar and set out on a road that would lead to his working with Pat Martino, Shakti and a host of other international musicians. Playing only rhythm guitar at first, Sagmeister soon developed a soft spot for Latin American music and, via the recordings of Carlos Santana, came under the influence of John Coltrane, Pat Martino and Wes Montgomery. Today, he is one of Germany's leading players, encompassing styles as diverse as neo-bop, fusion and the blues.

Norbert Scholly (b.1964) began playing in 1976, initially in acoustic guitar duos. In 1985, he won the prize for best soloist at the European Jazz Competition. Scholly really came to prominence, however, when he became the soloist for Germany's famous WDR Big Band, where he played alongside the likes of Benny Golson, Peter Erskine and Danny Gottlieb. Today, Scholly has his own group and has been playing and recording with the WDR in Madras and Bangalore with a host of prominent Indian musicians.

Bebop guitarist Heiner Franz (b.1946) can surely lay claim to being the

Christian Escoudé is always an interesting player, whether acknowledging his roots in the music of Django, following the bebop path or knocking on the door of the avant-garde. Escoudé recorded this 1994 CD (left) with a New York rhythm section and trumpeter Tom Harrell. Leading German guitarist Michael Sagmeister turns out an impressive set on acoustic guitar with a quintet featuring Dave Samuels on vibes and marimba for 1998's Here And Now (centre). Jaroslaw Smietana has been a leading figure on the Polish jazz scene for more than two decades, and the work of this good writer and interesting, versatile player is well represented on Sound & Colours (above) from 1987.

Guitarist Elek Bacsic at the Mars Club, Paris, with Art Simmons (piano) and Michel Gaudry (bass) in October 1960. A classically-trained violinist who switched to guitar, Bacsic had arrived from Budapest the previous year and worked in Paris until 1966, when he emigrated to the US.

only world-class jazz guitarist who started out as a Protestant cleric and theologian before turning to jazz, founding his own label (Jardis Records) and, most recently, making a line of fine arch-top jazz guitars. Franz is a melodic mainstream bebop player who has worked extensively with Ireland's Louis Stewart. Mainly at Franz's instigation, they founded the European Jazz Guitar Orchestra, which assembled and recorded for the first time in January 1993 in Franz's home town of Saarbrucken. Franz and Stewart have released a string of excellent CDs both as an acoustic duo and as a quartet.

Russ Spiegel was born in Los Angeles in 1962. After gaining a professional music scholarship from Berklee College in Boston, Massachusetts, he moved to Europe to live in 1988. Since then, he's worked tirelessly in Germany, culminating in his work with Barbara Dennerlein, Germany's best selling and most popular jazz artist. Very much in the jazz and blues vein, Spiegel has done arrangements for many of the leading German big-bands, as well as leading his own trio.

Paul Shigihara was born in Tokyo, Japan, in 1955. He started out learning classical guitar as well as Renaissance and Baroque lute music before moving to the US to study jazz guitar and composition at Berklee in 1983. Since then, Shigihara has worked extensively in the German studios as well as playing with world-class artists such as Charlie Mariano, Manfred Schoof, Sam Rivers and Klaus Doldinger. Today, Shigihara's musical direction has moved more towards finger-style jazz guitar and he has recently been appointed the new staff guitarist to the WDR Big Band in Cologne.

There has been a long tradition of jazz in what were the Eastern Bloc countries of Europe. Often suppressed by the authorities, the jazz movement nevertheless matured against the odds and has produced many fine players, including Hungary's Elek Bacsik, Jaroslaw Smietana in Poland and Rudolf Dasek in Czechoslovakia.

Elek Bacsik is undoubtedly the best known of the Eastern European players. Born in Hungary in 1926, he is another player of Gypsy stock. Initially trained on the violin, which he studied at the Budapest conservatory, it wasn't until the mid 1940s that he took up the guitar. Bacsik lived in Paris for a number of years before finally moving to the United States in 1966. Throughout a long career, he has proved that to be one of the best and most eclectic of all the players to have emerged from Eastern Europe.

In Poland, where jazz also became a symbol of rebellion, the name of Jarek Smietana has long been at the forefront of jazz guitar. Another player of diverse musical interests, Smietana has led many groups in Poland, including the excellent Extra Ball, the Symphonic Sound Orchestra and the Polish Jazz Stars Band, as well as playing with artists such as Freddie Hubbard, Joe Zawinul, John Abercrombie, Jack Wilkins and Mike Stern. A prolific writer, Smietana has composed over 200 jazz tunes and recorded 23 albums as leader.

At the heart of Europe, Czechoslovakia has produced a number of jazz artists of international repute. Guitarist Rudolf Dasek plays with a strong, urgent attack and an ear for "out" harmonies. Born in Prague in 1933, Dasek has gathered elements of classical Spanish guitar, Moravian folk music and contemporary classical music.

He first came to prominence in the early 1960s when he played in the progressive group S & H Quartet, which occasionally included pianist Joachim Kuhn. In the early 1970s, Dasek recorded a number of excellent albums for the Supraphon label with such luminaries as John Surman, Barre Phillips and Stu Martin. In the early 1980s, he worked in a duo with German guitarist Toto Blanke. Dasek remains Czechoslovakia's most famous jazz guitarist.

Given the huge ethnic mixture of the countries of Europe, it is inevitable that jazz guitar has so many varied styles and interpretations of the genre. In the US, jazz had its roots in the blues, from which sprang the elements of swing guitar, bebop and fusion. Today, the rise of the seven-string style is pushing the boundaries of the instrument as never before.

The Europeans have taken that heritage and added the romanticism of the Celts, the lyricism of the Gallic races, the drive and excitement of the Gypsies and the hard-edge of the Scandinavians to produce a distinctive offshoot – a mix of mainstream jazz with the many strands and diversities of ethnic folk music that pervade each individual country on the European continent.

Dave Brubeck's 'Blue Rondo A La Turk' builds up the tension in 9/8 time, only to release into a grooving 12-bar blues on Elek Bacsik's classic version. He is accompanied by the redoubtable rhythm section of Pierre Michelot (bass) and Kenny Clarke (drums).

THE AMERICAN SCENE

SOME OF THE NEW GENERATION OF AMERICAN PLAYERS ARE GOING TO EXTREMES IN THE INSTRUMENTS THEY USE. OTHERS, THOUGH, HAVE CHOSEN TO STICK WITH THE ESTABLISHED TECHNOLOGY AND MAKE THEIR INNOVATIONS PURELY MUSICAL.

The lure of TV and a regular wage has diverted the talented guitarist Kevin Eubanks (opposite) from a more precarious career in jazz.

The jazz guitar metamorphosises itself daily, breaking down barriers not only in music, but also as an instrument.

At one time jazz guitar meant the arch-top instrument, and the genre was bebop. But with jazz entering its second century, the old categories of style and type of guitar look all but redundant. Charlie Hunter and Steve Masakowski push the envelope with innovative instruments, while players such as Joe Diorio and Ron Affif stretch the musical boundaries of jazz using the same kind of guitars as Wes Montgomery and Charlie Christian.

When Wayne Krantz and Leni Stern play jazz, their Fender Strats offer a sonic pallette that blazes with signal processing. Wolfgang Muthspiel, meanwhile, divides his time between creating his own form of eclectic jazz and writing classical overtures. Kevin Eubanks burns the midnight oil with sounds that would have made Jimi proud, but on his albums it's the jazz guitarist that cuts through. Mark Whitfield and Royce Campbell are reminiscent of times gone by, but with that certain something that defines them as players who are a cut above the norm, heading in their own direction. Today's players have a style that gives us a foretaste of the jazz guitar of tomorrow.

Steve Masakowski's roots are firmly grounded in the jazz tradition, but a strong creative sense and innovative streak permeates his playing, his compositions and his arrangements. While so many jazz musicians gravitate to the East or West Coasts to build their careers, Masakowski has steeped himself in the fertile music scene of New Orleans, drawing from it and enriching it, both as a player and as an associate professor at the University of New Orleans. Since the early 1990s, his talents have brought him wider recognition, including accolades from *Downbeat* and *Jazz Times*, but his reputation dates back to the mid 1970s when he could be heard jamming with pianist Ellis Marsalis and other leading New Orleans musicians. Later he was to co-lead a quartet, Fourplay, with guitarist Emily Remler. And from the late 1980s he has performed or recorded with pianist Mose Allison, vocalist Dianne Reeves and saxophonist Rick Margitza, and tours internationally with the New Orleans group Astral Project.

His 1993 release *What It Was* placed him firmly on the map, highlighting his considerable skills as a composer and arranger. But it took *Direct AXEcess*, from 1995, to reveal the true scope of his instrumental powers and the varied elements of his style, for instance his creative use of harmonics and his fluent octave passages in homage to Wes Montgomery, with the occasional tip of the hat to Joe Pass. Using a baritone seven-string guitar built for him by master luthier Jimmy Foster, Masakowski creates textures and lush chordal voicing that simply could not be achieved on a conventional six-string instrument. He

With roots in the work of Montgomery and Benson, Mark Whitfield (right) gained solid experience with organist Brother Jack McDuff's combos. A series of albums for Warner and Verve have enabled him to establish his own identity as a jazz artist, and on Forever Love (above) from 1997 Whitfield – sometimes sensitive, sometimes swinging – more than justifies the orchestral accompaniment while exploring a set of classic songs of love and loss.

doesn't flaunt the seven-string, however, but employs it creatively in a way that makes the listener realise something special and different is going on.

Charlie Hunter is a jazz innovator, both for the music he plays and for the instrument he plays it on. His guitar is a unique eight-string invention, built and co-designed by Ralph Novak, a master luthier from the San Francisco Bay Area. The bottom three strings are the low EAD of the bass guitar and the top five are the ADGBE of the standard six-string guitar. With individual pickups for each set, he runs the three bass strings through one amplifier and the five guitar strings through another. Another unusual feature is that the frets are not laid straight across the neck but are arranged in an oblique pattern like a fan, giving each string its own unique scale length. The aim is to enhance the bass tones at the bottom end and retain the tonal qualities of a normal guitar on the top strings. More recently he has added a similar ten-string instrument to his working collection.

With Charlie Hunter in the band, a bass player is quite superfluous, as this unusual guitarist lays down the bass lines as well as the chords and the single-note lines. His initial interests on the guitar centred on the finger-style concepts of Joe Pass and Tuck Andress, but he became intrigued by the ability of jazz organists to maintain a bass line with their feet while simultaneously playing chords and melodic lines with their hands. Setting out to emulate this approach, he was influenced by the organ stylings of Jimmy Smith, John Patton and Larry Young, and he experimented first with a seven-string guitar before settling for the eight-string and later the ten-string varieties. Hunter uses his right-hand thumb to play the bass lines and his four fingers for the chords and melodic line. He views his instrument from an organ perspective rather than from a guitarist's point of view. While this split musical orientation may seem somewhat bizarre, for this jazz guitar innovator it not only makes sense, it is the only way he practices, performs and creates.

With an approach that combines an awareness of the dance styles of the late 1990s with the clamouring, bluesy, gospel-flavoured organ jazz of the 1960s, Hunter's initial appeal was to younger audiences. But his popularity soon spread to a larger and more diverse jazz audience. His maxim is "to put on a good live show and play music people can groove to". The policy has clearly worked for him as he moves to a new millennium, still in his early thirties and one of Blue Note Records' best-selling artists, with four successful album releases in the late 1990s and more than 200 live dates a year.

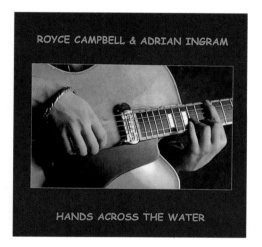

Hunter's 1998 album *Pound For Pound* sets the standard for the music he wants to create. Moving that year from Berkeley, California, to Brooklyn, New York, he had teamed up with New York vibraphonist Monte Croft and drummer Willard Dyson. Together they blend the new with the traditional and serve it up with a fresh jazz guitar sound that might be mistaken for a Hammond B3 organ, but could actually only come from Charlie Hunter. His music may be technically demanding to play, but it is easy to listen to.

As guitarist on NBC's *The Tonight Show* since 1992, Kevin Eubanks has one of the highest profiles of any guitarist in America, performing to an audience of millions, five nights a week. In 1995, with Branford Marsalis's departure to pursue other professional interests, he was promoted to musical director and sidekick to the programme's host, comedian Jay Leno.

Although this demanding position has effectively pushed his jazz career into second place, Eubanks was already a seasoned jazz veteran with 14 albums behind him, not to mention stints with jazz luminaries like Art Blakey, Roy Haynes and McCoy Tyner. Born in 1957 into a musical family (his uncle Ray Bryant is a distinguished jazz pianist and his brother Robin Eubanks is a leading jazz trombonist), he started on violin before switching to

On his 1992 album Turning Point (left) Kevin Eubanks performs his own compositions with two different rhythm teams, showcasing his individual approach on both acoustic and electric guitars. One of the few women in jazz guitar, Leni Stern has developed her own individual voice. On Like One (centre) from 1993 she is teamed with Bob Malach (tenor sax), Didier Lockwood (violin), Russ Ferrante (keyboards), Alain Caron (bass) and Dennis Chambers (drums). Former Henry Mancini sideman Royce Campbell and British jazz guitar guru Adrian Ingram trade solos on Hands Across The Water (above), a 1998 set of standards and originals, accompanied by bass and drums.

guitar. He soon came under the influence of John McLaughlin, and later Wes Montgomery. Like Wes, Kevin chooses to play without a pick. His use of his thumb on melodic passages gives him his trademark sound – a beautiful, clear, round tone – and he makes effective use of classical finger-style in his compositions. That does not, however, stop him from doing Hendrix covers and playing with a fierce intensity that John McLaughlin would admire.

Eubanks has performed with artists as varied as bassists Dave Holland and Ron Carter, trombonists Slide Hampton and Robin Eubanks, composer Mike Gibbs and drummers Marvin Smitty Smith and Mark Mondesir. The breadth of this guitarist's jazz artistry is displayed on his CD, *Turning Point*.

Wolfgang Muthspiel's original improvisations on his own harmonically adventurous compositions make him a fresh, distinctive voice in jazz guitar. Born in Austria in 1965, the young Wolfgang, like Kevin Eubanks, studied violin for several years before switching to classical guitar. The music of Pat Metheny and Keith Jarrett brought him to jazz, although his main influences were to be Bill Evans, Keith Jarrett and Miles Davis. After studying at the Musichochschule in his native Graz, he enrolled at the New England Conservatory and then at Berklee College of Music, where his mentors were to be guitarist Mick Goodrick and vibraphonist Gary Burton.

At the urging of John Scofield and Pat Metheny, Burton auditioned Muthspiel for his own band and was so impressed that he invited him to fill the guitar chair that had been vacant since the departure of Pat Metheny, 12 years previously. Burton also produced Wolfgang's next album *The Promise*, which remains a landmark Muthspiel recording with its all-star cast: Peter Erskine, John Patitucci, Richie Beirach and Bob Berg.

A Muthspiel performance is a journey through the mind of an unusual composer who is also a brilliant guitarist. He brings to his music a vocabulary that extends far beyond the boundaries of jazz and indeed he has composed music for the Schubert String Quartet and the Ensemble of New Music of Zurich. His *Drei Tonspiele For Guitar* have been published by Doblinger, Vienna. According to Mark Small of *Berklee Today* magazine,"The guitar has still not witnessed a counterpart to the brass world's Wynton Marsalis – a virtuoso musician equally adept at jazz and classical. Perhaps that will change as more of Wolfgang Muthspiel's ambitions become a reality."

Leni Stern was born Magdalena Thor in Munich, Germany, and started playing guitar as a teenager drawn to the sounds of Jimi Hendrix, Joni Mitchell and the Beatles. Even though music was always part of her life during these years, drama was her focal point. She achieved some success as an actress appearing in German television and many theatrical productions. As her acting career flourished, her penchant for composition was taking root.

In 1976 she entered Berklee College of Music where she was introduced to the styles of Wes Montgomery, Jim Hall, Keith Jarrett, Bill Evans and Pat Metheny. Bill Frisell, a fellow-student at this time, introduced her to Mike Stern, whom she married in 1980, moving to New York City when Mike joined Miles Davis's band. Since that time Leni has established herself as a formidable contender in the New York jazz scene and recorded a series of well-received albums including *Clairvoyant*, *Secrets* and *Ten Songs*. Her sophisticated harmonic style and strong melodic sense, and her use of a Fender Stratocaster, contribute to her distinctive playing.

Leni Stern has also made her mark as a composer and singer/songwriter, most notably on her 1999 album *Recollections*. Her book-and-CD text

Seeking the facility of an organist to play basslines, chords and melody simultaneously, Charlie Hunter (opposite) added two strings to his guitar to give him three bass strings and five treble. Hunter's eight-string guitar wizardry is evident on 1998's Return Of The Candyman (above) as this compelling innovator lays down the grooves and provides his own bass lines.

Composing And Composition casts light on her musical concepts. A career highlight was her duo with guitarist Wayne Krantz on the album *Separate Cages*, in which the innovative pair explored the outer reaches of contemporary jazz harmony.

Wayne Krantz, the polyrhythmic chord-melody fusion guitarist, is in a league all his own. On all his albums he plays high-intensity rhythmic solos that would make Thelonious Monk nod in approval, but his tour de force was his 1995 release, *2 Drinks Minimum*. He often solos in a chord-melody style, not in the usual jazz tradition but with more of a contrapuntal groove. "My chords are always melodically driven and the voicings that happen are really being developed on the spot from multiple notes in the scale of the moment," he says. "Because of my pick-and-fingers technique I can get a type of counterpoint going that many times will sound chordal, but I am thinking of it in a melodic way as opposed to a more block or grip style approach."

In 1986 Krantz joined Carla Bley's band and in 1991 he released *Signals*, his first album as leader. He joined forces with Leni Stern for the critically acclaimed duo album *Separate Cages* and two more as leader, *Long To Be Loose* and *2 Drinks Minimum*. Active internationally as a teacher throughout the 1990s, he also performed and recorded with a range of artists including the Brecker Brothers, Billy Cobham and Michael Formanek. Wayne was the guitarist for the 1996 Steely Dan world tour, and in November 1997 he began working on the first Steely Dan studio album in 20 years. In spite of this high-profile activity, his own trio remains his priority.

Mark Whitfield's jazz guitar roots lie in the mainstream genre of Wes Montgomery and George Benson, but with an added twist that informs the listener that his style is still developing and there is still more to come. His parents were big-band aficionados and the sounds of Duke Ellington and Count Basie were familiar to him at an early age. In 1983, at 16, he entered Berklee College of Music where he honed his craft and jammed with Branford Marsalis. In 1987 he headed for New York City to develop his career.

Whitfield established a mentor/protege relationship with George Benson which opened doors to the more established jazz players of the Big Apple. Since 1987 he has been a sideman with Brother Jack McDuff, Art Blakey, Donald Harrison and of course George Benson himself. As a leader he recorded three albums on the Warner Brothers label and four more with Verve. In 1998 he released an instructional video.

Mark is able to deal effectively with a wide range of musical contexts. On his album *Forever Love*, which features inventive string arrangements, he masterfully adapts a large orchestral setting to a swinging improvisational groove. With bassist Christian McBride and trumpeter Nicholas Payton he interprets the challenging compositions of Herbie Hancock on the trio album *Fingerpainting*. Still young, Mark is now a fixture in the jazz guitar community with much more in store.

Ron Affif is truly one of the young lions of the jazz guitar scene, with fire-breathing technique and a voracious passion for his music. His original inspirations were his uncle Ron Anthony, an established West Coast jazz guitarist, and legendary trumpeter Miles Davis, a personal friend of his professional prizefighter father. With these two influences, his destiny was shaped at a very early age. In 1984 he moved to California, performing with Jack Sheldon and many Californian jazz stalwarts. In 1992 he joined the Pablo record roster and now has five albums as leader.

Since moving to New York in 1989, Anthony has had a gig at the famed Manhattan Zinc Bar, and has worked with pianist Billy Mays and vocalist Sheila Jordan. With the soul of an artist and the heart of a prizefighter, Ron Affif is quickly making his mark in jazz guitar.

Royce Campbell is best known as Henry Mancini's guitarist, holding that prestigious position from 1975 until Mancini's death in 1994. Although he cites Wes Montgomery as his main influence, horn players such as Dexter Gordon and Chet Baker are easily recognised in Royce's warm, fluid sound and horn-like approach to changes. In 1998 he became a Benedetto Player, performing with other guitarists who use the celebrated luthier's instruments.

Campbell's forte is to bring together the cream of the jazz guitar world

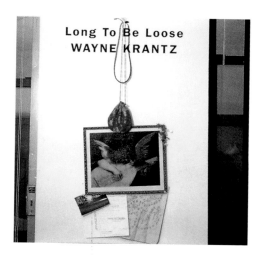

and to produce and perform in albums with them. In 1993 he produced *Project G-5, A Tribute To Wes Montgomery* which also featured legendary guitarists Tal Farlow, Jimmy Raney, Herb Ellis and Cal Collins. His 1994 album *6X6* featured guitarists Pat Martino, John Abercrombie, Larry Coryell, Dave Stryker and Bucky Pizzarelli.

With *Project G-5, A Tribute To Joe Pass*, in 1999, he combined the talents of Charlie Byrd, Gene Bertoncini, Mundell Lowe and John Pisano. With nine albums as leader and more than 30 as a sideman, his personal favourite is *A Tribute To Henry Mancini*. "It was such a wonderful experience playing with Mancini all those years," he says. "He was a kind, generous man and a great musician. Playing his music all those years helped make my composing and improvising more melodic, since Mancini was such a master of melody."

Joe Diorio has always been the consummate creative guitarist, often eschewing commercial projects for those of a more artistic nature. With almost 20 albums as leader, he is also a much sought-after sideman, garnering credits on hundreds of others. From his first successful album in the early 1960s, *Exodus In Jazz* with Eddie Harris, to the delightfully understated 1998 release *To Jobim With Love*, Joe displays the provocative sound and essence that is his trademark. Joe is not only a masterful player, but also a thoughtful and inspiring teacher who does not forget tradition, but expands upon it.

In his intructional book-and-CD *Fusion* he demonstrates, over a series of standard chord progressions, two solos – the first along conventional bebop lines and another that utilises an intervallic approach and contemporary harmonic devices. This is a unique resource for students, but also an insight into the mind of one of jazz guitar's most radical thinkers.

Wayne Krantz has gradually brought to centre stage an unusual chord-melody styling set in a contemporary context, as on this 1993 album Long To Be Loose (left). Joe Diorio is always a sophisticated improviser with a different spin when compared to other players, and on To Jobim With Love (centre) from 1996 applies his considerable solo guitar powers to 17 of Jobim's best. Ron Affif has the chops and uses them to good effect on this stimulating 1995 bebop workout (above).

RECOMMENDED LISTENING

This is a list of recommended records, compiled by the contributors to this book. It is certainly not a complete discography: rather, it is designed to help your quest for new listening pleasures and to supplement the information to be found in the body of *Masters Of Jazz Guitar*. Many entries are self-explanatory, some come with a note or two. Check the index to find more about a particular artist.

The guitarists are arranged in alphabetical order. The recommended recordings are listed in the following order: first, recommended records made by that player as leader; then recommended records made as co-leader ("With..."); then appearances on recommended records by other artists. Everything is alphabetical.

The listings show artist (where relevant), then album title (in *italics*) or, rarely, piece title (in 'single quotes'). In brackets are given the label and where available a date or dates. The date given is generally the date of the recording(s) and/or original release, although occasionally (and we hope obviously) it is a reissue date. A number of records have of course been available on different labels over the years. Where we know about these, multiple label names are separated by slashes. But always be on the look-out for the same artist or a specific title on a label other than those listed.

JOHN ABERCROMBIE
Getting There (ECM 1987)
Speak Of The Devil (ECM 1993)
Timeless (ECM 1974)
With Royce Campbell *6X6* (1994) See the Royce Campbell entry for more.
Jack DeJohnette New Directions *In Europe* (ECM 1979)
Gateway *Gateway 2* (ECM); *Homecoming* (ECM 1994)
Ron McClure *McJolt* (SteepleChase 1989)

RON AFFIF
Ringside (Pablo 1997)

HOWARD ALDEN
With George Van Eps *13 Strings* (Concord 1991)
With Frank Vignola & Jimmy Bruno *Concord Jazz Guitar Collective* (Concord 1995)

OSCAR ALEMAN
Speciales Guitares Volume 1 1937-1945 (Jazz Time 1992)
Swing Guitar Legend (Rambler 1938-45)

LAURINDO ALMEIDA
Braziliance Volume 1 (Pacific 1953)
Bud Shank *Baa-Too-Kee* (Giants Of Jazz)

FRANK ANASTASIO
With Serge Camps & Angelo Debarre *Gypsy Guitars* (Hot Club Records 1989)
Exciting French Gypsy guitar trio.

TUCK ANDRESS
Reckless Precision (Windham Hill 1990)
Recorded solo (no overdubs), Andress's 'Grooves Of Joy' and 'Stella By Starlight' are awesome.
With Tuck & Patti:
Paradise Found (Windham Hill 1998)
Celebrates the 20th year of the partnership of guitarist Andress and vocalist Patti Cathcart. The formula hasn't changed, but the music is as strong as ever.
Tears Of Joy (Windham Hill 1988)
Their debut release embraces finger-popping funk and beautiful jazz balladry, and raised the stakes for every jazz-inclined guitar-and-vocals duo.

ELEK BACSIK
The Electric Guitar Of The Eclectic Elek Bacsik (Fontana 1962)
His best: a virtuostic and truly inventive display, mixing bebop with Gypsy and pure acoustic guitar.

BADEN POWELL
Afro Sambas (JSL 1991)
Canto on Guitar (MPS 1970)
Live At The Rio Jazz Club (Caju 1990)
Live In Hamburg (Acoustic Music 1983)
Seresta Brasileira (Caju 1991)
Three Originals: Tristeza On The Guitar; Poema On Guitar; Apaixonado (MPS Master Series 1968/75)

DEREK BAILEY
Solo Guitar Volume 1 (Incus 1971)
Solo Guitar Volume 2 (Incus 1991)
With Arcana (Tony Williams and Bill Laswell) *The Last Wave* (DIW 1995)
With Tony Oxley *Tony Oxley Quartet* (Incus 1992)

DUCK BAKER
Clear Blue Sky (Acoustic Music Records 1995)

GEORGE BARNES
Plays So Good (Concord 1994)
Two Guitars And A Horn (Stash 1962)
With Carl Kress *Town Hall Concert* (United Artists 1963)
Ruby Braff & The George Barnes Quartet *Play Gershwin* (Concord 1974)

BILLY BAUER
Lenny Tristano 'Crosscurrent' (Capitol 1949)
Bauer's most successful collaboration with the iconoclastic Cool School pianist Tristano, this is an often mesmerising example of the guitarist's independence of approach and melodic conception as well as his sensitivity to very demanding surroundings.

BILLY BEAN
With John Pisano *Makin' It Again* (String Jazz Recordings 1999); *Take Your Pick* (Decca 1958)

JEFF BECK
Blow By Blow (Epic 1975)
Wired (Epic 1976)
Stanley Clarke *Journey To Love* (Nemperor 1975)
John McLaughlin *The Promise* (Verve 1995)
Stevie Wonder *Talking Book* (Tamla Motown 1972)

GEORGE BENSON
All Blues (Prestige 1973)
Blue Bossa (Prestige 1973)
Breezin' (Warner Brothers 1976)
Benson's passport to stardom, this jazz-funk record took the guitarist out of the jazz clubs and put him into stadiums. The technique he developed for playing in unison with his Stevie Wonder-like voice gave a familiar idiom a warm and mellow atmosphere. But if the jazz edge is missing, those guitar lines still duck and weave intriguingly.
The New Boss Guitar (Original Jazz Classics 1964)
Benson in his organ-band overdrive, working with his old boss Jack McDuff. The title is an intentional reference to a Wes Montgomery classic; the pieces motor along irresistibly, the blues feel is almost constant, and Benson's sharp yet swinging soloing continually adds sparkle.
White Rabbit (CTI/Epic 1992)
With Earl Klugh *Collaboration* (Warner Brothers 1987)

PIERRE BENSUSAN
Bamboule (Acoustic Music Records 1993)

WILL BERNARD
Medicine Hat (Antilles)

PETER BERNSTEIN
With Ed Cherry, Russell Malone, Dave Stryker, Mark Whitfield *A Tribute To Grant Green* (Evidence 1996)

ED BICKERT
At Toronto's Bourbon Street (Concord 1983)
Ed Bickert (CCD/PM 1975)
Mutual Street (Innovation/Jazz Alliance 1984)
Third Floor Richard (Concord 1989)
Ruby Braff *With The Ed Bickert Trio* (Sackville 1979)
Paul Desmond *Like Someone In Love* (Telarc 1975)
Largely demonstrating Bickert's ability to create attractive, intimate music with small groups: *Mutual Street* pairs him with valve-trombonist Rob McConnell (shades of Jim Hall and Bob Brookmeyer); on others Bickert's trio backs two supreme melodic improvisers, Paul Desmond and Ruby Braff.

LUIZ BONFA
The Bonfa Magic (Caju 1971)
Non Stop To Brazil (Chesky 1989)
Sambolero (Blue Moon)

JOSHUA BREAKSTONE
Let's Call This Monk! (Double-Time 1997)
9 By 3 (Contemporary 1990)
Self Portrait In Swing (Contemporary 1989)

LENNY BREAU
The Legendary Lenny Breau ... Now! (Soundhole 1979)
Breau unaccompanied and recorded in Chet Atkins's house. All the extraordinary technical advances the guitarist had explored are clearly audible, along with an understanding and creative development encompassing a wide variety of different genres, including jazz and flamenco.

TEDDY BUNN
Complete Pete Johnson/Earl Hines/Teddy Bunn (Blue Note)
The Port of Harlem Jazzmen (Blue Note 1994)
The Spirits Of Rhythm *The Spirits Of Rhythm 1933-34* (JSP)

KENNY BURRELL
The Concord Jazz Heritage Series (Concord 1977-96)
Ellington is Forever (Fantasy 1975)
Another brilliant Burrell set with an expanded band, this one specialising in Ellington classics – recorded the year after the maestro's death. 'Caravan', 'Take The A Train' and 'C-jam Blues' are all there, plus a blues medley that's precisely up the guitarist's street. Joe Henderson is present on tenor, and Jimmy Smith adds to the excitement on organ.
Guitar Forms (Verve 1965)
One of the finest and most ambitious of all Burrell albums, with charts arranged by Gil Evans, and in the company of an illustrious big-band including saxophonists Lee Konitz and Steve Lacy. Fine balance between the ambiguities and atmosphere of Evans's writing and Burrell's direct and bluesy feel.
Live At The Village Vanguard (Muse/Charly 1959)
Midnight Blue (Blue Note 1963)

CHARLIE BYRD
Brazilian Byrd: Music Of Antonio Carlos Jobim (Columbia 1965)
Great Guitars (Concord 1976)
Byrd, Barney Kessel and Herb Ellis
Latin Byrd (Milestone 1962-3)
The Return Of The Great Guitars (Concord 1996)
Byrd, Mundell Lowe, Herb Ellis, plus Larry Coryell on some tracks.
Stan Getz & Charlie Byrd *Jazz Samba* (Verve 1962)
With Royce Campbell *Project G-5: A Tribute To Joe Pass* (1999) See the Royce Campbell entry for more.

ROYCE CAMPBELL
Project G-5: A Tribute To Joe Pass (1999)
With Campbell, Gene Bertoncini, Charlie Byrd, Mundell Lowe, John Pisano.
Project G-5: A Tribute To Wes Montgomery (1993)
With Campbell, Cal Collins, Herb Ellis, Tal Farlow, Jimmy Raney.
6X6 (1994)
With Campbell, John Abercrombie, Larry Coryell, Pat Martino, Bucky Pizzarelli, Dave Stryker.

SERGE CAMPS
With Frank Anastasio & Angelo Debarre *Gypsy Guitars* (Hot Club Records 1989) See the Frank Anastasio entry for comment.

STEVE CARDENAS
Tom Coster *From The Street* (JVC 1996)

LARRY CARLTON
Larry Carlton (Warner Brothers 1978)
Larry Carlton Collection (GRP 1990)
Representative compilation from *Alone/But Never Alone*, *Sleepwalk*, *Discovery*, *Friends* and *On Solid Ground*.
The Crusaders *Those Southern Knights* (MCA 1976)
Steely Dan *The Royal Scam* (ABC 1976)

GREG CARMICHAEL
Acoustic Alchemy *Back On The Case* (GRP 1991); *Positive Thinking* (GRP 1998); *Red Dust And Spanish Lace* (MCA 1987). See the Nick Webb entry for comments.

AL CASEY
Buck Jumpin' (Prestige/Original Jazz Classics 1960)
Fats Waller *The Last Years 1940-43* (Bluebird)

OSCAR CASTRO-NEVES
More Than Yesterday (JVC)

PHILIP CATHERINE
Catherine-Escoudé-Lockwood Trio (Grammavision 1983)
I Remember You (Criss Cross 1991)
Live (Dreyfus 1997)
Sleep, My Love (CMP 1979)
With Chet Baker *There'll Never Be Another You* (Timeless 1997)

EUGENE CHADBOURNE
With Shockabilly *Shockabilly Live...Just Beautiful* (Shimmy Disc)
With 2000 Statues *The English Channel* (Parachute)

ED CHERRY
With Peter Bernstein, Russell Malone, Dave Stryker, Mark Whitfield *A Tribute To Grant Green* (Evidence 1996)

PETE CHILVER
Bebop In Britain (Esquire 1948-53)
Fluent, boppish lines from Chilver on four 1948 tracks with a young Ronnie Scott on tenor sax.

CHARLIE CHRISTIAN
Christian lived before the invention of the long-playing album and all his recordings were made for 78rpm shellac discs. Over the years since his death innumerable selections from these have been issued around the world in a variety of formats. Find all the pieces listed below (across several discs) and you will have a collection of some of his finest recorded work. Many of the Goodman tracks are on the excellent Charlie Christian *Genius Of The Electric Guitar* CD (Columbia/CBS 1987).
Benny Goodman & His Orchestra 1941 'Solo Flight'.
Benny Goodman Sextet 1939-40: 'AC/DC Current'; 'Flying Home'; 'Gone With "What" Wind'; 'Rose Room'; 'Stardust'; 'Seven Come Eleven'; 'Soft Winds'; 'Till Tom Special'.
Benny Goodman Septet 1940: 'As Long As I Live'; 'Benny's Bugle'; 'Breakfast Feud'; 'Royal Garden Blues'; 'A Smooth One'; 'Waiting For Benny'; 'Wholly Cats'.
Benny Goodman Septet (With Lester Young) 1939: 'Ad-Lib Blues'; 'Charlie's Dream'; 'Lester's Dream'; 'I Never Knew'.
Edmond Hall Celeste Quartet 1941: 'Jammin' In Four'; 'Profoundly Blue'.
Kansas City Six (*Spirituals To Swing* concert at Carnegie Hall): 'Good Morning Blues'; 'Paging The Devil'; 'Way Down Yonder In New Orleans'.
Metronome All-Stars 1941 'Bugle Call Rag'.
Minton's Playhouse Sessions 1941: 'Charlie's Choice'; 'Down On Teddy's Hill'; 'Stompin' At The Savoy'; 'Up On Teddy's Hill'.

DAVE CLIFF
Sipping At Bells (Spotlite 1995)
When Lights Are Low (Zephyr 1997)

JOHN COLLINS
The Incredible John Collins (Nilva)
With the Nat King Cole Trio *The Complete Capitol Trio Recordings* (Mosaic 1942-61)

LARRY CORYELL
Spaces (Vanguard 1970)
Listen on the memorable 'Spaces (Infinite)' for Coryell and John McLaughlin jousting against a background of rock textures and rhythms.
With Royce Campbell *6X6* (1994) See the Royce Campbell entry for more.
The Gary Burton Quartet *Duster* (RCA 1967)
Eleventh House *Introducing Eleventh House* (Vanguard 1972); *At Montreux* (Vanguard 1974)
Mike Mantler *Movies* (Watt 1980)

PEPPINO D'AGOSTINO
A Glimpse Of Times Past (Acoustic Music Records)

BILL DE ARANGO
Bill De Arango (EmArcy 1954)
Anything Went (GM 1993)

ANGELO DEBARRE
With Frank Anastasio & Serge Camps *Gypsy Guitars* (Hot Club Records 1989) See the Frank Anastasio entry for comment

AL DIMEOLA
Cielo e Terra (Manhattan/One Way 1985)

Inspired by Julian Bream, focuses on the acoustic guitar and combines excellent performances with some highly original writing.
World Sinfonia – Heart of the Immigrants (Tomato/Mesa 1993)
Celebrates his friendship with Astor Piazzolla and features several of the tango master's compositions including 'Nightclub 1960' and 'Tango 11'. A landmark in DiMeola's recording career.
With John McLaughlin & Paco de Lucia *Passion Grace And Fire* (Philips/Columbia 1982) See the John McLaughlin entry for comment.

JOE DIORIO
To Jobim With Love (RAM 1995)

LATCHO DROM
Live In Madrid (Scalen)
La Verdine (Musiques du Soleil)
One of the new Gypsy sensations: pure, exciting gypsy music in the Hot Club Quintet style.

MARC DUCRET
Un Certain Malaise (ScrewU 1997)
In the Grass (Enja 1996)

CHARLES ELLERBEE
Ornette Coleman *Body Meta* (Artists House 1975); *Dancing in Your Head* (A&M 1975); *Of Human Feelings* (Antilles 1979)

HERB ELLIS
Concord Jazz Heritage Series (Concord 1998)
Great Guitars (Concord 1976)
Byrd, Barney Kessel and Herb Ellis.
Herb Ellis Meets Jimmy Giuffre (Verve 1959)
Man With A Guitar (Dot)
The Midnight Roll (Epic 1962)
Nothin' But The Blues (Verve 1957)
The Return Of The Great Guitars (Concord 1996)
Byrd, Mundell Lowe, Herb Ellis, plus Larry Coryell on some tracks.
Roll Call (Justice 1991)
Softly, But With That Feeling (Verve 1961)
Soft Shoe (Concord 1974)
With Royce Campbell *Project G-5: A Tribute To Wes Montgomery* (1993) See the Royce Campbell entry for more.
With Stan Getz & Oscar Peterson *Stan Getz & The Oscar Peterson Trio* (Verve 1957)
With Freddie Green *Rhythm Willie* (Concord 1975)
Jazz At The Philharmonic Volume 17 (new Volume 10) (Verve)
With Joe Pass *Seven Come Eleven* (Concord Jazz 1973); *Two For The Road* (Pablo/Original Jazz Classics 1974)
With Oscar Peterson Trio *At the Concertgebouw* (Verve 1957); *Eloquence* (Limelight 1965); *At The Stratford Shakespearean Festival* (Verve 1956)
With Stuff Smith *Together!* (Epic/Koch 1963)
Various Artists *Jazz Giants 1958* (Verve 1958)

RON ESCHETE
Rain Or Shine (Concord 1995)

CHRISTIAN ESCOUDE
Catherine-Escoudé-Lockwood Trio (Grammavision 1983)
Hell's Kitchen (Verve Gitanes 1995)
Plays Django Reinhardt With Strings (Verve Gitanes/Emarcy)
One of the top world-class Gypsy players offers lovely workings of a host of Django tunes with a string backing.

JOHN ETHERIDGE
Ash (Voiceprint 1994)
Sweet Chorus (Dyad 1998)
Django-inspired stylings with some fine acoustic solo performances.

KEVIN EUBANKS
Spirit Talk (Blue Note 1993)
Spirit Talk 2: Revelations (Blue Note 1995)
Turning Point (Blue Note 1992)
With Mino Cinelu & Dave Holland *World Trio* (VeraBra/Intuition 1995)

TAL FARLOW
Autumn In New York (Verve 1954)
Chromatic Palette (Concord 1981)
Fuerst Set (Xanadu 1957)
Interpretations Of Tal Farlow (Verve 1955)
Poppin' & Burnin' (Verve)
The Return of Tal Farlow (Original Jazz

Classics 1969)
A Sign Of The Times (Concord 1977)
The Swinging Guitar Of Tal Farlow (Verve 1956)
Just as its title suggests, Tal is in bubbling form: this is a jazz-guitar classic.
Tal (Verve 1956)
Tal Farlow: Verve Jazz Masters 41 (Verve 1995)
CD compilation from several albums 1954-8 presenting an excellent overview.
Tal Farlow Quartet (Blue Note 1953)
This Is Tal Farlow (Verve 1958)
A recent and welcome CD reissue: Farlow at his peak.
With Royce Campbell *Project G-5: A Tribute To Wes Montgomery* (1993) See the Royce Campbell entry for more.
Red Norvo Trio *Move!* (Savoy 1951); *Legendary Trio Volume 2: The Norvo- Mingus-Farlow Trio* (Vintage Jazz Classics 1943-50)
Artie Shaw *The Last Recordings* (Music Masters 1954)

RAPHAEL FAYS
La Nuit des Gitans (Sony)
Superb CD from one of the hottest Gypsy players of recent years.

BOULOU FERRE
With Elios Ferré *Pour Django* (SteepleChase)
Excellent CD from the brothers Ferré which has become a classic of the genre.

ELIOS FERRE
With Boulou Ferré *Pour Django* (SteepleChase) See the Boulou Ferré entry above for comment.

BARRY FINNERTY
Space Age Blues (Hot Wire 1982-96)
Straight Ahead (Arabesque 1994)
The Brecker Brothers *Heavy Metal Bebop* (Arista 1978); *Straphangin'* (Arista 1981)
The Crusaders *Street Life* (MCA 1979)

ANTONIO FORCIONE
Dedicato (Naim 1996)
This mix of solo acoustic guitar performances and band tracks with sax and vocals offers a satisfying variety of contexts and moods.
Acoustic Mania *Talking Hands* (Naim 1997)
Two virtuoso players, Forcione and Neil Stacey explore everything from Zawinul's 'Birdland' and McLaughlin's 'David' to Gismonti's 'Karate' and Monti's 'Czardas' with wit, depth and imagination.

ROBBEN FORD
Handful Of Blues (Blue Thumb 1995)

HEINER FRANZ
Louis Stewart *In A Mellow Tone* (Jardis 1992) See the Louis Stewart entry for comment.

BILL FRISELL
Before We Were Born (Elektra Musician 1988)
Bill Frisell Quartet (Nonesuch 1996)
Rambler (ECM 1984)
Ginger Baker *Falling Off The Roof* (Atlantic 1996); *Going Back Home* (Atlantic 1994)
Joey Baron *Down Home* (Intuition 1997)
Marc Johnson *Bass Desires* (ECM 1985)
Paul Motian *Bill Evans* (JMT 1990); *On Broadway Volume 2* (JMT 1989)

FRED FRITH
Gravity (Ralph Records 1980)
Guitar Solos (Caroline 1974)

BARRY GALBRAITH
After Hours Jazz (Epic)
Guitar And The Wind (Decca 1958)
Tal Farlow *The Tal Farlow Album* (Norgran 1954)
Instructional book/CD sets *Guitar Comping* (Jamey Aebersold); *Guitar Improv* (Jamey Aebersold)
Gil Evans *Into The Hot* (Impulse 1961)

FRANK GAMBALE
Chick Corea's Elektric Band *Beneath The Mask* (GRP 1991)
Tom Coster *Let's Set The Record Straight* (JVC 1993)
GRP Super Live In Concert (GRP 1987)
Mark Varney Project *Centrifugal Funk* (Legato 1991); *Truth In Shredding* (Legato 1990)

JERRY GARCIA
Ornette Coleman *Virgin Beauty* (Columbia Portrait 1988)

ARV GARRISON
Charlie Parker *The Legendary Dial Masters Volume 1* (Stash 1945-7); *On Dial - The Complete Sessions* (Spotlite/Dial 1945-7)

EGBERTO GISMONTI
Dansa dos Escravos (ECM 1989)
Sol Do Meia Dia (ECM 1977)

MICK GOODRICK
Biorhythms (CMP 1990)
In Pas(s)ing (ECM 1978)
Jack DeJohnette *Audio-Visualscapes* (MCA 1988); *Irresistible Force* (MCA 1987)
Goodrick+Liebman+Muthspiel *In The Same Breath* (CMP 1995)
Gary Thomas *By Any Means Necessary* (JMT 1989)

GRANT GREEN
Born To Be Blue (Blue Note 1962)
Ike Quebec is on tenor saxophone on this terrific session which shows how emotional and at the same time economical in effect Green could be. As well as Green and the redoubtable Quebec, the sensitivity and variation of the young Sonny Clark on piano is a standout.
Green Street (Blue Note 1961)
Idle Moments (Blue Note 1963)
Some of the best jazz guitar-playing of the early 1960s is here in Green's mixture of muscular force, confidence and melodic ingenuity. In long improvised outings Green doesn't repeat himself –as he was to later and his interpretation of John Lewis's 'Django' is superb. The sidemen include the great saxophonist Joe Henderson and vibraharpist Bobby Hutcherson.
Street Of Dreams (Blue Note 1964)

TED GREENE
Solo Guitar (Professional Music Products)

TINY GRIMES
Callin' The Blues (Prestige/Original Jazz Classics 1958)

MARTY GROSZ
Songs I Learned At My Mother's Knee And Other Low Joints (Jazzology 1994)
With Wayne Wright *Goody Goody* (Aviva 1979)

HARALD HAERTER
Intergalactic Maidenballet Gulf (Tiptoe 1992-4)

JIM HALL
Alone Together (Original Jazz Classics 1972)
Concierto (CBS/Columbia 1975)
Jazz Guitar (Pacific 1957)
Panorama – Live At The Village Vanguard (Telarc 1997)
With Bill Frisell & Mike Stern *Dialogues* (Telarc 1995)
With Pat Metheny *Jim Hall & Pat Metheny* (Telarc 1999)
Paul Desmond Quartet *East Of The Sun* (Discovery 1959)
Bill Evans *Undercurrent* (Blue Note 1962); *Intermodulation* (Verve 1966)
Jimmy Giuffre *Trav'lin' Light* (Atlantic 1958)
Interesting combination of sax, trombone and guitar.
Chico Hamilton Quintet *Spectacular* (Pacific 1955)
Sonny Rollins *The Bridge* (RCA/Bluebird 1962)
George Shearing *First Edition* (Concord 1981)

MICHAEL HEDGES
Aerial Boundaries (Windham Hill 1984)

SCOTT HENDERSON
Dog Party (Mesa 1994)
Tom Coster *The Forbidden Zone* (JVC 1994)
Tribal Tech *Face First* (Bluemoon 1993); *Illicit* (Bluemoon 1992); *Nomad* (Relativity 1988); *Reality Check* (Mesa/Bluemoon 1995); *Spears* (Passport 1986); *Tribal Tech* (Relativity 1990)
Zawinul Syndicate *The Immigrants* (CBS/Columbia 1988)

JIMI HENDRIX
Are You Experienced (Polygram 1967)
Axis: Bold As Love (Polygram 1967)
Electric Ladyland (Polygram 1968)
Listen out for Hendrix's authentic blues playing, his Wes Montgomery-like use of octaves (on the single 'Purple Haze') and his avant-garde use of feedback or using a solo played backwards as accompaniment

(on 'Are You Experienced', or 'Castles In The Sand' on *Axis*). There has always been more to Hendrix than meets the ear, and Miles Davis was one of the first jazz musicians to reap the benefit of this.

ALLAN HOLDSWORTH
Metal Fatigue (Enigma 1985)
None Too Soon (Cream 1996)
Bill Bruford *Feels Good To Me* (Polydor Deluxe 1977)
Mark Varney Project *Truth In Shredding* (Legato 1990)
Chad Wackerman *Forty Reasons* (CMP 1991)

CHARLIE HUNTER
Pound For Pound (Blue Note 1998)

IKE ISAACS
Intimate Interpretations (IIM 1992)
Superb solo performances of standards that showcase his harmonic depth.

RON JACKSON
Guitar Thing (Muse 1991)
Song For Luis (Master Mix)

LONNIE JOHNSON
Blues In My Fingers (Indigo 1920s/30s)
Hot Fingers (Catfish 1920s/30s)
Each of these compilations contains some (but neither has all) of the Johnson-Eddie Lang duets; both have the fine guitar solos 'Playing With The Strings' and 'Away Down In The Alley Blues'.
Playing With The Strings (JSP 1927-40)
Bypasses the duets but includes Johnson's collaborations with Armstrong, Ellington and The Chocolate Dandies.
Steppin' On The Blues (Columbia 1925-32)
Another useful compilation.

LAURENCE JUBER
LJ (Acoustic Music Records)

VIC JURIS
The Music Of Alec Wilder (Double Time 1996)

BARNEY KESSEL
Autumn Leaves (Black Lion 1969)
Feeling Free (Contemporary/Original Jazz Classics 1969)
Great Guitars (Concord 1976)
Byrd, Barney Kessel and Herb Ellis.
Just Friends (Sonet 1973)
Let's Cook! (Contemporary 1957)
The Poll Winners (Contemporary/Original Jazz Classics 1957)
The Poll Winners Ride Again (Contemporary/Original Jazz Classics 1958)
Some Like It Hot (Contemporary/Original Jazz Classics 1959)
To Swing Or Not to Swing (Contemporary/Original Jazz Classics 1955)
Hampton Hawes *Calendar Girl* (Liberty)
Julie London *Julie Is Her Name* (Capitol/Liberty 1955)
With Red Mitchell *Two Way Conversation* (Sonet 1973)
Charlie Parker *The Legendary Dial Masters Volume 1* (Stash 1945-7)
On Dial - The Complete Sessions (Spotlite/Dial 1945-7)

STEVE KHAN
Crossings (Verve Forecast 1993)
Evidence (Arista Novus 1980)
Eyewitness (Antilles 1981)
Tightrope (CBS 1977)
With Rob Mounsey *Local Colour* (Denon 1987)
Steely Dan *Gaucho* (MCA 1980)

EARL KLUGH
The Best Of Earl Klugh (Warner Brothers 1991)
A good representative collection spanning Klugh's period with Warners from 1984.
Fingerpainting (Blue Note 1977)
One of Klugh's strongest albums from early in his early recording career, both for his writing and his guitar work.
With George Benson *Collaboration* (Warner Brothers 1987)
Superb album: the presence of Benson and the rhythm-team of Marcus Miller and Harvey Mason inspire Klugh to some of his most creative work on record.

RECOMMENDED LISTENING (*continued*)

NICLAS KNUDSEN
Human Beat Boxer (Stunt 1997)

WAYNE KRANTZ
2 Drinks Minimum (Enja 1995)
With Leni Stern *Separate Cages*

CARL KRESS
Two Guitars And A Horn (Stash 1962)
Various Artists *Pioneers Of The Jazz Guitar* (Yazoo 1928-37)
With George Barnes *Town Hall Concert* (United Artists 1963)
With Dick McDonough *Guitar Genius In The 1930s* (Jazz Archives 1934-7)

VOLKER KRIEGEL
Volker Kriegel Trio (Atlantic)
Excellent album from one of Europe's top fusion players.

FAPY LAFERTIN
Fleur de Lavende (Hot Club Records 1991)
Hungaria (Le Jazzetal 1996)

BIRELI LAGRENE
Live In Marciac (Dreyfus 1994)
Routes To Django (Jazzpoint/Antilles 1980)
Standards (Blue Note 1992)

EDDIE LANG
A Handful Of Riffs (ASV Living Era 1927-8)
Jazz Guitar Virtuoso (Yazoo 1927-32)
Good introductions to Lang's work as a soloist; the former is less well remastered.
Joe Venuti *Violin Jazz 1929-1934* (Yazoo)
Has some of Lang's delectable work with the violinist's Blue Four and Blue Five – music as redolent of the 1920s as Betty Boop.

NGUYEN LE
Million Waves (ACT 1994)
Tales From Vietnam (ACT 1996)
Three Trios (ACT 1996)

PHIL LEE
Twice Upon A Time (Cadillac 1987)

PETER LEITCH
Colours And Dimensions (Reservoir 1995)
A Special Rapport (Reservoir 1993)

MUNDELL LOWE
California Guitar (Famous Door 1974)
The Incomparable Mundell Lowe (Dobre)
The Mundell Lowe Quintet (Riverside)
Mundell Lowe Presents Transit West (Pausa 1983)
The Return Of The Great Guitars (Concord 1996)
Lowe, Herb Ellis, Charlie Byrd, plus Larry Coryell on some tracks.
Souvenirs (Concord/Jazz Alliance 1977/92)
With Royce Campbell *Project G-5: A Tribute To Joe Pass* (1999) See the Royce Campbell entry for more.
Andre Previn Trio *Jazz At The Musikverein* (Verve 1995)
Sarah Vaughan *After Hours* (Blue Note 1961)

REGGIE LUCAS
Miles Davis *Agharta* (Columbia 1975); *Pangaea* (Columbia 1975)
Here Davis glimpses the far side of the moon with these two misunderstood yet key albums that took the essence of Hendrix's avant-garde urges to the limit.

IVOR MAIRANTS
Duets And Guitar Group – Focus On Ivor Mairants (Zodiac cassette only)

RUSSELL MALONE
Black Butterfly (Columbia 1993)
Russell Malone (Columbia 1992)
Sweet Georgia Peach (Impulse 1998)
With Peter Bernstein, Ed Cherry, Dave Stryker, Mark Whitfield *A Tribute To Grant Green* (Evidence 1996)
Diana Krall *Love Scenes* (Impulse 1997)

PAT MARTINO
All Sides Now (Blue Note 1997)
Footprints (Muse/32 Jazz 1975)
Strings! (Original Jazz Classics 1967)
One of Martino's earliest, confirming his lineage from Grant Green and Wes Montgomery, and rarely far from the blues. But familiar material and instrumentation do not hamper Martino's fresh voice.
Head And Heart (32 Jazz 1974)
A compilation from two of Martino's sets for Muse records, working with trios. The materials are simple and uncluttered, but that's just the formula Martino likes and is able to fill with his dynamism and clarity of line. His work on Coltrane's 'Impressions' is startling, and he slices the blandness out of guitar samba with his Latin account of 'Along Came Betty'.
With Royce Campbell *6X6* (1994) See the Royce Campbell entry for more.

STEVE MASAKOWSKI
Direct AXEcess (Blue Note 1995)

DICK McDONOUGH
Various Artists *Pioneers Of The Jazz Guitar* (Yazoo 1928-37)
With Carl Kress *Guitar Genius In The 1930s* (Jazz Archives 1934-7)

JOHN McLAUGHLIN
Extrapolation (Polydor 1969)
A neglected classic of jazz-rock that pointed to how McLaughlin would help shape the music of Miles Davis and Tony Williams's Lifetime.
My Goal's Beyond (CBS/Douglas 1970)
Playing on an Ovation over his own pre-recorded accompaniments, McLaughlin turns out impassioned performances on Mingus's 'Goodbye Pork Pie Hat', Miles Davis's 'Blue In Green', Chick Corea's 'Waltz For Bill Evans' and his own 'Follow Your Heart'.
The Promise (Verve 1995)
Time Remembered (Verve 1993)
Interesting if perhaps not wholly successful project presenting the music of pianist Bill Evans with McLaughlin playing solo acoustic guitar to the accompaniment of four classical guitarists, the Aighetta Quartet.
With Miles Davis *Aura* (Columbia 1985); *Bitches Brew* (Columbia 1969); *In A Silent Way* (Columbia/CBS 1969); *Jack Johnson* (Columbia/CBS 1971).
With Al DiMeola & Paco de Lucia *Passion Grace And Fire* (Philips/Columbia 1982)
The trio at its peak with a truly collaborative performance and strong individual statements. Highlights are de Lucia's 'Sichia', McLaughlin's 'David' and the title track penned by DiMeola.
With The Mahavishnu Orchestra *The Inner Mounting Flame* (Columbia/CBS/Legacy 1971); *Birds of Fire* (Columbia/CBS 1973); *Between Nothingness & Eternity* (Columbia/CBS 1974)
Inner Mounting Flame set a blueprint of jazz-rock in stone, as McLaughlin changed the face of modern guitar-playing with his blitzkreig technique. But he also set in motion the Guitar Olympics – where speed and flash were exploited at the expense of content – that eventually undid the promise of jazz-rock.
With Tony Williams Lifetime *Emergency!* (Verve 1969); *Turn It Over* (Verve 1970)
Emergency is one of the great albums in jazz, not only for its apocalyptic vision of what the music could become but for some seat-of-the-pants playing that is the very essence of improvisation.

PAT METHENY
As Falls Wichita, So Falls Wichita Falls (ECM 1981)
Bright Size Life (ECM 1976)
Pat Metheny Group (ECM 1979)
Question And Answer (Geffen 1989)
Rejoicing (ECM 1984)
Another biting improvisatory jazz outing in a trio with strong Ornette connections, featuring Charlie Haden (bass) and Billy Higgins (drums).
Secret Story (Geffen 1992)
An ambitious themed project that does not always quite work, but provides an important directional pointer in his work.
Song X (Geffen 1985)
No pastel shadings here. This take-no-prisoners meeting with Ornette Coleman, one of the icons of free jazz, blasts away any stereotypes of Metheny's playing that the Group may have created.
Travels (ECM 1982)
A good showcase for the way the Group was evolving as an international phenomenon, with the strong Brazilian accent now more readily apparent.
80/81 (ECM 1981)
The first real taste of Metheny as a straight jazz improviser, showing his stuff in some serious company.
Charlie Haden *Beyond The Missouri Sky* (Verve 1997)
Some listeners find this too understated, but the delicate and nostalgic interplay of Metheny's guitar and Haden's bass is hauntingly beautiful.

FRANCIS-ALFRED MOERMAN
Passion (Iris Musique)
The best to date from an under-exposed player in the true Gypsy tradition.

WES MONTGOMERY
Bumpin' (Verve 1965)
The best of his more pop-inclined recordings.
The Complete Riverside Recordings (Riverside 1959-63)
Only for those with a hefty wallet, but this 12-CD set contains a disproportionately high proportion of his greatest jazz recordings.
Far Wes (Pacific Jazz 1958-9)
A good taster of his early work with brothers Monk and Buddy.
Full House (Riverside 1962)
The first of his great live albums, teamed with saxman Johnny Griffin and the Wynton Kelly Trio.
Fusion! Wes Montgomery With Strings (Riverside 1963)
Has more of a genuine jazz feel than the later orchestral albums.
Impressions: The Verve Jazz Sides (Verve 1964-6)
A valuable two-CD survey of his releases for the label, with the emphasis on jazz.
The Incredible Jazz Guitar Of Wes Montgomery (Riverside 1960)
The essential studio album. Captures his style and sound on ballads, blues and up-tempo bop to perfection.
Movin' Along (Riverside 1960)
The middle release in a trio of classic studio sets, this quintet album has suffered a little by comparison, but should not be passed over.
Smokin' At The Half Note (Verve 1965)
Another essential live set, again with the Wynton Kelly Trio.
So Much Guitar! (Riverside 1961)
Features the guitarist in a fine quintet, and on a rare solo ballad outing.

OSCAR MOORE
Oscar Moore & Friends (Fresh Sounds)
With the Nat King Cole Trio *The Complete Capitol Trio Recordings* (Mosaic 1942-61)

TONY MOTTOLA
Various Artists *Fun On The Frets* (Yazoo)

JIM MULLEN
Rule Of Thumb (EFZ)
Morrissey-Mullen *Badness* (Beggars Banquet 1981)

WOLFGANG MUTHSPIEL
Loaded, Like New (Amadeo 1995)
The Promise (Verve)

NICHOLAS
Love Cry Want *Love Cry Want* (New Jazz 1972)

BERN NIX
Ornette Coleman *Body Meta* (Artists House 1975); *Dancing in Your Head* (A&M 1975); *Of Human Feelings* (Antilles 1979)

ROBIN NOLAN
Robin Nolan Trio *Street* (RNT)

ROBERT NORMANN
Best Of Robert Normann (Hot Club)

MARY OSBORNE
A Memorial (Stash 1959-81)

REMO PALMIER
Remo Palmier (Concord 1978)
Dizzy Gillespie *Groovin' High* (Savoy 1945-6)
Various Artists *Small Groups: Night in Tunisia* (Giants of Jazz)

JOE PASS
Blues Dues (Original Jazz Classics 1984)
Interesting Pass solo date, partly because it proves how little live performance interfered with his remarkable musicality and focus, and partly for a rare concentration on the blues. In an interesting choice of pieces, Pass makes inventive use of the possibilities of Thelonious Monk's 'Round Midnight', a deceptive tune on which to improvise that suggests there could have been a more rugged and unsentimental Joe Pass trying to get out.
Chops (Original Jazz Classics 1978)
An accurately-titled record: "chops" is jazz-speak for virtuosity, and in this duo set with bassist Niels-Henning Orsted-Pedersen that's exactly what's on display. The revelling in technique can overpower the music, but the contrast in sound and texture between these two makes it work.
Finally (Emarcy 1992)
A late-period recording for both Pass and bassist Red Mitchell, and a resourceful and poignant guitar-bass duet. On ballads like 'I Thought About You' the reflective nature of the music almost suggests they'll disappear into a fascinating reverie and stop altogether.
Joy Spring (Pacific 1964)
A rare early Pass session and in his favourite pre-solo setting of a piano trio. The repertoire is bebop, and as well as the title track the disc includes bop anthems like 'Relaxin' At Camarillo' which Pass cruises through with sustained and eloquent ease. Though the guitarist's harmonically-rich and multi-layered style isn't required in a situation like this, it's evident that most of his skills are in place.
Virtuoso (Pablo 1973)
Pass's first and most famous journey into the world of unaccompanied guitar performance, delivering a set of standards with exquisite tenderness and care. The richness of texture, coupled with the sense of momentum imparted by his simultaneous rhythm effects, show just why this approach to the instrument hypnotised guitarists of all kinds.

LES PAUL
The Complete Decca Trios – Plus (MCA 1936-47)
The Legend & The Legacy (Capitol 1948-57)
Jazz At The Philharmonic *The First Concert* (Verve 1944)

JOHN PISANO
Among Friends (Pablo 1995)
Pisano teams up with guitar-playing buddies, including Joe Pass, Lee Ritenour and Phil Upchurch.
With Royce Campbell *Project G-5: A Tribute To Joe Pass* (1999) See the Royce Campbell entry for more.

BUCKY PIZZARELLI
With Royce Campbell *6X6* (1994) See the Royce Campbell entry for more.
With Scott Hamilton *The Red Door* (Concord 1998)
With John Pizzarelli *Complete Guitar Duos* (Stash 1980-4)
Zoot Sims *Elegiac* (Storyville 1980)

JOHN PIZZARELLI
All Of Me (BMG Novus 1992)
Dear Mr Cole (BMG 1994)
With Bucky Pizzarelli *Complete Guitar Duos* (Stash 1980-4)

BADEN POWELL
See under Baden

JOE PUMA
Shining Hour (Reservoir 1984)
With Chuck Wayne *Fourmost Guitars* (ABC Paramount ?date)

RAPHAEL RABELLO
Dois Irmãos (Caju)

DOUG RANEY
Raney 96 (SteepleChase 1996)
Raney turned 40 when this set was released, and sounds all the better for it.

JIMMY RANEY
The Complete Jimmy Raney in Tokyo (Xanadu 1976)
Guitaristic (Swing 1974)
Here's That Raney Day (Black & Blue 1980)
The Influence (Xanadu 1975)
Jimmy Raney (Jamey Aebersold Play-a-Long series Volume 20 1979)
Jimmy Raney Quartet (Prestige 1954)
Jimmy Raney Visits Paris Volume 1 (BMG 1953)

The Master (Criss Cross 1983)
Momentus (Pausa 1974)
Play Duets with Jimmy Raney (Jamey Aebersold
Play-a-Long series Volume 26 1981)
Strings & Swings (Choice/Muse 1957/69)
Too Marvellous For Words (Biograph 1954)
Two Jims & A Zoot (Mainstream 1964)
Wisteria (Criss Cross 1986)
With Royce Campbell *Project G-5: A Tribute To Wes
Montgomery* (1993) See the Royce Campbell entry
for more.
With Jim Hall *Street Swingers* (Pacific)
Stan Getz *The Complete Roost Recordings*
(Roulette/Roost 1950-4); *Early Stan* (Original Jazz
Classics 1949-53);
Phil Woods *Early Quintets* (Prestige/Original Jazz
Classics 1954)
Various Artists including Jimmy Raney Quintet
Americans In Sweden 1949-1954 Volume 2
(Metronome)

ERNEST RANGLIN
Below The Bassline (Island Jamaica Jazz 1996)
Caribbean classics like The Congos 'Congo Man',
Toots & The Maytals '54-46 (Was My Number)' and
Burning Spear's 'Black Disciples' show how close
Ranglin is to his roots in this vigorous set. But it
includes some of the world's leading jazz musicians,
including Ira Coleman on acoustic bass, Idris
Muhammad on drums and Monty Alexander on
piano. It's a measure of the breadth and generosity
of Ernest Ranglin's talents.

DJANGO REINHARDT
Over the years since his death innumerable
selections from Reinhardt's many, many recordings
have been issued around the world in a variety of
formats. We can but groan inwardly and quote *The
Penguin Guide To Jazz On CD*: "The Reinhardt
discography is now as mountainous as his native
Belgium is flat... There are huge numbers of
compilations on the market, some of them of
questionable authority and quality, often
inaccurately dated and provenanced and with only
notional stabs at accurate personnels." You might
try at the very least:
Django's Music (Hep 1940-2)
Django Reinhardt 1935-36 (Classics)
Djangology 1949 (Bluebird)
Pêche a la Mouche (Verve 1947/53)
Swing From Paris (ASV 1935-9)
Swing Guitar (Jass 1945-6)

LULU REINHARDT
With Titi Winterstein Quintet *Titi Winterstein
Quintet* (Boulevard)
Underexposed group featuring this excellent
guitarist: pure Gypsy music.

EMILY REMLER
Retrospective Volume One: Standards (Concord
1981-8)
Retrospective Volume Two: Compositions (Concord
1981-8)
This Is Me (Justice 1990)

LEE RITENOUR
Alive In LA (GRP 1997)
Ritenour pays tribute to one of his early influences,
the great Wes Montgomery.
Stolen Moments (GRP 1990)

HOWARD ROBERTS
Mr Roberts Plays Guitar (Verve 1981)
The Real Howard Roberts (Concord 1977)

ROMANE
Quintet (Iris Musique)
Samois-sur-Seine (Arco-Iris 1998)
Romane is still one of the few today who sticks
mainly to the Reinhardt tradition.

STOCHELO ROSENBERG
Seresta (Hot Club Records 1989)
Long acknowledged as one of the finest Gypsy
releases of recent years.

RAY RUSSELL
Rites And Rituals (Columbia 1970)

TERJE RYPDAL
Blue (ECM 1986)
The Chasers (ECM 1985)
Skywards (ECM 1996)

Terje Rypdal (ECM 1972)
Waves (ECM 1973-77)
Whenever I Seem Far Away (ECM 1974)
With David Darling *Eos* (ECM 1984)
With Jan Garbarek *Afric Pepperbird* (ECM 1970);
Sart (ECM 1971)
With The Lounge Lizards *Big Heart: Live In Tokyo*
(Antilles/Island)
Marc Ribot *Rootless Ballad For What's His Name*
(Disques Du Crépuscule); *Cosmopolitans* (Antilles);
Don't Blame Me (DIW); *Marc Ribot Y Los Cubanos
Postizos* (Atlantic)

MICHAEL SAGMEISTER
Here And Now (Acoustic Music Records 1998)

SAL SALVADOR
Boo Boo Be Doop (Capitol/Affinity 1954)
Sal Salvador Quartet/Quintet (Blue Note)
World's Greatest Jazz Standards (Stash 1983)
With Stan Kenton *New Concepts Of Artistry In
Rhythm* (Capitol 1952)

JOHN SCOFIELD
Blue Matter (Gramavision 1986)
Electric Outlet (Gramavision 1984)
Flat Out (Gramavision 1988)
Hand Jive (Blue Note 1993)
Meant To Be (Blue Note 1990)
Shinola (Enja 1981)
Still Warm (Gramavision 1985)
Who's Who (Arista Novus 1979)
Chet Baker *You Can't Go Home Again* (A&M
1977)
Billy Cobham *Funky Thide Of Sings* (Atlantic 1975)
Miles Davis *Decoy* (Columbia 1983-4)
Mike Gibbs *Big Music* (Virgin Venture 1988)
Marc Johnson *Bass Desires* (ECM 1985)
Gary Thomas *By Any Means Necessary* (JMT 1989)

BOLA SETE
Black Orpheus (Verve c1963)
Vince Guaraldi *Live At El Matador* (Fantasy 1966)

SONNY SHARROCK
Ask The Ages (Axiom 1991)
With Last Exit *The Noise Of Trouble - Live In Tokyo*
(Enemy 1987)
With Nicky Skopelitis *Faith Moves* (CMP 1989)

PAUL SHIGIHARA
Tears Of Sound (Nabel)

JOHNNY SMITH
Jazz Studio One (Decca)
A rarity: Smith in the company of several soloists
from the Count Basie Orchestra.
Johnny Smith (Verve 1967)
Johnny Smith Plays Jimmy Van Heusen
(Roost/Studio One/Decca)
Moonlight In Vermont (Roulette 1952)
Contains the famous collaborations between Smith
and saxophonists Stan Getz, Paul Quinichette and
Zoot Sims.
With George Van Eps *Legends* (Concord 1994)

NEIL STACEY
Acoustic Mania *Talking Hands* (Naim) See the
Antonio Forcione entry for comment.

LENI STERN
Clairvoyant (Passport 1986)
Closer To The Light (Enja 1989)
Recollections (1999)
Secrets (Enja 1988)
Ten Songs (Lipstick 1992)
Words (Lipstick 1995)

MIKE STERN
Between The Lines (Atlantic 1996)
Is What It Is (Atlantic 1994)
Upside Downside (Atlantic 1986)
Bob Berg *Cycles* (Denon 1988); *Short Stories*
(Denon 1987)
Miles Davis *We Want Miles* (CBS 1981)

LOUIS STEWART
Baubles, Bangles And Beads (Wave 1976)
Duets with bassist Peter Ind.
In A Mellow Tone (Jardis 1992)
Lovely acoustic jazz-guitar duets with Heiner Franz,
the empathetic pairing creating melodic, mainstream
jazz guitar.
Louis The First (Hawk Jazz 1975)

Recorded in Dublin, Stewart's debut as a leader
includes a stunning interpretation of 'Here's That
Rainy Day'.
Overdrive (Hep 1994)

JACQUES STOTZEM
Fingerprint (Acoustic Music Records 1997)

DAVE STRYKER
Blue To The Bone (SteepleChase 1996)
A strong example of the guitarist's hard-hitting style
in an expanded ensemble setting.
With Peter Bernstein, Ed Cherry, Russell Malone,
Mark Whitfield *A Tribute To Grant Green*
(Evidence 1996)
With Royce Campbell *6X6* (1994) See the Royce
Campbell entry for more.

GABOR SZABO
Spellbinder (Impulse 1966)
Szabo's unorthodox approach to melody and
enduring curiosity about jazz structure give a
unique flavour to this uneven but often intriguing
set of standards and originals.

MIROSLAV TADIC
J. Kühn/M. Nauseef/T. Newton/M. Tadic *Let's Be
Generous* (CMP 1990)

MARTIN TAYLOR
Artistry (Linn 1992)
Produced by Steve Howe. The confirmation of
Taylor's brilliance as a solo performer. 'Polka Dots
And Moonbeams' is explored with sensitivity and
harmonic depth; a funky backbeat is applied to
'Day Tripper'; and Taylor unleashes his total
approach to the guitar on an awesome 'They Can't
Take That Away From Me'.
Sarabanda (Gaia 1987)
Recorded in Nashville, Taylor sailing with relaxed
ease over a grooving rhythm section which includes
bassist John Patitucci. Also here, a duet with
Stephane Grappelli, and a beautiful solo version of 'I
Remember Clifford'.
Spirit Of Django (Linn 1994)
Reinhardt's music is here in spirit and fact, but this
is no mere Hot Club re-creation. The arrangements,
with guitar, saxophone and accordion frontlining,
are convincing, and the guitar solos find Taylor in
fine, melodic form.
Taylor Made (Wave 1979)
Taylor was 22 and, supported by with Peter Ind
(bass) and John Richardson (drums), this album
heralded the arrival of a major new guitar talent,
with all his musical skills already firmly in place.
A Tribute To Art Tatum (Hep 1984)
The watershed album, on which Taylor performs
superb, unaccompanied performances of standards
in his own distinctive and totally fresh way.
With Stephane Grappelli *Reunion* (Linn 1993)
Taylor coaxes some lively musical statements
from his former boss and throws in a beautiful
solo-guitar interpretation of Johnny Mandel's
'Emily'.

TOMMY TEDESCO
My Desiree (Discovery 1989)

RENE THOMAS
Guitar Groove (Jazzland 1960)
Strong lines from Thomas alongside J. R.
Monterose's tenor sax. recorded in
New York.
With Eddy Louiss & Kenny Clarke *Rene
Thomas/Eddy Louiss/Kenny Clarke* (RCA 1974)
Quintessential Thomas including his interpretation
of 'You've Changed', long regarded as one of the
best jazz-guitar ballad recordings.

TOQUINHO
Instrumental (AAD)

RALPH TOWNER
Open Letter (ECM 1992)
Towner on classical and 12-string guitars, Peter
Erskine on drums; features the standard 'I Fall In
Love Too Easily' and Bill Evans's 'Waltz for
Debby' alongside nine of Towner's compositions.
With Oregon *Always, Never And Forever* (veraBra
1990); *Music Of Another Present Era*
(Vanguard 1973)
At times introspective, at times uplifting, but always
interesting, with Towner's varied compositions and
playing well to the fore on *Always*.

JIMI TUNNELL
Trilateral Commission (101 South 1991)

JAMES BLOOD ULMER
Odyssey (Columbia/Legacy 1983)
With Third Rail *South Delta Space Age* (Antilles)

GEORGE VAN EPS
Mellow Guitar (Columbia/Corinthian 1956)
With Howard Alden *13 Strings* (Concord 1991) See
the Howard Alden entry for comment.
With Johnny Smith *Legends* (Concord 1994)

JESSE VAN RULLER
European Jazz Guitar Orchestra (Jardis)
One of the very best ensemble jazz guitar CDs. Five
superb players – Van Ruller plus Louis Stewart,
Doug Raney, Heiner Franz and Frederic Sylvestre –
produce a swinging, melodic rich orchestral
backdrop to some fine individual soloing.
European Quintet (Blue Music)
Debut CD from one of the young lions of modern
European jazz guitar. Hard-edged bebop played
with great style and facility.

ULF WAKENIUS
Ray Brown *Seven Steps To Heaven* (Telarc 1995)
Graffiti *Good Groove* (Lipstick 1993)

MIKE WALKER
Roy Powell *Big Sky* (Totem 1994)

CHUCK WAYNE
The Jazz Guitarist (Savoy)
George Shearing *Midnight On Cloud 69* (Savoy
1949-50)
With Brew Moore & Zoot Sims *Tasty Pudding*
(Savoy 1953-4)
With Joe Puma *Fourmost Guitars* (ABC Paramount)

NICK WEBB
Acoustic Alchemy *Back On The Case* (GRP 1991)
Classic mid-period Alchemy. No great profundities,
but plenty of enjoyable moments on a well-crafted
album.
Positive Thinking (GRP 1998)
Dedicated by Greg Carmichael to Webb, who was
seriously ill by the time and could still write but no
longer play. The album thus has its own particular
resonance.
Red Dust And Spanish Lace (MCA 1987)
This early album from the Webb/Greg Carmichael
duo is fresh, lively and sparkling with infectious
grooves and sparkling acoustic guitar.

SUSAN WEINERT
Crunch Time (veraBra 1994)

MARK WHITFIELD
Forever Love (Verve 1997)
True Blue (Verve 1994)
With Peter Bernstein, Ed Cherry, Russell Malone,
Dave Stryker *A Tribute To Grant Green*
(Evidence 1996)
With Christian McBride & Nicholas Payton
Fingerpainting: The Music Of Herbie Hancock
(Verve 1997)

JACK WILKINS
Call Him Reckless (Musicmasters 1989)
Alien Army (Musicmasters 1991)

STAFFAN WILLIAM-OLSSON
Smile (RT)
Three Shades Of Blue (RT)
An as-yet unsung player of modern bebop: attack,
taste, melodic invention and great sound.

ATTILA ZOLLER
Lasting Love (Acoustic Music Records 1997)
Solo guitar performances of his own compositions.
Overcome (Enja 1986)
Excellent live example of Zoller's lyricism and
delicacy, in a quartet including Kirk Lightsey on
piano. The guitarist's account of 'Sophisticated
Lady' is a thumbnail sketch of just how imaginative
he could be.
Zo-Ko-So (MPS 1965)
Zoller with saxophonist Hans Koller and French
piano virtuoso Martial Solal. Fine performances by
all three, with the guitarist creatively accompanying
Koller in duo format, and richly improvising
counterpoint with Solal's piano.

ACKNOWLEDGEMENTS

Charles Alexander would like to thank several people for their help and support with this project:

Bill Mulholland and Dougie Campbell for kindling my interest in jazz guitar many years ago in Edinburgh.

My wife Lesley Alexander for her patience and encouragement.

Stephen Graham (Editor, *Jazzwise Magazine*) for his advice and suggestions.

Nigel Osborne and Tony Bacon and their colleagues Sally Stockwell and Phil Richardson at Balafon, Outline Press, for allowing me the opportunity to develop this project.

My long-time radio partner Nick Freeth for practical help and advice.

Martin Taylor for his endless supply of inspiring music, good humour and helpful ideas.

Kerstan Mackness (New Note Distribution), Trevor Mainwaring (Harmonia Mundi) for providing CDs.

Jon Newey (Publisher *TOP Magazine*, Tower Records) for his discographical help.

Photographs were supplied by the following (number indicates page):
George Benson (**2**) Val Wilmer; *Danny Barker* (**5**) P. Vacher/Jazz Index; *Bud Scott* (**6**) P. Vacher/Jazz Index; *Bing Crosby* (**7**) P. Vacher/Jazz Index; *Lonnie Johnson* (**8**) Val Wilmer; *Freddie Green* (**11**) T. Cryer/Jazz Index; *Alan Reuss* (**12**) M. Jones/Jazz Index; *Marty Grosz* (**13**) David Redfern/Redferns; *Bucky Pizzarelli* (**15**) T. Motion/Jazz Index; *Teddy Bunn* (**16**) Peter Tanner/Val Wilmer; *John Kirby Sextet with Teddy Bunn* (**17**) P. Vacher/Jazz Index; *Al Casey* (**18**) William P. Gottlieb/Redferns; *Les Paul* (**21**) David Redfern/Redferns; *Ivor Mairants* (**23**) Ashley Mark/Jazz Index; *Django Reinhardt* (**25**) William P. Gottlieb/Redferns; *The Quintet of the Hot Club of France* (**26**) Max Jones/Jazz Index; *Stephane Grappelli* (**29** main) Max Jones/Redferns; *Stephane Grappelli* (**29** right) David Redfern/Redferns; *Charlie Christian* (**32**) Michael Ochs Archives/Redferns; *Eddie Durham* (**35**) Val Wilmer; *Charlie Christian* (**37**) Peter Symes; *Herb Ellis* (**39**) Val Wilmer; *Al Casey* (**41**) P. Vacher/Jazz Index; *John Collins* (**43**) Val Wilmer; *Mundell Lowe* (**45**) T. Motion/Jazz Index; *Jimmy Raney* (**47**) T. Motion/Jazz Index; *Tal Farlow* (**48**) Stuart Nicholson; *Tal Farlow* (**49**) M. Jones/Jazz Index; *Chuck Wayne* (**51**) P. Vacher/Jazz Index; *Jim Hall* (**57**) Val Wilmer; *Ernest Ranglin* (**64**) Val Wilmer; *Ernest Ranglin* (**65**) Christian Him/Jazz Index; *Atilla Zoller* (**67**) Christian Him/Jazz Index; *Wes Montgomery* (**69**) David Redfern/Redferns; *Wes Montgomery* (**71**) David Redfern/Redferns; *Kenny Burrell* (**75**) Val Wilmer; *Grant Green* (**76**) Val Wilmer; *George Benson* (**79**) Val Wilmer; *Brother Jack McDuff* (**80**) Christian Him/Jazz Index; *Joe Pass* (**83**) Stuart Nicholson; *Ella Fitzgerald* (**86**) P. Roberts/Jazz Index; *Miles Davis* (**89**) David Redfern/Redferns; *Larry Coryell* (**90**) Roger Coles/Jazz Index; *John McLaughlin* (**91**) David Redfern/Redferns; *Tony Williams* (**93**) David Redfern/Redferns; *L. Shankar* (**95**) Christian Him/Jazz Index; *Paco De Lucia & John McLaughlin* (**96**) Jazz Index; *Emily Remler* (**97**) T. Motion/Jazz Index; *Pat Metheny* (**99** left) Christian Him/Jazz Index; *Lyle Mays* (**99** right) Christian Him/Jazz Index; *Pat Metheny* (**101**) Bob Willoughby/Redferns; *John Abercrombie* (**104**) G. Walden/Jazz Index; *John Scofield* (**105** left) Peter Symes; *Bill Frisell* (**105** right) Brigitte Engl/Redferns); *Mike Stern* (**107**) Christian Him/Jazz Index; *Larry Carlton* (**108**) T. Motion/Jazz Index; *Jeff Beck* (**109**) Robert Knight/Redferns; *Yngwie Malmsteen* (**112**) Roberta Parkin/Redferns; *Scott Henderson* (**113**) Christian Him/Jazz Index; *Joe Satriani* (**115**) T. Motion/Jazz Index; *Allan Holdsworth* (**116**) Christian Him/Jazz Index; *Charlie Byrd* (**119**) Terry Cryer/Jazz Index; *Antonio Carlos Jobim* (**121**) Nancy Clen Daniel/Jazz Index; *Baden Powell* (**123**) Christian Him/Jazz Index; *Egberto Gismonti* (**124**) Peter Symes; *Jose Neto* (**125**) Christian Him/Jazz Index; *Tommy Tedesco* (**128**) P. Vacher/Jazz Index; *Lee Ritenour* (**129**) Christian Him/Jazz Index; *Robben Ford* (**130**) Stuart Nicholson; *Mark Ribot* (**132**) R. Andrew Lepley/Redferns; *Sonny Sharrock* (**134**) Stuart Nicholson; *James Blood Ulmer* (**136**) Christian Him/Jazz Index; *Derek Bailey* (**137**) Peter Symes; *Al DiMeola* (**141** left) Christian Him/Jazz Index; *Paco de Lucia* (**141** right) Peter Symes; *Earl Klugh* (**147**) Redferns; *John Pizzarelli* (**149**) T. Motion/Jazz Index; *Howard Alden* (**150**) Peter Symes; *Peter Leitch* (**151**) P. Vacher/Jazz Index; *Russell Malone* (**153**) Stuart Nicholson; *Babik Reinhardt* (**155**) T. Motion/Jazz Index; *Birelli Lagrene* (**156**) Christian Him/Jazz Index; *Fapy Lafertin* (**158**) Christian Him/Jazz Index; *Diz Disley* (**159**) Max Jones/Jazz Index; *Lauderic Caton* (**163** left) Val Wilmer; *Denny Wright* (**163** right) T. Motion/Jazz Index; *Ike Isaacs* (**164**) T. Motion/Jazz Index; *Jim Mullen* (**166**) T. Motion/Jazz Index; *John Etheridge* (**167**) Christian Him/Jazz Index; *Esmond Selwyn* (**168**) Mike Heard/Jazz Index; *Ronny Jordan* (**169**) Christian Him/Jazz Index; *Philip Catherine* (**171**) Christian Him/Jazz Index; *Louis Stewart* (**173**) Christian Him/Jazz Index; *Elek Bacsic* (**176**) Val Wilmer; *Kevin Eubanks* (**179**) Christian Him/Jazz Index; *Mark Whitfield* (**180**) Stuart Nicholson; *Charlie Hunter* (**182**) Christian Him/Jazz Index; *George Benson* (jacket front) David Redfern; *Freddie Green* (jacket rear above) T. Cryer/Jazz Index; *Charlie Byrd, Herb Ellis, Barney Kessel* (jacket rear middle) O. Noel/Jazz Index; *Tal Farlow* (jacket rear below left) Christian Him/Jazz Index; *John McLaughlin* (jacket rear below centre) Christian Him/Jazz Index; *Joe Pass* (jacket rear below right) T. Motion/Jazz Index.

Record sleeves came from the collections of Charles Alexander, Tony Bacon, Balafon and Nigel Osborne. The sleeves were guided to the page through the lens of Miki Slingsby.

Bibliography

Ian Carr et al *Jazz, The Rough Guide* (Rough Guides 1995)
Richard Cook & Brian Morton *The Penguin Guide To Jazz On CD* (Penguin 4th ed 1998)
Charles Delaunay *Django Reinhardt* (Ashley Mark 1981)
Michael Erlewine et al *All Music Guide To Jazz* (Miller Freeman 3rd ed 1998)
Richard Hetrick *Jazz Guitar On Record 1955 To 1990* (privately published c1991)
Barry Kernfeld (ed) *The New Grove Dictionary Of Jazz* (Macmillan 1994)
Allan Kozinn et al *The Guitar: History, Music, Players* (Columbus 1984)
Norman Mongan *The History Of The Guitar In Jazz* (Oak 1983)
Stuart Nicholson *Jazz-Rock - A History* (Canongate 1998)
James Sallis *The Guitar Players* (Bison/University of Nebraska Press 1994)
Mary Alice Shaughnessy *Les Paul - An American Original* (Morrow 1993)
Geoffrey Smith *Stéphane Grappelli - A Biography* (Pavilion 1987)
Maurice J Summerfield *The Jazz Guitar: Its Evolution, Its Players And Personalities Since 1900* (Ashley Mark 4th ed 1998)

Periodicals

Acoustic Guitar
Down Beat
Guitar International
Guitar Player
Guitarist
Jazz Journal International
Jazzwise Magazine
Just Jazz Guitar
The Guitar Magazine

"The good players have feeling. They are giving you a message, and the message is not how many notes they are playing, it's the feeling that they get. That's just the way it is."
Herb Ellis, 1980.